IDENTITY CAPTURED BY LAW

Identity Captured by Law

Membership in Canada's Indigenous Peoples and Linguistic Minorities

SÉBASTIEN GRAMMOND

McGill-Queen's University Press
Montreal & Kingston • London • Ithaca

© McGill-Queen's University Press 2009

ISBN 978-0-7735-3503-9 (cloth)
ISBN 978-0-7735-3504-6 (paper)

Legal deposit second quarter 2009
Bibliothèque nationale du Québec

Printed in Canada on acid-free paper that is 100% ancient forest free
(100% post-consumer recycled), processed chlorine free

This book has been published with the help of a grant from the
Canadian Federation for the Humanities and Social Sciences,
through the Aid to Scholarly Publications Programme, using funds
provided by the Social Sciences and Humanities Research Council of
Canada.

McGill-Queen's University Press acknowledges the support of the
Canada Council for the Arts for our publishing program. We also
acknowledge the financial support of the Government of Canada
through the Book Publishing Industry Development Program (BPIDP)
for our publishing activities.

Library and Archives Canada Cataloguing in Publication

Grammond, Sébastien, 1970–
    Identity captured by law : membership in Canada's indigenous
peoples and linguistic minorities / Sébastien Grammond.

Includes bibliographical references and index.
ISBN 978-0-7735-3503-9 (bnd)
ISBN 978-0-7735-3504-6 (pbk)

1. Native peoples – Legal status, laws, etc. – Canada. 2. Native
peoples – Canada – Ethnic identity. 3. Indians of North America –
Canada – Band membership. 4. Linguistic minorities – Legal status,
laws, etc. – Canada. 5. Human rights – Canada. I. Title.

KE4395.G73 2009   342.7108'72   C2008-906381-3
KF4483.C58G73 2009

Typeset by Jay Tee Graphics Ltd. in 10.5/13 Sabon

Contents

Acknowledgments

This book is a substantial revision of my doctoral dissertation, defended at the University of Oxford in 2004. I would like to thank, first and foremost, Sandra Fredman, my Oxford supervisor, for her critical and insightful guidance, as well as my examiners, Timothy Endicott, Paul McHugh, Christopher McCrudden, and Peter Oliver, for their useful comments. I would also like to express my appreciation to my colleagues Nathalie Des Rosiers, Ghislain Otis, Dwight Newman, Muriel Paradelle, Karen Eltis, and Lucie Lamarche, whose feedback helped me at various stages of the project. Thanks also to Karole Dumont-Beckett of the Métis Nation of Ontario, Martin Dunn of the Congress of Aboriginal Peoples, and Juanita Taylor of Nunavut Tungavik, who gave me useful information or allowed me access to their organisations' records.

The research for this book was made possible by funding received from the Fonds québécois pour la recherche sur la société et la culture and the Social Sciences and Humanities Research Council of Canada. Its publication was funded by a grant from the Aid to Scholarly Publications Programme of the Canadian Federation for the Humanities and Social Sciences, using funds provided by the Social Sciences and Humanities Research Council of Canada. Certain parts of chapter 1 appeared in an article entitled "Disentangling Race and Indigenous Status: The Role of Ethnicity," published in (2008) 33 *Queen's Law Journal*, and are reprinted with permission.

Finally, thanks to Christiane, Catherine, and Magali for their patience and unwavering support.

Introduction

I live in an area called the Gatineau Hills. While it is only a short drive away from Ottawa, the beautiful scenery and the quiet countryside make for a welcome break from the city's activity. The region lies within the province of Quebec but is inhabited by Francophones and Anglophones alike. While some villages are predominantly English-speaking and others are more French-speaking, no sharp linguistic border divides the area, as most people are bilingual and routinely bridge the linguistic divide in various social contexts. The apparent linguistic harmony makes it hard to believe that one of the area's favourite picnic destinations, Meech Lake, has become a codeword for Canada's inability to come to terms with its multiple identities. We are far removed from the controversy that surrounded the failed constitutional agreement reached at the prime minister's cottage on Meech Lake in 1987. It seems that it does not matter much whether you are an Anglophone or a Francophone.

Yet the area was the backdrop to recent controversies in which individual identity mattered, not only from a social but also from a legal perspective. When Michael Parasiuk wanted to send his son Cohen to the English elementary school in Wakefield, he ran against Quebec's Charter of the French Language[1] (popularly known as Bill 101), which requires everyone in Quebec to send their children to French schools, except where they are able to demonstrate their membership in the Anglophone community through the language of their own elementary schooling. As Michael's wife had been schooled in English outside Canada and Michael himself went to a French immersion primary school in Manitoba, Quebec's Education Department took the stance that Cohen did not meet Bill 101's criteria and was not entitled to attend English school, despite the fact that English was spoken at home and was the only language in which Cohen was able to go to school. It took a judgment of the Quebec Court of Appeal criticising the government's literal application of the law to open the doors of the local English school to him.[2]

Another facet of Canada's ethnic diversity took the stage during the 2006 federal election. The incumbent MP for the area, David Smith, became embroiled in a controversy regarding contracts awarded to his firm by the federal government in the years prior to his election.[3] Another candidate denounced the fact that Smith's consulting firm had obtained contracts reserved for "aboriginal businesses" even though Smith did not have Indian status under the Indian Act. Smith replied that although he did not hold Indian status, he considered himself a Métis because his great-grandmother was native. Thus, he was asking voters to go beyond the usual equation between aboriginal identity and government-recognised Indian status. The Grand Chief of the Native Alliance of Quebec, Carl Dubé, came to his rescue and explained to the media that, even though they lack governmental recognition, Métis communities are no less aboriginal than First Nations (or "Indian bands") and that the Alliance maintained its own system of membership control whereby applicants must prove their aboriginal ancestry before they obtain their card. According to Dubé, Smith's indigenous identity was confirmed by the fact that he was a card-carrying member of the Alliance. As it happened, however, Smith lost his election, and we cannot say for sure what role this controversy over his identity played in his defeat.

These two stories reveal instances of what I have just called "membership control," which is the subject of this book. I use this expression to describe rules, procedures, or systems whereby the law classifies individuals in ethnic categories for the purposes of granting them special rights or imposing special obligations on them. In the first story, Bill 101 contained criteria to identify the members of the Anglophone community who were entitled to have their children instructed in their own language, rather than in French. Although the definition serves only a specific purpose (regulating access to English schools), it amounts to a definition of Quebec's English-speaking minority and, by a mirror effect, of its French-speaking majority. The second story highlights the parallel existence of several definitions of indigenous identity: the rules of

Indian status found in the Indian Act,[4] a federal statute, which Smith did not meet, and the membership systems put in place by various Métis organisations, under which Smith qualified.

I have selected those two cases, the indigenous peoples and official-language minorities (English in Quebec, French elsewhere in Canada), as the object of my study because they are the two main instances in Canada where membership in an ethnic group is regulated by law and results in a different set of rights and obligations. In contrast, membership in ethnic or linguistic groups arising from more recent immigration, such as Ukrainians, Italians, or Vietnamese, is not regulated: individuals are entirely free to hold themselves up as members of those groups, and no legal consequences or special rights and obligations attach to that identity. Religion used to be a different matter, as the Canadian constitution affords certain Christian denominations a right to run their own schools, but those guarantees are slowly fading away and courts are highly reluctant to test individual assertions of religious identity.[5]

The most obvious question that springs to mind when one considers the practice of membership control is its compatibility with human rights. When we mention to a foreign audience that Canada regulates membership in certain ethnic groups, we are politely reminded that similar schemes were pivotal to the apartheid regime in South Africa or to segregationist laws in the United States. Hence, any study of membership control must explain how it is compatible with individual rights and set forth what conditions it must comply with in order to avoid discrimination. But if native persons are asked what they think of the fact that the state controls membership in the indigenous peoples, the answer is likely to be different: "What right does the state have to say who is indigenous and who is not? *We* should be the ones deciding that!" Thus, membership control must also be measured against collective rights, in essence the right of ethnic groups to define themselves, a component of their right to self-determination.

Therefore, this book will be structured as an inquiry into how the rules that control membership in Canada's indigenous peoples and official-language minorities interact with human rights in their individual and collective dimensions. Stated briefly, my main conclusion is that the two are indeed compatible and that minorities have no greater tendency to discriminate than the majority of the population. Thus, one need not fear the autonomy of minorities in defining their own membership. Conversely, minorities should not be wary of judicial review of their membership decisions according to human rights standards. Judicial review may help to correct some questionable rules, but it does not result in the systematic invalidation of decisions made by minorities.

However, this study cannot remain strictly within the confines of traditional legal scholarship. Analysing the various statuses created by the law without regard for the social realities they purportedly describe would be playing with empty boxes. Hence, I will relate legal membership rules to the conceptions of ethnic identity revealed by the social sciences. This will provide us with illuminating insights into the law's ability to reflect accurately concepts such as ethnicity, culture, and identity and into the role of human rights in assessing discrepancies between legal categories and social realities.

One major objection to this project must be disposed of at the outset. Studying the indigenous peoples and linguistic minorities together might seem to be an unusual endeavour. The conditions of the two groups seem far removed from one another, as are the rights afforded to them, and indigenous leaders have consistently objected to the description of indigenous peoples as being "minorities." The specificity of the indigenous peoples lies in their immemorial occupation of their territories, which lays firm ground for claims to self-determination and land rights.[6] In the result, indigenous peoples usually enjoy a broader array of rights than linguistic minorities. Yet I am not comparing apples and oranges. The rights of indigenous peoples and linguistic minorities have overlapping, although not identical, philosophical foundations.[7] Research in anthropology and sociology has shown that the concept of ethnicity explains the processes of identity formation in both indigenous peoples and linguistic communities,[8] although the markers of each kind of identity are obviously different. More to the point, the issue of membership control arises in both cases and involves the same questions of respect for individual and collective human rights. Those common threads make possible a comparative study of membership control. Indeed, Canada provides a rare instance of a country where two very different minorities have both been defined in legal terms under the constraint of a charter of human rights entrenched in the constitution and of international human rights treaties. The remainder of this book will show that their parallel study is worthwhile.

The boundaries of the inquiry must also be made clear. In analysing membership controversies, I assume that a decision has already been made, on contingent or principled grounds, to recognise certain groups and not others or to grant particular rights to certain groups and not to others. Thus, I will not scrutinise the rightfulness of the differential treatment of First Nations and Métis groups,[9] or the selection of French and English as Canada's only two official languages. Those issues could be the subject of a whole book in itself.

Chapter 1 of the book is devoted to the clarification of three concepts that are central to my argument: ethnicity, equality, and minority rights. Ethnicity is a social science concept that describes how people conceive of themselves as belonging to groups identified by their cultural differences. Understanding the modern conception of ethnicity is a precondition to any analysis of the classification of indigenous or linguistic groups in Canada. Equality and minority rights theory, for their part, form the normative framework of the thesis. I will contrast "formal" and "substantive" conceptions of equality, showing how the latter is necessary for the analysis of minority rights regimes.

Chapter 2 operationalises these concepts in the legal sphere and sketches the main legal issues raised by membership control. First, collective minority rights, most importantly the right to self-determination, provide a legal foundation for the establishment of membership rules. Second, individual rights, chiefly the right to equality, act as a substantive limit on the membership criteria selected for a particular group. In this regard, the analytical framework developed by courts to analyse alleged breaches of the relevant individual rights calls for a certain degree of correspondence between legal membership criteria and actual conceptions of the group's ethnicity; in other words, status must mirror ethnicity.

In chapters 3, 4, and 5, I use that framework to analyse the membership control systems in Canada's indigenous peoples and linguistic groups. Chapter 3 deals with the "old" Indian Act, prior to its reform in 1985. The rules it contained were fundamentally flawed, as they ran afoul of both the individual and collective aspects of human rights. Their purpose was not to benefit the indigenous peoples but rather to further their assimilation by gradually reducing their population. Those rules were developed and applied by the federal bureaucracy in total disregard of the autonomy of the indigenous peoples, whose objections were ignored. They breached equality in many distinct ways, especially by making Indian status flow through the male line only and by excluding women who married non-Indians. The latter rule was contested unsuccessfully in the Canadian courts,[10] but the United Nations Human Rights Committee held, in the famous *Lovelace* case,[11] that it violated the right to enjoy one's own culture. This led to the entire overhaul of the rules of Indian status in 1985.

Chapter 4 is devoted to the four main legal types of definitions of indigenous identity that exist today in Canada: the new rules of Indian status, the rules identifying the beneficiaries of the modern treaties signed with certain indigenous peoples, the membership codes adopted by Indian bands, and the definition of Métis identity. First, I rank those systems in terms of the autonomy recognised for the indigenous peoples in their adoption. That autonomy is never complete. The power of Indian bands to control their own membership was made conditional on the reintegration of women who had "married out" and who had been excluded by the old rules. Even in the case of the Métis, in which there is no legislative intervention on the part of the state, the Supreme Court, in the recent *Powley* case,[12] has set conditions for the recognition of the definitions adopted by Métis political organisations. Second, I assess the compliance of those rules with equality and individual rights. While the situation has improved considerably, there is still "residual" discrimination in the rules of Indian status, and certain band membership codes contain provisions of doubtful validity. However, I show that there is no correlation between autonomy and violations of individual rights. Indigenous groups do not have a greater tendency to discriminate than the rest of the population. Rather, the remaining breaches of equality are mostly related to the manner in which the former exclusion of women who had "married out" was corrected.

My second case study, a study of the linguistic minorities, is found in chapter 5. I first describe the very different purposes that animate the language laws enacted by Quebec and the provisions of the Canadian constitution dealing with minority-language education. While the former aims at the promotion of the French language and the prevention of the slow assimilation that is thought to be a potential consequence of market forces, the latter focuses on the preservation of individual choice. Evaluating respect for self-determination in this case raises difficult problems. A given group, such as Quebec Francophones, can be considered as a minority within Canada and as a majority in Quebec. Hence, the definition of a minority must be sensitive to context. I will show that the autonomy of Quebec Francophones to define themselves was curtailed by the provisions of the 1982 constitution, although this was done in a manner broadly consistent with the definition enacted by Quebec before 1982. The membership definitions found in Quebec legislation and in the Canadian constitution are generally compatible with equality and individual rights. Even though Quebec Francophones are required to send their children to French schools, this does not result in a breach of their right to equality or to enjoy their own culture, as these rights do not entail, in the circumstances, a "right of exit" or a right to assimilate into the Canadian English-speaking majority.

IDENTITY CAPTURED BY LAW

I

Ethnicity, Equality, and Minority Rights

The main argument of this book is that the rules that control membership in Canada's indigenous peoples and official language minorities need not violate equality rights and that much of the controversy that exists about membership control measures may be explained as the result of a disagreement over fundamental concepts. Thus, some people think that the indigenous peoples should be treated equally with other citizens, meaning that there should be no Indian status and special rights, whereas others would argue that true equality requires state-sponsored measures to improve their condition. Are French-speaking Quebeckers treated unequally when they are not given the choice to send their children to English schools, while their Anglophone counterparts may choose between English and French? It is quite difficult to answer that question without a clear conception of the right to equality and the reasons behind minority rights. Moreover, there is much confusion about what exactly makes a minority different and deserving of special rights: is it ancestry, culture, language, education, or history? The social sciences have developed the concept of ethnicity as an analytical tool to understand how people view human diversity. Thus, in order to gain a better grasp of membership control issues, it is necessary to refine our conceptions not only of equality and minority rights but also of ethnicity. This chapter is dedicated to the study of those three theoretical concepts that are central to the remainder of this book.

A major difference between those concepts should be noted at the outset. The concept of ethnicity was developed by social scientists to analyse human diversity. It is descriptive concept: it aims at describing how things *are*, by figuring out categories into which the social reality, with its irreducible complexity, can be sorted. The discussion that follows will thus be focused on the various ways in which social science has attempted, through ideas such as race, culture, and identity, to give an accurate account of human diversity. In contrast, equality and minority rights are normative (or prescriptive) concepts. They describe not the actual state of things but how things *should be*. Both concepts may be viewed from a moral or a legal perspective. The moral perspective, which draws mainly upon political theory, aims at developing a conception of equality or minority rights that can be justified by an appeal to widely accepted philosophical principles. The legal perspective, in turn, describes the legal norms that implement those moral conecptions. While positivist conceptions of law would separate law and morality, modern theories of legal interpretation readily admit that moral views play their part in giving actual meaning to rules of law.[1] Hence, it makes sense to study both the legal and the moral dimensions of equality and minority rights. Beyond that, however, an accurate application of those concepts to membership control issues must take into account the descriptive concept of ethnicity. In other words, any normative proposition about what membership control systems *should* look like must be based on a sound understanding of what ethnic groups and ethnic identity actually *are*. This is where law and the social sciences meet.

ETHNIC GROUPS AND ETHNIC IDENTITY

The reality of human diversity is very hard to grasp. Over the ages, people have taken various stances as to what characteristics of human beings should be relevant when we attempt to classify them into groups. Skin colour, culture, and language are but a few examples of markers that have been in common use. However, other human characteristics, such as hair colour, have rarely been suggested as a basis for defining groups. We thus need an account of how such "identity markers" are selected and how we can judge their morality or legitimacy.

The first step in clarifying this thorny question is to recognise that most, if not all, of the concepts that we use to describe human diversity are "constructed" concepts. To understand what this means, I will resort to an example from the natural sciences. Not long ago, we heard on the news that there was one less planet in our solar system. However, this was not the result of a large-scale natural catastrophe. Pluto, the planet in question, did not suddenly explode or leave its orbit to chart a lonely course in outer space. What happened was that an international convention of astronomers held in Prague adopted a new definition of "planet."[2] For technical reasons, Pluto did not fit the new criteria and was expelled, not from the solar system, but from the list of objects that astronomers call planets. Obviously, the reality did not change, only our manner of describing it. This is why the concept of planet is a constructed one. It has no purely objective existence. Objects in space do not have labels affixed to them saying, "this is a planet" or "this is not a planet." Rather, astronomers, for their own purposes, have constructed definitions that are not intrinsically true or false. One of them may gain wide acceptance or may even be adopted by some official body. But the recent replacement of the formerly widely accepted definition (which included Pluto) by a more restrictive one (which excludes it) shows that the concepts that we use to describe the reality have no necessary or inherent meaning, just the one that we choose to give them. Their meaning is constructed by the human mind.

The conceptions of ethnicity that we are about to study share their constructed nature with the definition of "planet." Ethnicity is a creation of the human mind: it does not exist "out there" in nature. But there are some notable differences. First, the definition of "planet" was adopted by an official international body, and it seems that astronomers are happy to go along with the new version. Ethnicity, in contrast, does not conform to the stipulations of a centralised defining authority. It is a diffuse or fluid concept, in the sense that individuals hold their own conceptions of what makes up a particular ethnicity, so that the social scientist may discern only general tendencies in the markers that are used to describe a group's ethnicity. Second, Pluto's exclusion from the select club of planets has no moral or political consequences. No one is disadvantaged by that exclusion. The selection of a conception of human diversity, however, is not innocent. One such conception, race, has been used to justify the grossly unjust policies of slavery and apartheid. Identity, when it is imposed from the outside, has the potential to buttress oppression.

I cannot, in the few pages that follow, give a full account of such complex and controverted concepts as race, culture, or ethnicity.

These notions have spawned an immense body of literature, and they have been deployed in support of oppression or liberation alike. My modest aim here is to give the reader an idea of the most recent conclusions of the social sciences regarding the manner in which people see their own diversity. In doing so, however, I need to step back a little bit and discuss conceptions, such as race, that are now discredited. As my focus here is on the descriptive aspects of ethnicity, I will leave normative questions (what conceptions are acceptable or not) for later.

Racial Conceptions of Ethnicity

Most scientists today believe that the concept of race is seriously flawed and should be abandoned. They now see race as a socially constructed category. Yet ordinary people who employ the concept of race think that it refers to an objective reality, although they would be hard-pressed to define it. Official discourse sometimes echoes this popular conception.[3] In other words, people form their own views as to what races are and how to allocate individuals to a particular race, irrespective of what science considers to be the objective reality. Hence, to be able to detect racial conceptions at work in membership control systems, it is necessary to give some thought to the main components of that notion.

What, then, does race mean in popular discourse? What is the content of this social construction? Again, the answer is not easy to find, as the social conceptions of race have evolved over time and differ from place to place.[4] What a nineteenth-century American understood by the word "race" may have little in common with the meaning ascribed to the same word by a seventeenth-century Frenchman. Nevertheless, it is possible to identify the most frequently recurring components of the concept of race. Audrey Smedley, in her historical analysis of this concept in the English-speaking world, points to five interlocking beliefs: (1) that humanity is divided into discrete biological groups; (2) that those groups are ranked in hierarchical fashion so that some are superior and others inferior; (3) that the physical characteristics associated with those groups are the indicia of psychic or behavioural realities, such as intelligence, laziness, and promiscuity; (4) that those characteristics are transmitted by heredity; and (5) that those groups were created different by God and their difference is immutable.[5]

For the purposes of this book, it is not necessary to rely on the idea of divine origin of the races. Although this is necessarily a simplification, I am content to assume that when people use racial concepts, they refer to the fact that human beings can be classified into discrete groups recognizable by their physical appearance, that these differences are relevant in social interactions, and that membership in a race is hereditary – you cannot change your race. More synthetically, race can be defined as a "socially constructed immutable difference."[6]

For a long time the socially constructed meaning of race was backed by science. Well into the twentieth century, researchers endeavoured to classify human beings according to objective information (for example, cranial or teeth measurements, skin colour), in an attempt to find a scientific basis for commonly accepted racial categories. For instance, as late as 1939, when the Supreme Court of Canada was asked to determine if "Eskimos" (the Inuit) were to be included in the legal category of "Indians," it was presented with a wealth of evidence describing the physical similarities and differences between the Inuit and the other indigenous peoples of Canada.[7] The judges wisely declined to give any weight to racial arguments, preferring to rely on evidence that the Inuit were counted as Indians in the official discourse in Canada at the time the relevant statute was enacted.

The demise of the "science of race" came from the realisation that scientific observation falsified, rather than supported, the main beliefs that constituted the social conception of race. This led to the gradual acknowledgment of the absence of biological reality behind the concept of race,[8] to the point where some well-known academics today claim flatly that "there are no races."[9]

The first racial belief proved wrong by modern biology is that humanity can be divided into discrete groups according to physical characteristics. We now know that humanity has a common origin and that diversity in physical characteristics is continuous: there are no sharp breaks between the supposed races. To be sure, modern genetics has shown that there is a "genetic structure" in human populations, or, in other words, that genetic diversity tends to follow geography.[10] Thus, one is likely to be more similar genetically to one's neighbour than to someone who lives on another continent. Yet this is only a matter of statistics and probabilities. Intermarriage between different populations has always existed, and there are no "pure" populations. There is also no objective method for identifying a discrete number of racial groups. If you ask a computer loaded with genetic data to sort individuals into four groups according to genetic similarity, you will obtain four "races." And if you ask for six groups, you will get six "races." Discrete and closed racial categories exist only in the eyes of the beholder, not in nature.

The second discredited belief is that membership in a race carries with it certain intellectual, behavioural, or cultural characteristics. This belief is incompatible with modern conceptions of the relative importance in human beings of the innate and the acquired, or of heredity and the environment. The findings of modern genetics do not alter the picture: while certain diseases have been traced to a particular gene that is more frequent (again, a question of probabilities) in individuals who identify with a particular population, it has never been shown that complex behavioural traits depend on one's genotype in a manner that would draw a correlation between one's supposed race and one's behaviour. According to a recent account of genetic variation, "[h]uman behavior is complicated, and it is strongly influenced by nongenetic factors. Thousands of pleiotropic genes are thought to influence behaviour, and their products interact in complex and unpredictable ways. Considering this extraordinary complexity, the idea that variation in the frequency of a single allele could explain substantial population differences in behavior would be amusing if it were not so dangerous."[11]

The concept of race can thus be seen in a new light. Races do not exist "out there" in nature. They are not objective realities or classifications. There is no objective method for ascribing a specific race to an individual on the basis of his or her physical characteristics. While some physical characteristics may be transmitted by descent, ancestry does not determine behaviour or culture. Yet because some people do believe otherwise and act upon such beliefs (for example, they would not hire dark-skinned people, because they perceive them to be less intelligent), race as a social construct is relevant to the analysis of racism and to the framing of responses to it. The term "racialisation" is sometimes used to describe the process through which racial categories are constructed. The phrase "racialised group" is increasingly employed to describe groups that are victims of racism without acknowledging the scientific validity of the concept of race. In short, there are no races, but some people are racist.

Cultural Conceptions of Ethnicity

If race is an invalid concept to describe human diversity, the instinctive substitute seems to be the concept of culture. While race emphasises aspects of the human being that are presumed to be transmitted genetically, culture refers to human conduct or human values that are learned or acquired, rather than inherited, that are transmitted by processes of social interaction.

A classic definition of the concept of culture was given by E.B. Tylor, a British anthropologist, who described it as "that complex whole which includes knowledge, belief, art, morals, law, custom, and any other capabilities and habits acquired by man as a member of society."[12] This wide conception of culture is still accepted today. For instance, Bhikhu Parekh proposed to define culture as a "historically created system of meaning and significance or, what comes to the same thing, a system of beliefs and practices in terms of which a group of human beings understand, regulate and structure their individual and collective lives."[13]

Given such definitions of culture, an obvious manner of delineating cultural groups would be to isolate certain observable cultural characteristics that appear to be common to all group members. Each cultural group would be identified by a small set of cultural traits (ways of dressing, foundational myths, language, etc.) in such a way that each group's culture would be different, in some essential respects, from the culture of its neighbours. Thus, for a long time anthropologists attempted to isolate and describe the *essential elements* of a group's culture. For that reason, that conception of ethnicity and culture is now called "essentialism." The assumption is that each member of the group must share those essential cultural traits, forming a cultural mould of sorts.

The law seldom attempts to define culture or cultural groups, perhaps recognising the inherent difficulties of such a task. When it does so, however, it tends to resort to an essentialist vision of culture, premised on the idea that minorities and indigenous peoples are composed of individuals who share certain cultural characteristics and who can be readily classified as members or non-members of the group based on the presence or absence of the relevant characteristics. Thus, cultural groups would have an objective existence and composition that could be ascertained by an external observer and defined in legal tems. For instance, Convention 169 of the

International Labour Organisation gives a definition of "indigenous peoples" that stipulates that they must have retained "some or
all of their own social, economic, cultural and political institutions."[14] The focus is on specific cultural elements that are thought
to have been distinctive of indigenous peoples since the first con-
tacts with European colonists. With respect to the concept of
"minority," international law does not provide an accepted definition. However, most writers on the subject usually accept the following working definition given by Francesco Capotorti, who
authored a United Nations report on the subject: "a group numeri-
cally inferior to the rest of the population of a state, in a non-domi-
nant position, whose members – being nationals of the state –
possess ethnic, religious, or linguistic characteristics differing from
those of the rest of the population and show, if only implicitly, a
sense of solidarity, directed towards preserving their culture, traditions, religion or language."[15] This emphasis on specific cultural
traits found a Canadian parallel in the 1992 Charlottetown Accord,
which proposed a constitutional amendment recognising Quebec's
distinct society, the main features of which were "French language,
a distinctive culture and the civil law."[16]

While these definitions may appear intuitively right, the attempt
to implement them in practice has proved highly controversial.
Faced with the necessity of defining the "aboriginal rights" protected in section 35 of the Constitution Act, 1982, the Supreme
Court of Canada decided that section 35 covered only practices that
were "integral to the distinctive culture" of the indigenous people
asserting the right and that in order to be distinctive, a present-day
cultural practice must be related to historical practices that existed
prior to contact with European settlers.[17] The adoption of that test
was severly criticised on several fronts.[18] It "freezes" indigenous
culture in a distant past: if culture evolves too much as a result of
European influence, it loses its constitutional protection. This has
the effect of stereotyping members of an indigenous culture in the
terms in which the dominant society has always seen them, that is,
as people who hunt, trap, and fish. Everything else is deemed to be
non-indigenous and not deserving of legal recognition. Thus, it is
very difficult to assert rights related to commercial activities or self-
government,[19] as current indigenous practices cannot be divorced
from the evolution of indigenous society over the last two hundred
years. The application of the "integral to a distinctive culture" test

by judges also gives rise to considerable practical difficulties. Aboriginal rights trials end up being contests between expert witnesses in history or anthropology trying to figure out what were the cultural practices of indigenous peoples in a distant past. Almost always, the issue ends up being decided by non-aboriginal judges, whose authority to decide what is integral to a culture unfamiliar to them is highly questionable. To illustrate the absurdity of the approach, Russel Barsh and Sakej Henderson imagined a scenario whereby, had Quebec's distinct society been recognised in the constitution, the Supreme Court of Canada would have attempted to figure out what was integral to contemporary Quebec society by reference to the practices of French Canadians at the time of the British conquest.[20]

Relational Conceptions of Ethnicity

While the essentialist vision of culture and ethnic groups still prevails today in some areas of the law, its use in anthropology has faded away since the 1960s, and it has been replaced with a new, "constructivist" conception of cultural groups and ethnicity.[21] This means that ethnic groups are no longer defined on the basis of the supposedly essential elements of their culture, as determined by external observation and classification, but rather by the cultural features, or "markers," that group members use in identifying themselves with the group in the course of social interaction; this is why we will call this conception "relational."

   In modern anthropology and sociology, the terms "ethnic" and "ethnicity" are used to refer to groups who construct a definition of themselves that relies on (real or perceived) cultural differences. While the world's cultural diversity cannot be divided into discrete, mutually exclusive cultural groups, individuals interacting with other persons who are culturally different ascribe significance to some (but not all) of those differences. They create "ethnic boundaries" through the selection of relevant cultural "markers" that will be used to distinguish members of different ethnic groups. Language, religion, traditions, and ways of life are examples of what may become ethnic markers. But they need not be so in any given case: for instance, many indigenous peoples define themselves in a manner that is compatible with adherence to a Western religion. Thus, Catholics, Anglicans, and Pentecostals may coexist within an indigenous community. And these markers need not be fixed in time: the relevance of religion, to use that example again, may gradually fade as members of an ethnic group come to accept religious diversity in their midst.

While Catholicism was once an essential element of French Canadian identity, Quebec nationalism now avoids any reference to religion. Notice also how the "ethnic label" itself has gradually changed from "French Canadian" to "*Québécois*." The selection of the relevant markers may flow from a historical situation of oppression of the members of one group by another. The oppressor group may try to justify its domination by the fact that some cultural traits of the dominated group are signs of inferiority. The latter group may then internalise those traits as particularly relevant to its own identity. In turn, ethnic consciousness values and strengthens the cultural differences that demarcate ethnic identity, thus closing the circle between ethnicity and culture. This model of ethnicity is now widely accepted. For instance, Eriksen defines ethnicity as follows: "[e]thnicity is an aspect of social relationships between agents who consider themselves as culturally distinctive from members of other groups with whom they have a minimum of regular interaction. It can thus also be described as a social identity (based on a contrast vis-à-vis others) characterized by metaphoric or fictive kinship ... When cultural differences regularly make a difference in interaction between members of groups, the social relationship has an ethnic element."[22]

The definition of ethnic groups thus derives from what the actors themselves subjectively consider to be relevant cultural characteristics of group members. Cultural similarity is a result, rather than a cause, of this group formation process. Fredrik Barth, a Norwegian anthropologist who pioneered this approach, pointed out that "much can be gained by regarding this very important feature [the sharing of a common culture] as an implication or result, rather than a primary and definitional characteristic of ethnic group organization."[23] Moreover, it is now accepted that the cultural markers that define an ethnic group may evolve over time: in this regard, everything depends on the group members' changing views. Ethnic identity is thus a fluid concept, since it ultimately depends on individual perceptions of the cultural markers that distinguish the members of an ethnic group. Because individuals within an ethnic group may disagree as to the relative importance of various markers, the social interactions that give rise to ethnic groups do not create clear and permanent boundaries between them. Observation by social scientists can reveal only the variety of views held by group members and the relative preponderance of some of them. This conception bears little resemblance to legal definitions as we are accustomed to see them, and we can already foresee that it will be a challenge for lawyers to define ethnic identity according to this identity-based conception.

It is true that the indigenous peoples have sometimes rejected the classification of ethnic minority because it does not duly recognise their status of first occupiers of the territory.[24] Yet, the anthropological concept of ethnicity is wide enough to include the indigenous peoples.[25] Indigenous peoples have their own culture, language, way of life, spirituality, relationship with the land, and so on, and for those reasons, they consider themselves to be distinct from the rest of the population of the countries in which they live. Moreover, there is evidence that indigenous difference conforms to the non-essentialist, identity-based model of culture and ethnicity. Thus, anthropologist Joane Nagel shows that American Indian identity has been flexible and has responded to external factors over the last forty years.[26] From a theoretical standpoint, the case of the indigenous peoples and that of other ethnic minorities (e.g., linguistic minorities) raise the same issues of equal treatment and cultural difference. In recent cases, the Supreme Court of Canada has recognised that constitutional provisions dealing with official-language groups and indigenous peoples share the same basic objective (or constitutional value) of "minority protection,"[27] while noting that first occupancy of the land distinguishes the indigenous peoples from other minorities.[28] It is thus appropriate to use the concept of ethnicity to understand what underlies indigenous identity and what political consequences flow from it. Of course, the characteristics of indigenous peoples' ethnicity may be quite different from those of immigrant groups that are often labelled as "ethnic." Indigenous peoples' prior relationship with the land may justify land rights and rights to self-government that immigrant ethnic groups have no claim to.[29] Thus, one must bear in mind that I am using the concept of ethnicity in its anthropological sense, not in its popular reference to visible immigrant communities. Nor by employing that label am I prejudging the legal characterisation of certain ethnic groups: they may at the same time constitute "peoples" who in international law are entitled to self-determination.

We can now appreciate more fully the theoretical and practical advantages of relational conceptions of ethnicity in comparison to conceptions based on race or essentialised culture. The first and most obvious point, as we will see later in this chapter, is that it is much easier to attribute moral relevance to culture than to skin colour. Racial conceptions cannot explain why linguistic minorities and indigenous peoples are granted special rights, while culture can. Second, while racial conceptions view the classificatory features they use as immutable, cultural conceptions acknowledge that culture is not beyond the individual's control. In other words, one can change his or her culture: culture is not innate but acquired. Third, contrary to racial conceptions, but contrary also to essentialist cultural conceptions, relational ethnicity does not assume the existence of discrete groups of people objectively identified by the essential elements of their culture. Rather, modern theorists of ethnicity see group formation and identity ascription as fluid processes. Moreover, the concept of ethnic identity allows for diversity within a cultural group, especially where the ethnic markers that define identity do not cover all aspects of culture. It also recognises that cultures evolve over time and cannot be defined by their supposedly essential elements. Groups can thus define their own ethnic identity from the inside, rather than having it imposed from the outside. Fourth, relational conceptions do not carry, as such, any value judgment to the effect that one ethnic group's culture is superior to that of another. Fifth, ethnic identities may overlap, in particular as a result of processes of intermarriage or immigration. For instance, immigrants from many countries learn French and integrate into Quebec society while retaining cultural bonds to their country or region of origin. If they identify with and are recognised as members by both groups, they may have overlapping ethnic identities. Ethnic identity may also coexist with other identities, such as citizenship in a state: many Francophone Quebeckers feel a strong attachment to Canada, even though they identify themselves primarily as Quebeckers.

Nevertheless, we must be aware that relational conceptions of ethnicity may, in some cases, be morally condemnable. It might be the case that in a given group, a majority of individuals view themselves as members of a specific race. That situation shows that relational identity may be racial, depending on what group members think. Recent media reports concerning the use of genetic testing to assert indigenous identity show that some people still associate ethnic identity and genetic heritage.[30] Moreover, relational ethnicity may very well be imposed by dominant sub-groups within a minority or indigenous people. Relational conceptions of ethnicity may in fact be used to foster prejudice or oppression. As we saw above, ethnicity is a descriptive concept carrying no inherent normative value, so it needs to be assessed against a moral standard. However, before we study the theories that will enable us to perform such a normative assessment, we need to clarify the relationship between ancestry and the conceptions of ethnicity that we have just analysed.

Ancestry and Ethnicity

Another intuitive means of describing ethnic groups and ethnic identity is provided by ancestry. We usually assume that ethnicity is transmitted by parents to their children. But if we link ethnicity and genealogy, are we not embracing racist ideologies? Are we not saying that culture is genetically inherited? Not necessarily.

From a cultural essentialist perspective, it makes sense to define ethnicity by trying to follow the processes by which culture is acquired by individuals. In this regard, the most important process of socialisation by which culture is transmitted to children is provided by the family.[31] Parents teach their children the language, the religion, the customs, the traditions, and the founding myths of their group. They give them a sense of group identity. They show them who their fellow group members are, what land they can call their homeland, and so on. Thus, ancestry would seem to be a logical predictor of a person's identity. If your parents are indigenous, you are very likely to be indigenous as well.

The same holds true when one turns to a relational conception of ethnicity. For the reasons just reviewed, ancestry is likely to be one of the markers that individuals use to identify their fellow group members. Typically, when we seek to determine someone's ethnicity, we ask who that person's parents were (in terms of ethnicity). In such a case, the modern theory of ethnicity would acknowledge that ethnic identity is defined, at least partly, in genealogical terms, without necessarily giving effect to racist ideology.

How can we ascertain whether the use of ancestry reveals a racial conception of ethnicity? Anyone adopting a cultural perspective would readily admit that ancestry is not the sole factor involved in

defining a group's identity. Culture is transmitted in many places
other than the family. Schooling provides another obvious process
of socialisation that contributes to the formation of ethnicity.
Through the teaching of a first language, geography, history, and
literature, the school will make children internalise the distinctive
characteristics of their ethnic group. The acquisition of ethnic identity may also take place in other contexts, such as the work environment, voluntary associations, cultural activities, and so on.
Moreover, ancestry is not a very good predictor where the parents
of a child come from different cultural backgrounds. Thus, where
ancestry is complemented by other factors that define ethnic identity, we are not confronted with a racist conception. To the contrary, the rigid use of ancestry may indicate a racial outlook. Yet
other factors may be at play, especially where a legal definition is
analysed: as we will see in the next chapter, the selection of ancestry
as a criterion of ethnicity may be explained by the fact that other
potential criteria are difficult to assess in a legal process.

THE PRINCIPLE OF EQUALITY

So far, I have set the stage, so to speak, by analysing various conceptions of ethnicity. Ethnicity is a descriptive concept as it relates to
the actual state of things. I will now move to the realm of the normative and study what political theory and law have to say about
equality and minority rights and what basic implications they have
for legal translations of ethnic identity. Let us start with equality.

The concept of equality is central to many philosophical theories
of justice.[32] It is also one of the most important rights guaranteed by
the constitutions of several countries and by widely ratified international treaties. In the few pages that follow, I can give only a
short account of the debates raised by the idea of equality and its
application in the field of law. To structure the discussion, it will be
useful to distinguish between formal and substantive conceptions
of equality.[33]

Formal Equality

A formal conception of equality focuses on how people are treated.
It is not concerned with results, outcomes, or how different individuals fare when they are treated the same. According to Aristotle,

likes must be treated alike: this is the ideal of consistent treatment. The principle of formal equality guarantees that the state does not treat one category of persons more favourably than others; it upholds, in that sense, the ideal of state neutrality and impartiality. It also promotes individual autonomy, in the sense that the actual outcomes that individuals achieve when treated equally are thought to depend exclusively on individual choices or merit.[34]

However, laws are bound to make distinctions of some sort if they are to be effective. For instance, laws directed at relieving victims of industrial accidents define what such accidents are and apply only to persons who fall within that definition. Consumer protection laws give rights only to consumers, not to merchants. The legal classification of situations is therefore inescapable. Hence, when applied in the legal sphere, the principle of equality translates into the prohibition of discrimination: decisions concerning individuals must not be made on certain "suspect" grounds, such as race, sex, religion, age, and so on, unless the use of such a distinction has a valid justification related to the specific decision at issue. The law focuses on decisions or on rules applied to individuals and not on the actual situation of the individual before or after the application of a particular decision or rule.

The fact that the antidiscrimination principle forbids distinction on certain specified grounds generates two sets of problems. First, by requiring that individuals be consistently treated, the principle relies on a comparison: is A treated in the same manner as B? In order to ascertain whether different treatment is based on a prohibited ground, one must select a B who is different, with respect to that ground, from A, but otherwise similarly situated. Thus, to detect sexual discrimination, one must compare the treatment afforded to women with the treatment afforded to men placed in a similar situation. Yet there is a significant risk that the comparison will fail because of a judgment to the effect that unequal treatment flows not from the gender of the victim but rather from a factual difference in the victim's situation that is relevant to the decision to treat her differently. In other words, if the comparator is not shown to be similarly situated, an unfavourable treatment will apparently be explained. This approach was used to obstruct pregnant women's claims to equal treatment. In the *Bliss* case,[35] the Supreme Court of Canada refused to strike down a rule that denied unemployment insurance benefits to pregnant women. As men cannot

become pregnant, said the Court, the differential treatment at issue
was not based on sex, but "on nature." The Court later overruled
itself, noting that the fact that only women could become pregnant
proved that a distinction based on pregnancy was really a distinction based on gender and that it was unjust to require women to
bear all the costs associated with pregnancy.[36]

Second, the comparative methodology requires victims of discrimination to conform to dominant norms if they want to be
considered "alike" and deserving of equal treatment.[37] The antidiscrimination principle constructs pairs of groups identified by the
prohibited grounds. One member of the pair (men, white persons,
Christians, heterosexuals, and so on) is deemed to be normal, the
standard, the baseline for comparison, whereas the other member
(women, indigenous peoples, persons of colour, Jews or Muslims,
gays and lesbians, and so on) is considered abnormal or different.
For instance, if they have children, women who compete with men
in the business or professional sectors may have much trouble conforming to the male norm of working long hours. They may thus be
denied promotions or equal pay. Under a formal-equality approach,
that differential treatment could be said to be based on the number
of hours they work, not on their sex, obscuring the fact that it may
be legitimate for men and women to have career patterns that are
different but of equal value. Formal equality therefore represses difference and induces assimilation to the dominant norm. Such an
impact may be felt more strongly by cultural minorities or indigenous peoples, whose values may be very different from those of a
comparator chosen from the dominant society.[38]

Beyond the methodological problems arising from the search for
a comparator, the actual benefits of formal equality remain limited
in that it forbids only the disparate treatment of individuals and
excludes from consideration disparate results flowing from identical treatment. Yet, even where persons are treated consistently,
considerable social inequality may flow from the historical subordination or domination of a group or from the prejudices that are
ingrained in the fabric of society.[39] As those inequalities are in no
way related to the personal choices of the individuals concerned,
they cannot be just. Recent reformulations of the liberal doctrine
recognise the necessity of redistribution schemes that aim, at least,
to redress the consequences of unchosen disadvantage.[40] Hence,

justice requires the state to equalise, to a certain degree, the fortunes of different individuals.

Substantive Equality

A conception of equality can be called "substantive" when it scrutinises results (the actual situation of individuals) rather than treatment (the decisions or rules applied to individuals). Thus, the goal of equality would be not to treat people consistently but to ensure that the application of the law leaves them in similar situations. Substantive equality is thus a concept that involves an element of redistribution.[41] Yet, it is an open-ended concept, because there is no obvious means to select the object to be equalised (total wealth, income, education). It is beyond the scope of this book to canvass the debate between theories of "equality of results," "equality of opportunity," "equality of resources," or "equality of capabilities."[42]

As the primary goal of substantive equality is to equalise certain results, it follows that in certain cases this might require unequal treatment, contrary to the principle of formal equality. This unequal treatment may pursue two kinds of goals: facilitating the integration of the minority into the majority through the remediation of pre-existing disadvantage or legitimating the minority's difference. I will analyse those two possibilities in turn.

The first of those two strands proceeds from the premise that members of the minority suffer a disadvantage if they wish to integrate into the majority or to compete with majority members on a level playing field. To take the example of the United States, it is well known that Blacks who seek employment face systemic disadvantage and that non-English speakers have very limited opportunities of employment. That disadvantage is not the result of individual choice, as one does not select his or her skin colour or mother tongue. Thus, justice calls for compensation in order to redress this imbalance. This line of argument can justify programs of affirmative action, which give a preference to members of disadvantaged groups (such as Blacks or women) in training, hiring, and so forth. Those programs usually aim at incorporating a significant number of minority members into certain areas of the workforce where they have previously been underrepresented, in order to break the circle of systemic discrimination and prejudice.[43]

The remedial aspect of substantive equality can also come into play where knowledge of the majority language is essential for various forms of social interaction. For instance, the United States Supreme Court held that the absence of programs to teach English to non-English speaking pupils violated those pupils' right to the equal protection of the laws.[44] While the Court did not specify what remedial measures were needed, there are presently in the United States various programs seeking to provide pupils with the required fluency in English to be able to benefit from English-language instruction.[45] Thus, by subsidising the learning of English, the state attempts to remove the burden borne by children whose mother tongue is different.

Yet programs of affirmative action or programs of language acquisition are assimilative in purpose. They seek to achieve a better integration of the minority into the majority.[46] They view sexual, racial, linguistic, or ethnic difference as something that must be overcome in order for disadvantaged groups to be able to participate fully in society. Their ultimate aim is to make gender or racial difference no more socially relevant than, say, differences in hair or eye colour. But as we saw above, they take social rules, institutions and practices as givens. The majority is the norm. For instance, the attitude towards minority-language groups in the United States rests on the assumption that the bulk of social interaction in that country will take place in English, so that it is necessary that non-English speaking pupils become fluent in English. (A controversy rages over whether English immersion or bilingual education is the best manner of achieving that goal.) Policies of preferential hiring for women or for members of racial or ethnic minorities do not seek to modify the organisation or structure of workplaces. They simply try to achieve a better distribution of positions within the existing labour market. In both cases, the goal is for minority persons to become like the majority. This is entirely unsatisfactory to minorities, such as the Francophones and the indigenous peoples of Canada, who have successfully resisted assimilation and who now wish to retain their distinctive identity.

In contrast, a second strand of substantive equality calls for the adaptation of society to sexual, linguistic, or cultural difference.[47] Contrary to affirmative action policies, this adaptation would not be viewed as temporary, to remain in effect only until the minority becomes fully integrated. Rather, minorities would be allowed to retain and express their difference without suffering from disadvantage as a result.

This approach is the basis for the concept of indirect discrimination: a rule or a practice that treats everyone consistently may nevertheless be considered discriminatory if it has a particular impact on a disadvantaged group.[48] One solution may be to create exemptions to the rule for members of that group. Thus, American and Canadian courts have held that employers must try to adapt the work schedules of employees whose religion mandates a day of rest other than Sunday (the day of rest of the Christian majority).[49] Yet, this approach might have the effect of perpetuating stereotypes against the minority, who could be viewed by other workers as benefiting from better treatment than that afforded to members of the majority. It also stops short of questioning the validity of the impugned rule. Hence, a better solution is to strike down rules that disproportionately affect members of a disadvantaged group, if the person who made the rule is unable to offer a non-discriminatory justification for it. This was what the United States Supreme Court did in the famous *Griggs* case,[50] where an employer's hiring practices included literacy tests that bore no relationship to the duties of the work and that disproportionately affected African-Americans, who for a long time had had schools of inferior quality. Physical strength and height requirements are other examples of rules that have been struck down, as they constituted indirect discrimination against women.[51]

Nevertheless, the concept of indirect discrimination remains limited, as it focuses on the relative impact of a rule on certain groups. Applying that concept does not lead to substantial changes in the structure of society. It may equalise certain burdens borne by minorities, but it does not modify the global distribution of power between dominant and disadvantaged groups.[52] Therefore, a substantive conception of equality may be thought of as requiring the adoption of different rules to address the special situation of minorities or disadvantaged groups.[53] For instance, it might require that paid maternity leave be made available to women in order to compensate for the burdens associated with pregnancy and childbirth,[54] that an interpretation service be offered to deaf people who must receive medical services[55] or that minority-language education be offered to pupils whose mother tongue is not that of the majority.[56] In all those cases, the majority and the minority are treated differently, allowing both groups to express their particularities without incurring burdens or disadvantage. The condition of the minority is not seen as a deviation from the majority norm; rather, both are deemed equally deserving of respect, thus requiring a different legal treatment.

One of the challenges common to doctrines of formal and substantive equality is to avoid the construction of fixed categories of persons who are presumed to suffer from discrimination. The basic problem is that equality is usually implemented by reference to categories that have been proved by social science to be without basis (race) or that are now understood as constructed concepts (ethnicity). The challenge is to promote the equality of a disadvantaged minority without imposing a rigid view of that minority's culture or identity, which might happen if we are unaware of the constructed nature of the elements we use to define the group. This is illustrated by the related problems of essentialism and failure to respond to intersectionality.

Essentialism flows from the failure of the comparative methodology to take into account differences among members of those categories. Rather, there is a tendency to essentialise the characteristics of the group: all women are presumed to share the problems of the typical woman, all Francophones are presumed to have identical interests, and so on. However, lumping together all persons who share one characteristic may not lead to the accurate description of an individual's situation.[57] To the contrary, it may lead to further stereotyping, in the sense that this method of categorising people assumes that all persons possessing one characteristic are similar for the purposes of equality analysis. Thus, all women would be presumed to work in so-called "women employment ghettos" and to have primary responsibility for child care, ignoring the situation of women who hold managerial positions, of women without children, of immigrant women, and so on. If a given measure has a particular impact on the latter groups, it will be difficult for them to prove discrimination, because their experience is not that of the "typical woman."

The problem of intersectionality arises where describing discrimination as involving distinctions based on one particular ground would obscure the specific situation of groups defined by the intersection of two (or more) such grounds,[58] like black women in the United States or, as we will see in chapter 3, indigenous women in

Canada. The situation of indigenous women cannot be assimilated to that of indigenous men nor to that of non-indigenous women; rather, they suffer from specific disadvantages flowing from their specific social situation defined by both race and gender. It is not possible, in those cases, to isolate one ground (either gender or race) as the basis of the unfavourable treatment that the victims receive, and antidiscrimination laws that focus on single grounds will not afford a full remedy.

Of course, affording a different legal treatment to the members of a minority may be reminiscent of the infamous "separate but equal doctrine," whereby the segregation of Blacks in the United States was held to be consistent with equality. To be consistent with substantive equality, differential treatment must not be a disguised manner of imposing burdens or furthering stereotypes. In the same fashion, it has been pointed out that early-twentieth-century legislation aimed at protecting women (for example, through the prohibition of night work) also had the effect of imposing certain burdens on women (for example, by restricting employment opportunities for women).[59] Thus, while substantive equality calls for the different legal treatment of minorities, there may sometimes be a fine line between a measure that fosters substantive equality and one that imposes burdens and gives effect to prejudice.

The foregoing discussion should have made clear that adopting a substantive conception of equality is necessary for the promotion of the interests of minorities. Formal equality, with its emphasis on sameness and integration, cannot respond to the needs of minorities who wish to retain their cultural or linguistic differences. Thus, I will adopt a substantive perspective in the remainder of this book, while pointing out, where relevant, the shortcomings of a formal approach. A substantive conception of equality now enables us to study the third main element of my theoretical framework, the theory of minority rights.

MINORITY RIGHTS THEORY

Minority rights have existed for a long time in many countries, going back to antiquity or the Ottoman Empire. Well-known examples of the last century were the "minority treaties" concluded after the First World War, which guaranteed certain rights to minority populations in the new countries of Eastern Europe. The failure of those treaties and their role in paving the way for the Second World War fostered much suspicion of the concept and led the architects of the human rights guarantees put in place after 1945 to emphasise universal rights rather than minority protections. From a theoretical standpoint, it was assumed that equality called for the end of the distinct treatment of ethnic minorities. The interest for minority rights theory resurfaced in the early 1990s, after the collapse of the Berlin Wall underscored the need for ethnic accommodation in many Eastern European countries. Minority rights theory provides a philosophical basis for the protections enacted in several countries and by the Council of Europe. It also helps to rationalise political compromises that have been in place for a long time in Western countries such as Belgium, Switzerland, Italy, or Canada.

Based broadly on liberal philosophy, most strands of minority rights theory embrace individual autonomy and a substantive conception of equality as their normative foundations. Yet, as mentioned above, there is no consensus about what elements of a person's circumstances must be equalised. How access to culture can or should be equalised is not self-evident. The contribution of minority rights theorists has been to prove why members of minority cultures suffer certain disadvantages that must be remedied to ensure justice. Authors are not in agreement, however, about exactly what aspects of a person's cultural identity are sources of injustice. In the following pages, I will attempt to describe and classify the most common theories according to the conception of ethnicity that they appear to rely upon (race, essentialised culture, or relational ethnicity). I will also mention group-based theories of minority rights and explain their relationship to conceptions of ethnicity.

Ensuring Racial Equality?

The injustices committed in the name of race over the last centuries have been so monstrous that today any mention of laws that single out persons of one particular race only revives memories of slavery, apartheid, and the Holocaust. It has now become widely accepted that race is morally irrelevant: we should make decisions about individuals irrespective of their race, and any consideration of a person's race is morally wrong. To use an oft-quoted phrase, laws must be colour-blind.[60] This view has become reflected in the most basic precepts of our legal system. The Universal Declaration of

Human Rights opens with an article proclaiming that "all human beings are born free and equal in dignity and rights" and that they are all "are endowed with reason and conscience," thus implicitly rejecting racist ideologies.[61] This rejection is made explicit in the International Convention on the Elimination of All Forms of Racial Discrimination, which states in its preamble that "any doctrine of superiority based on racial differentiation is scientifically false, morally condemnable, socially unjust and dangerous, and that there is no justification for racial discrimination, in theory or in practice, anywhere."[62]

One exception to this moral irrelevance occurs when a society is so ridden with racial injustice that it is necessary to take measures to redress the situation of persons who are victims of racial oppression. Legal prohibitions on racial discrimination usually make an exception for programs aimed at improving the condition of a disadvantaged racialised minority.[63] Those programs are considered valid even though they employ a racial distinction and make, contrary to the general rule, race morally (and legally) relevant. The aim of those programs may be to offer compensation for past injustice. It may also be to root out systemic forms of racial discrimination in a society.[64] Yet, this exception to the moral irrelevance of race is limited in scope and duration. The special treatment of a racial group must be linked to an identifiable injustice that was or is done to them.[65] It cannot be justified by the wish to maintain a degree of separateness between racial groups. Thus, self-government schemes would not fall within the scope of the exception. Moreover, because separate treatment cannot last longer than would be necessary for the attainment of equality,[66] advocates of affirmative action programs in the United States usually make the point that these programs will be discontinued when African-Americans no longer suffer from discrimination. (Of course, the larger the injustice, the more time it will take to reach that point.)

A racial conception of indigenous identity may, in some circumstances, provide some explanation of and redress for the injustices visited upon the indigenous peoples. It is certainly true that many people in the mainstream society do hold racist views against the indigenous peoples. The Supreme Court has stated accurately that such racism has led to systemic discrimination (presumably racial) against them in the criminal justice system.[67] And laws such as the one that was struck down in the *Drybones* case are based on racist thinking.[68] Showing the racist basis of such mistreatment is essential to their powerful denunciation: you then prove that the law is based on mistaken social conceptions that have no scientific foundations.

However, viewing the indigenous peoples exclusively through a racial lens leaves little room for granting them special rights. If a specific injustice against an indigenous people can be identified, reparation or restitution is in order. This is simply an application of the idea that when a wrongful action has impacted a racialised group, reparation or restitution must, of necessity, benefit the same racialised group that was harmed in the first place. Yet, this simple case of corrective justice captures only a small subset of the contemporary rights of the indigenous peoples in countries such as Canada or in emerging norms of international law. Rights of self-government, cultural rights, and several forms of land rights are intended to protect indigenous distinctiveness for the future, rather than to remedy a specific racist injustice of the past. In those cases, the principle of the moral irrelevance of race would dictate that the indigenous peoples cannot have a separate government or a separate territory on the basis of their racial difference only. Because race is now seen as a mistaken social construction devoid of biological basis, indigenous self-government would perpetuate a scientific error. Thus, Tom Flanagan, a prominent critic of Canada's current indigenous policy, argues that aboriginal self-government "makes race the constitutive factor of the political order" and would "redefine Canada as an association of racial communities."[69] In the same vein, the United States Supreme Court struck down legislation benefitting native Hawaiians because it employed distinctions that the Court viewed as "racial."[70]

Equalising Cultural Burdens

If we must abandon race as a defining factor of rights-bearing minorities, the usual reflex is to turn to culture. One of the most popular accounts of minority rights, that of Canadian philosopher Will Kymlicka, is an attempt to reconcile cultural difference with liberal philosophy. As a liberal, Kymlicka starts from the moral principle of individual autonomy, which allows individuals to live their lives according to their own values. Moreover, everyone should have an opportunity to revise his or her own views about what a good life is. This is where culture comes into play. Cultures give their members a range of options and a set of possible meanings for their actions, enabling them to exercise a meaningful choice as to how to conduct their lives.[71] Therefore, being a member of a culture is a precondition to the realisation of liberalism's main goal and is thus a primary good, a basic need of all individuals.

Having proved the importance of culture, we may then ask why it is important that people be allowed to be members of their *own* culture. Can the state simply not insist that minority cultures assimilate into the majority? The majority culture, after all, could provide shared meanings and a frame of reference for the actions of minority members, and it would satisfy the individual's basic needs. While the following account may not do justice to Kymlicka's rich argument, the justification of minority rights based on culture focuses on the burdens or costs associated with requiring persons to function in a culture other than their own. Asking minority members to forego, in whole or in part, their own culture in order to function in the country's majority culture imposes a heavy burden. To take only language as an example, it means that minority members will be required to learn the language of the majority, while the reverse is not true. The cost (financial, personal, or otherwise) of learning a second language is a differential burden imposed on the minority only. It is an injustice inherent in situations of cultural difference.[72]

How should the state (and its legal system) react to those differential burdens? One view, known as "benign neglect," considers culture as a purely private matter. Cultures rise and fall when individuals invest in them or decide to assimilate in another one. State intervention in matters of culture would be tantamount to the imposition of a particular conception of the good life, which cuts against the grain of liberal philosophy. Yet benign neglect leaves market forces at work, and the market favours the majority culture. For example, Spanish-speaking Americans must learn English if they want to have significant work opportunities.

But beyond the effect of market forces, benign neglect fails to take into account that States cannot be neutral between cultures.[73] Even though states may purport to adopt laws, institutions, doctrines, and symbols that are culturally neutral, they are bound to reflect the values of the majority culture. Majorities tend to consider their values as universal, which can be oppressive to minorities who do not share them.[74] Language is the best example. Every state has a limited set of official languages, most often one or two.

The state bureaucracy functions in that or those languages, and so do the schools. The state thereby gives a powerful advantage to members of the majority culture.[75] State-funded schools are certainly the most important institutions for the transmission of culture and language. For instance, if Francophones in the English-speaking provinces of Canada had to send their children to English schools (as was usually the case during most of the twentieth century), it would be much more difficult for them to transmit their culture and language to their children than for members of the majority. The same is also true of national holidays and weekly days of rest, which generally coincide with the majority's religious holidays. In addition, in the case of the indigenous peoples, the state implicitly or explicitly sanctions an economic model that favours the accumulation of wealth through extraction and sometimes overuse of natural resources, which is a significant obstacle for those who wish to maintain a traditional indigenous way of life. Another example is the majority school calendar, which does not allow for the indigenous peoples' traditional hunting periods, thereby interfering with the transmission of hunting traditions to children. Moreover, even assuming those issues are raised and debated in the political process of the state, there is no reason to believe that minorities will not be systematically outvoted.

Being a member of a minority culture within a state therefore comes with burdens not shared by members of the majority. State inaction will in fact reinforce them. Hence, there is a powerful argument that the state should attempt to equalise those burdens by granting special rights to the minority. While such special treatment would appear to violate the principle of formal equality, because all citizens are not formally treated equally, it furthers the principle of substantive equality.[76] Members of the minority are in a different situation than members of the majority. Their identical treatment would amount to inequality. Some measures must be adopted to take into account their cultural difference.

Because they are based upon individual autonomy, cultural justifications lead to measures that safeguard the individual's liberty to make cultural choices. Kymlicka, for one, views unfavourably "internal restrictions" that a group might impose on its members to ensure a form of cultural conformity.[77] Other theorists insist that members of the group should be afforded a "right of exit," that is, a right to dissociate from the group and no longer be subject to its potentially oppressive rules.[78] These arguments would suggest that membership control is at odds with liberal theory, at least insofar as membership rules would deny individuals the right to leave the group. However, more recent analyses, such as those of Dwight Newman and Alan Patten, suggest that some collective interests may justifiy restricting the individual's right to exit the group or replacing it with an opportunity to influence the group's decisions.[79] They may do so if some of the group's interests are non-individualisable or if exit by one member would create "free-riding" problems, that is, if it would adversely affect those who stayed in the group. Under appropriate circumstances, these analyses would support membership rules that limit the exercise of individual will. In other words, groups can prevent exit to some extent. This possibility will be further studied in chapter 5.

Equal Respect for Identity

Kymlicka's theory of minority rights as protections for the autonomy interests of minority members has sparked much interest and discussion. However, the popularity of that theory should not make us forget that there are individual interests beyond autonomy that may also justify minority rights. For instance, Charles Taylor has underlined the importance of the recognition of one's identity.[80] In the same vein, philosophers such as Joseph Raz, Yael Tamir, and Bhikhu Parekh have asserted that membership in one's own cultural or national group provides the individual with a sense of personal stability and a frame of reference.[81] Raz, for one, points out that membership in a cultural group is a matter of belonging, not achievement, and that this allows the individual to be anchored in an identity irrespective of what one does and of whether one is successful in one's endeavours or not.[82] Parekh, for his part, underlines the fact that cultural membership gives one's identity "a social basis, emotional energy and a measure of stability and objectivity."[83]

The common thread in these theories is their reliance on a relational conception of ethnicity. It is not culture per se that produces self-esteem or stability. It is, rather, membership in a group that is respected by outsiders that makes those goods available to the individual. That has nothing to do with culture or the promotion of individual autonomy. Suppose, for example, that a fellow Quebecker wins an Olympic gold medal. The sense of pride that I may feel derives from my perception that the athlete and I share a common identity. When I meet other people who identify me as a Quebecker, they may show increased respect for me (or for Quebeckers in general) because they associate me with the medalist.

The nuance between protecting culture and protecting identity is made explicit by Tim Schouls in his study of representations of indigenous identity in Canada. He rejects culture as the basis of the rights of the indigenous peoples. According to him,

> Rather than stress distinctive cultural elements or the preservation of nations as central to Aboriginal identity, a relational pluralist stresses that a healthy Aboriginal identity is the outcome of Aboriginal communities and the members within them having control over their lives in ways consistent with their own aspirations ... According to this approach, then, key from the point of view of justice is that Aboriginal communities possess the right to develop and give expression to any element of communal identity, whether culturally distinctive or otherwise.[84]

In this context, membership control may be a tool employed by a group to define its own identity. According to Schouls, indigenous peoples "need access to political space fenced in by boundaries so that they can develop their identities free from external interference."[85] Thus, specific cultural traits are not protected from the outside. Rather, the group is given the freedom to develop its own culture without interference. But preventing such interference requires the exclusion of non-members. In the same vein, Margaret Moore argues that while changes within a culture should not be discouraged, the speed and direction of those changes should be controlled by the members of that culture and not imposed from the outside.[86]

Equal Respect for Pre-existing Groups

Another strand of political theory puts the emphasis on justice between groups rather than on culture or identity. Insisting on the collective aspect of justice brings relationships of colonialism, conquest, and dispossession under scrutiny. Several indigenous scholars have championed this approach, often under the name of "treaty federalism."[87]

Group justice arguments are usually made on two rather different planes. The first category of arguments relates to private rights or interests that are usually thought to be compensable in monetary terms. Most land claims of the indigenous peoples are based on the idea that past dispossession was wrongful and calls for compensation. The Supreme Court of Canada has made prior presence, or the "right of the first occupier," one of the main bases of its aboriginal rights jurisprudence.[88] To be sure, prior presence, or what philosophers call "original acquisition," is not a unanimously accepted moral theory.[89] It may be difficult to assess who the original possessor of a particular piece of land is. Most importantly, too heavy a reliance on the past may prevent distributive justice: resources would be allocated according to history rather than current needs.[90] Trying to correct injustices of a distant past also raises the difficulties associated with counterfactual reasoning: no one really knows what would have happened if an unjust act had not taken place a long time ago. Other people may have formed legitimate bonds to the lands in the meantime. Claims for compensation fade over time.[91]

Despite these shortcomings, the doctrine of original acquisition provides a powerful justification for the land claims of the indigenous peoples.[92] When it is applied at a general, collective level and when it is used to compare two claims, rather than to judge one claim in the abstract, much of the criticism can be deflected. Relative to the European colonists, indigenous peoples were certainly the first occupiers of America, Australia, and other parts of the world. They had formed bonds with the land over many generations. Hence, as between the indigenous peoples taken globally and the colonists, indigenous peoples no doubt had a better right. Moreover, historical arguments may gain strength from their combination with arguments based on culture.[93] In this regard, Dwight Newman has recently argued that prior occupation may in fact be a proxy for community connections to land; that is, it may be a proxy for the fact that a particular land may be a significant component of a group's identity, so that recognizing rights to the land would actually make members of that group more secure in their identity.[94]

The second version of the historical argument focuses not on property rights but on sovereignty. Indigenous peoples were sovereign before the arrival of the European colonisers in the sense that they were identifiable populations living independently of one another on definite territories under their own political arrangements. Many scholars have shown that international law provides no convincing justification for the later denial of the sovereignty of the indigenous peoples.[95] Again using the framework of compensation for past wrongs, it can be said that denial of sovereignty is an injustice that calls for reparation.[96] Authors within this current generally base their arguments on the principle whereby dealings between different peoples should be based on mutual consent.[97] The legal translation of this moral requirement is the right to self-determination: every people should be free to determine its political status, through autonomy arrangements or perhaps even independence.

Group-based historical arguments suggest that the institutions of the minority should have the power to enact their own membership criteria. This is simply a mirror image of the citizenship criteria that the state, presumably controlled by the majority group, enacts for itself. Equality of peoples would require that if states have the power to enact their own citizenship laws, national minorities and indigenous peoples should be allowed to do the same.[98] However, equality of peoples does not have much to say about a particular people's conception of its own identity. In practice, that identity will obey one of the three conceptions outlined above (a racial, cultural, or relational conception). Moreover, if pushed to the extreme, arguments about group autonomy may have the effect of legitimating discrimination.[99] For that reason, I will not stress group-based justifications of minority rights in the remainder of this book, except to argue in favour of the power of minorities to define their own membership criteria themselves.

The concepts studied in this chapter provide us with the analytical tools required to refine our understanding, from descriptive and normative perspectives, of the laws that purport to regulate membership in linguistic minorities or indigenous peoples. First, we have seen that there are various conceptions of the bonds between such groups and their members. In social science this is known as the theory of ethnicity, and for my purposes I have classified conceptions of ethnicity in three categories: racial, cultural, and relational.

We then saw how the principle of equality is now generally understood in a substantive sense, which opens the door to the principled recognition of special rights to certain minority groups. Racial conceptions of identity do not justify special rights, except perhaps measures aimed at combating racism. (I noted, however, that defining a group through ancestry does not necessarily evince a racist conception.) Today, minority rights are mainly justified in cultural or historical terms. Cultural arguments stress the importance of equalising the burdens borne by members of cultural minorities, while historical arguments focus on the reparation of past injustice. As we will see in the next chapter, both strands of justification may, in the proper circumstances, ground systems of membership control.

2

Assessing Membership Control

Minority rights have received much theoretical attention over the last few decades. As we have seen in the last chapter, several lines of argument have been put forward to explain what constitutes an apparent breach of equality. Moreover, these theories are increasingly taking into account the current perspectives of social science on the treatment of human diversity. Yet as one would expect, many aspects of minority rights remain highly controversial. In this chapter, I will focus on one of those controversial aspects: membership control. The analysis will be based on legal concepts, marking the transition from the philosophical perspective of the previous chapter towards the case studies of chapters 3, 4, and 5.

The first part of this chapter is devoted to collective rights, such as the right to self-determination in international law or minority rights that are found in Canada's constitution. These rights provide the justification of membership control. In practical terms, this means that minorities have a legal argument to assert jurisdiction over the definition of their own membership rules. Justifications of membership control are also highly relevant to the legal analysis of alleged conflicts between membership rules and individual rights, which will be the focus of the second part of this chapter. Equality is the individual right most likely to be invoked against particular membership criteria. I will explain the framework employed by courts when dealing with claims of breaches of equality, showing how that framework forces membership criteria to correspond to social or "actual" conceptions of the ethnicity of the group involved. I will also demonstrate that the right to culture, which is sometimes used to challenge membership rules, leads to similar conclusions.

It is true that self-determination or equality have not always been recognised as fundamental rights. The law presented here is the current one. Its application to past situations, such as the "old" Indian Act analysed in chapter 3, may be anachronistic to some degree. However, the exercise is worth pursuing, because it reveals the injustice of past legal rules and the flaws of past decisions.

RESPECT FOR GROUP RIGHTS OR INTERESTS

Our gradual transition from the philosophical sphere to the legal sphere will begin with the question of group rights or interests. I will outline the rights recognised for groups in international and Canadian law and then evaluate whether such rights necessarily imply that group membership should be controlled. Assuming a positive answer to the latter question, I will also discuss whether the power to control membership should be exercised by the group itself, and under what conditions, or whether the state retains an interest in the matter.

The issue of group rights remains shrouded with controversy, especially on the international plane, and in many respects there is a lack of legal precedent. Hence, the discussion below necessarily appeals more to general principles than to positive legal rules. Yet it is useful to review the interplay between group rights and membership control, first because it helps in understanding the rationale behind membership control and second because it helps in identifying the legislative objective that courts scrutinise when they assess alleged human rights violations according to the framework that is analysed in the second half of this chapter.

The Law of Self-determination and Collective Cultural Rights

The most celebrated, if not controversial, legal source of group or minority rights is the right of all peoples to self-determination guaranteed by, among other legal instruments, article 1 of the International Covenant on Civil and Political Rights. If an ethnic group or a minority qualifies as a "people," it is a beneficiary of that right, and it may freely determine its political status. However, the evolution of the right to self-determination over the last forty years has been a history of backtracking, with states and international bodies trying to forestall any attempt at secession that might be defended as an exercise of self-determination.[1] In practice, self-determination has lost much of its legal force, being transformed more or less into a right to participation[2] or a right to democracy, and international bodies have adopted quite different norms with respect to indigenous peoples, on the one hand, and national or linguistic minorities, on the other hand.[3]

Indigenous Peoples. Indigenous peoples are increasingly recognised as "peoples" possessing the right to self-determination under article 1 of the Covenant,[4] especially in article 3 of the United Nations Declaration on the Rights of Indigenous Peoples.[5] Nevertheless, the scope of self-determination is generally thought to exclude secession and to be limited to "internal" self-government within existing states.[6] Yet emerging norms of international law suggest that self-determination, even in its internal aspects, comprises the right of peoples to define their own membership.

The clearest support for an indigenous jurisdiction over indigenous identity is found in the United Nations Declaration on the Rights of Indigenous Peoples, which states, at article 33, that "Indigenous peoples have the right to determine their own identity or membership in accordance with their customs and traditions." Because this is a collective right, it is a right of the group itself to control its membership, not a right of the individual to claim membership irrespective of the criteria enacted by the group. While it expressly refrains from any pronouncement about self-determination, International Labour Organisation Convention No. 169 states that the most important factor in the determination of indigenous identity is the opinion of the groups concerned.[7] This suggests that membership is a particularly important jurisdiction in the context of self-determination or self-government. The power of the indigenous peoples to control their membership also flows from the principle, put forward by the influential Martínez Cobo report, that a person is a member of an indigenous people where two conditions are met: (1) the person identifies with the group (subjective identification) and (2) the group recognises him or her (objective identification).[8]

In Canada, the federal government has accepted that the aboriginal rights protected by sections 25 and 35 of the Constitution Act, 1982, include a right of self-government.[9] Still, the precise content of the rights so protected remains unclear. Indigenous peoples have argued that defining their own membership is one of the most central aspects of the right to self-government.[10] American case law also provides support for the proposition that defining membership is an inherent power of indigenous groups.[11] Yet Canadian case law on the subject remains unclear. There is only one case at the trial level in which the issue was discussed. The judge concluded that indigenous peoples, in pre-contact times, did not control their membership and were constituted of small groups under the informal leadership of respected hunters, groups that anyone could join or leave at will.[12] Hence, there could be no aboriginal right to control membership. The Supreme Court has not dealt with this specific issue, but it did state in a 1996 case that it would recognise self-government rights only on a piecemeal basis, according to the test applied for other aboriginal rights, that is, that the practice or custom in question must have been an integral part of a distinctive indigenous culture before contact with European colonists.[13] This test, which was designed in the context of hunting and fishing rights, is inadequate because it freezes indigenous culture in a distant past,[14] and it is difficult to understand why practices of a distant past should be used to define the rights of the indigenous peoples in a modern context. More recent decisions suggest that courts are moving away from that approach and would be ready to recognise a more general right to self-government that would not require proof of particular pre-contact practices or customs.[15] For the reasons that follow, such a general right should include a right to control membership.

National or Linguistic Minorities. Where a minority does not qualify as a people and is not entitled to self-determination, its members still have the right to enjoy their own culture, under article 27 of the International Covenant on Civil and Political Rights. Yet despite some suggestions to the contrary, when applying to groups other than indigenous peoples, article 27 has been interpreted as providing only for a very limited bundle of rights,[16] excluding any form of group autonomy.[17] Moreover, international bodies have insisted that article 27 guarantees rights to individuals, not to groups. The United Nations Declaration on the Rights of Persons Belonging to National or Ethnic, Religious or Linguistic Minorities,[18] which purports to provide guidelines for the implementation of article 27, refers only to individual rights. Thus, many states in which there is a significant ethnic or linguistic minority have been able to resist calls for group autonomy.

The focus on individual rights in the interpretation of article 27 makes it difficult to suggest that minorities have a right to define their own membership, because the right to control membership is in essence a group right. Most writings about minority rights in international or European law are based on the premise that minority membership is a matter of individual choice and should be subject to minimal state regulation.[19] The Human Rights Committee cases dealing with membership issues provide no support for a group right to control membership under article 27.[20] This cautious attitude towards membership control is also apparent in the international instruments on the subject. Contrary to the Declaration on the Rights of Indigenous Peoples, which readily admits membership control, the United Nations Declaration on the Rights of Persons Belonging to National or Ethnic, Religious or Linguistic Minorities contains only one provision dealing with membership control, and it implies that no one may be considered a member of a minority against his or her will or be forced to exercise minority rights.[21] Such a principle does not exclude membership control altogether but makes self-identification a necessary part of any set or criteria employed to attribute membership.

The Council of Europe Framework Convention for the Protection of National Minorities adopts a more confused position.[22] While its article 3 suggests that membership in a minority is an individual choice, its explanatory memorandum states that the "individual's subjective choice is inseparably linked to objective criteria relevant to the person's identity."[23] No details are provided, however, as to what those objective criteria are and who has the power to decide those issues. For its part, the United Nations Committee on the Elimination of Racial Discrimination has issued a recommendation to the effect that racial or ethnic identity should be based, if no justification exists to the contrary, upon self-identification by the individual concerned.[24] This leaves little space for membership control.

Canadian law does not recognise any right of linguistic minorities to self-determination. Those minorities do not have norm-enacting political institutions and cannot control their own membership. It is only where a provincial government can be said to represent a minority, such as in the case of Quebec, that the minority has, through the provincial political process, the power to enact membership criteria for purposes that are within the province's jurisdiction. (This explains why Quebec was able to enact membership criteria with respect to education, a provincial jurisdiction.)

Membership Control as a Consequence of Collective Minority Rights

Whether they do it as a result of international obligations or on grounds of political expediency or justice, many states, such as Canada, do provide significant group or collective rights to indigenous peoples or ethnic or linguistic minorities. When this is so, the collective nature of those rights or the collective aspect of the interests they seek to further may require a membership control system. In other words, the realisation of those collective rights would be jeopardised if membership in the group were not regulated.

Rights to Scarce Resources. The most obvious case where membership must be controlled occurs when particular resources are set apart for use by members of a minority. In Canada, the best example is, of course, the land rights of the indigenous peoples. Indian reserves are parcels of land, the use of which is granted to particular Indian bands. Bands, in turn, can allocate portions of their reserves to their members.[25] Non-members are not entitled to any form of permanent rights on a reserve.[26] Therefore, it is necessary to distinguish members from non-members of Indian bands.

Indigenous land rights also comprise rights respecting natural resources, such as the right to harvest wildlife. Sometimes commercial rights are recognised and the stakes can be high.[27] The state or the indigenous people, depending on whether the resource is allocated on an individual or a collective basis, will want to control the membership of those who claim a share of those resources. When petroleum or gas was found under the reserves of a few Indian bands in the Canadian West, it was not surprising that membership in those bands became the object of litigation.[28]

Indigenous people also receive benefits other than land from the state. One of the most important of those benefits is a tax exemption for income earned or goods purchased on a reserve.[29] Certain public services available to everyone are also provided on different terms to indigenous persons. For instance, they are entitled to the reimbursement of university tuition fees and to a wider range of free medical services than the rest of the population. For the individual, those benefits may be very significant, whereas their cost to the state cannot be discounted.

The common thread of those situations is that there is a limited pool of resources available to the indigenous peoples. Justice and fairness require that these resources be used only by their intended beneficiaries. If there is no independent control of the ethnic identity of the individuals who draw resources from that pool, persons who have no legitimate claim to be members of an indigenous people will be tempted to avail themselves of a portion of those resources, thereby leaving a reduced portion for the legitimate members. As anthropologist James Clifton says, "every time the value of being Indian increases, the number of persons of marginal or ambiguous ancestry who claim to be Indians increases."[30]

A decision of the United Nations Human Rights Committee shows how the scarcity of resources can justify important controls on membership.[31] Ivan Kitok was a Swedish citizen of Sami origin whose family had traditionally engaged in reindeer breeding, an activity central to Sami culture. However, Kitok engaged in other activities for a period of more than three years and, according to Swedish legislation, he thereby lost his right to participate in reindeer breeding. The Human Rights Committee was concerned by the fact that someone who was "objectively" an ethnic Sami was not treated as such under Swedish law. However, given that the land available for reindeer breeding was very limited, that it was necessary to restrict the number of people who engaged in that activity, and that Kitok could still exercise other rights important to Sami culture, such as hunting and fishing, the committee found that the restriction was reasonable and that there was no violation of article 27 of the International Covenant on Civil and Political Rights.

Defining Personal Jurisdictions. Certain aspects of the political autonomy that is recognised for indigenous peoples require that membership be controlled. This political autonomy is exercised by bodies elected by the adult population of indigenous communities. Communities governed by the Indian Act elect "band councils" that are vested with powers of local government with respect to their reserves.[32] Other self-government regimes also provide for the election of a governing body.[33] As these self-government regimes are closely related to the management of reserved lands, it is logical that only members of the band, who are the "collective owners" of the reserve, be allowed to vote in the elections of the band council. If it were otherwise, non-members could participate in the decision to surrender part of a reserve, to allocate reserve lands to band members, to lease reserve lands, and so on.

Some of the more recent self-government regimes also vest indigenous governments with powers defined on a personal basis. While the powers of local governments are usually defined in territorial terms (for example, in terms of the territory of a municipality or an Indian reserve) and apply to all persons found within that territory, personal powers can be exercised only with respect to the class of persons subject to the jurisdiction of that government. For instance, First Nations in the Yukon Territory may enact laws regarding the adoption of their members, the custody and care of their members' children, wills and estates of their members, and some forms of taxation of their members, even where those members do not reside on their First Nation's exclusive territory.[34] Again, that situation necessitates membership control. Certain authors argue that the powers of indigenous governments will increasingly be recognised on a personal, rather than on a territorial, basis, which will make membership issues even more important.[35]

Individual Burdens and Collective Interests. As discussed in the previous chapter, it is sometimes considered necessary to restrict to some degree the freedom of minority members to engage in conduct that would be detrimental to the preservation of their culture. Burdens are imposed on individuals in order to promote certain collective interests, in particular to preserve culture and identity. Where the imposition of such burdens is justified, it is necessary to enact membership criteria, for the law must set out clearly on which individuals those burdens are imposed. The failure to do so may result in members of the minority unfairly trying to avoid the burdens that their fellow members are bearing and jeopardising the purpose of the law. In other words, if the possibility of exit is too easily available, the achievement of collective objectives may become more difficult. Membership control can regulate exit, by making the status of group member independent of one's will, with the aim of ensuring that individual choice does not jeopardise collective goods. Of course, restricting exit from an ethnic group may put individual freedom in danger,[36] but these issues can be managed if the group serves the interests of its members and allows its members to participate in group decisions.[37]

The regulation of access to English schools in Quebec, which is in effect a form of membership control, provides an example of a burden imposed on individuals to safeguard collective interests. Bill 101 requires Francophones to send their children to a French school, in order to ensure the predominance and long-term survival of the French language in Quebec. Only Anglophones are allowed a choice between English and French school for their children. In order to implement such a policy, the law must identify the Anglophones who benefit from the possibility of choosing the language of instruction of their children. As we will see in chapter 5, the absence of well-defined criteria in the early 1970s constituted an occasion for many Francophones and immigrants to attempt to circumvent the law.

International law provides a striking analogy with Bill 101: the case of Upper Silesia.[38] A part of that region, which formerly belonged to Germany, was ceded to Poland after the First World War. Poles in Polish Upper Silesia had formed for centuries a subordinated segment of the population of that region, even though they may not have constituted a numerical minority. They can therefore be considered, for the purposes of this analysis, as a minority within the larger context of Germany's former area of influence. When it acquired Upper Silesia, the Polish state considered that the promotion of the Polish character of its new Polish subjects required that education be provided to them in Polish. At the same time, the minority treaty between Germany and Poland required that German-language education be made available to members of the German minority, although initially, there were no legal norms to determine who was a member of the German minority. This lack of rules led many Poles to register their children in German schools, as they thought that this would provide them with better opportunities. The situation was of great concern to the Polish government, which was not willing to let important numbers of the Polish people have their children educated in a language other than Polish. It wanted to impose on Poles the "burden" of sending their children to Polish schools. Could Poles decide instead to send their children to German schools? Could they freely "choose their own culture"?

The German minority and the Polish state had very different views of the matter: whereas the German minority believed that parents could decide without constraints whether to send their children to minority schools, the Polish government maintained that the assertion of membership in the German minority had to be substantiated by objective facts. The government therefore rejected the applications of many pupils whom it considered not to be members of the German minority. The German minority brought the matter before the Permanent Court of International Justice, which ruled that in principle an individual's claim to belong to the German minority had to be based on objective facts but that in practice the treaty expressly forbade any inquiry into the grounds of such an assertion on the part of the individual.[39] This decision did not put an end to the controversy, however, and the Polish government and the German minority eventually agreed that only children who already had a sufficient knowledge of German could be admitted to German-language schools, thus showing the practical necessity of some forms of membership control.

To return to Canada, another example of a burden imposed in order to further collective goals is the fact that members of an Indian band cannot transfer their land rights on a reserve to non-members of the band.[40] Alienability is severely restricted so that non-members of the band cannot acquire rights on the reserve. The goal is to preserve the integrity of the reserves and to ensure that reserves remain places where indigenous cultures can flourish without too much influence from mainstream culture. If the right of possession of reserve land could be freely sold, reserves, especially those located near urban centres, would lose their indigenous character. In fact, the protection of Indian reserves against encroachment by non-Indians was one of the main purposes behind the initial versions of the Indian Act. Again, achieving this objective requires a definition of who a band member is.

Group Governance and Membership Control

Saying that membership control is required in certain circumstances is one thing; deciding who should exercise that control is a separate issue. For instance, the federal Parliament has assumed the power to define indigenous identity since the latter part of the nineteenth century, and indigenous peoples have sought to regain that power since at least the middle of the twentieth century. Similarly, the conflict between Bill 101 and section 23 of the Canadian Charter of Rights and Freedoms may be seen as a contest about who will define linguistic groups in Quebec.

There are moral grounds in favour of the attribution of the power to define membership criteria to the political institutions of the minority concerned. As we saw in chapter 1, ethnic identity is a social construct. Members of the group choose cultural markers that differentiate them from non-members. Each individual may have his or her own view of the distinctive features of the group's ethnicity. Thus, social definitions of ethnic identity are bound to be blurred and imprecise. The best way to aggregate them into a fixed legal definition is through a political process involving the members of the group and allowing them to define their own ethnicity. On the one hand, this approach respects their autonomy, as group members are allowed to decide for themselves what cultural characteristics are relevant to them. On the other hand, it ensures a higher degree of conformity between the legal definition and the social conception of ethnicity than would occur if membership criteria were imposed from the outside. Self-definition also helps to avoid stereotyped definitions of identity and constitutes a guarantee that membership control will not be used as a tool of oppression by the majority.

Self-definition of membership criteria, however, assumes that the minority possesses norm-enacting political institutions. This is not always the case. A minority may exist even in the absence of any institution or organisation. There may be voluntary associations that purport to represent the minority, but there is no guarantee that those associations would be representative of, or recognised by, most members of the minority. Those associations do not have the power to enact norms that bind all members of the minority. This usually prevents them from adopting membership criteria that will attract a consensus of the members of the minority or that will be recognised by the state.

Thus, in order to justify the attribution to the minority of the power to enact membership criteria, its political institutions must allow for the participation of all members in the political debate. If that were not the case, the advantages of self-definition of membership, outlined above, would vanish. For instance, if only men were entitled to vote in the election of the governing body of a given minority, there would be no assurance that the criteria enacted by that body would reflect the social perceptions of the minority's population (or at least half of it) or that they would not result in oppression. Of course, this requirement is somewhat circular: in order to ascertain whether the political process of the minority allows for the participation of all members, you must have, at the outset, an idea of who those members are. Yet in most cases, a preliminary judgment about membership will not be necessary to assess whether there is a sufficient degree of participation: there is no doubt that participation is lacking where the leaders are elected by male members only or chosen according to a hereditary system or a system of co-optation. It is only in borderline cases (such as the case of the Métis, studied in chapter 4) that the state will have to make a decision about representativity.

There are also circumstances where the state is justified in enacting minority membership criteria. First, where a minority does not have representative political institutions, the state is justified, as a second-best solution, in enacting its own membership criteria. Second, if the state grants benefits directly to individual minority members, it may also determine for itself who is entitled to those benefits. For instance, the fact that the Indian Act contains a definition of Indian status is justified by the tax exemption granted to individual Indians, regardless of their membership in a particular Indian band or other indigenous community.[41]

Minority Rights and Equality

The potential conflict between invididual rights and membership control will be studied in the next section of this chapter. However, I shall now discuss, because of its collective implications, the perceived conflict between the very existence of minority rights and the principle of equality. A formal conception of equality has often led courts to consider minority rights as antithetical to equality. However, as minority rights are protected by the constitution, courts usually conclude that they constitute an "exception" to equality and refrain from applying equality rights to laws implementing minority rights. The shift from formal equality towards substantive equality should bring about the demise of that "exception to equality" approach and its replacement with a perspective that stresses the compatibility, rather than the conflict, between equality and minority rights. Both perspectives will be studied in turn.

A Hierarchy of Rights? Where the constitution guarantees the right
to equality, while simultaneously recognising special rights for certain groups or mandating the separate treatment of those groups, one
is tempted to apply the principle of interpretation embodied in the
Latin maxim *generalia non specialibus derogant* (particular provisions prevail over general ones) and to conclude that the right to
equality must be construed as not applying at all to that special treatment. For instance, section 6 of the Charter guarantees the right of
Canadian citizens, but not of permanent residents, to enter and to
remain in Canada. Thus, a law providing for the deportation of permanent residents (but not citizens) who committed serious offences
was held not to violate the right to equality guaranteed by section 15,
even though it employed a distinction based on national origin.[42]
Sometimes this hierarchy of rights is made explicit in the text of the
constitution. Hence, section 29 of the Charter makes it clear that the
Charter does not invalidate the right to denominational schools set
forth in section 93 of the Constitution Act, 1867.[43]

A similar doctrine is apparent in certain decisions of the United
Nations Human Rights Committee. Laws defining marriage as the
union of a man and a woman have been held not to discriminate
against homosexuals (under article 26 of the International Covenant), because article 23 expressly contemplated that marriage was
the union of a man and a woman.[44] Laws governing pension
entitlements of citizens of one country, which varied according to
the country of residence of the pensioner, reflecting different bilateral agreements with different countries, were also held not to constitute discrimination.[45] The fact that in international law those
bilateral treaties had the same legal force as the Covenant probably
led the committee to attempt to reconcile the two through an atten-
uated interpretation of the right to equality. Although the committee has not yet considered the issue, the same reasoning could be
applied to the relationship between articles 26 and 27 of the Covenant: national laws that purport to give effect to article 27 by recognising special rights for members of religious, linguistic, or ethnic
minorities would be deemed not to violate article 26.

The Supreme Court of Canada has applied this doctrine to the
case of the indigenous peoples. Section 91(24) of the Constitution
Act, 1867 expressly gives to the federal Parliament the power to
legislate concerning "Indians, and lands reserved for the Indians."
In *Lavell*,[46] the majority of the court stated that the right to equality

before the law, guaranteed by the Canadian Bill of Rights,[47] did not have the effect of repealing the Indian Act or of nullifying Parliament's powers under section 91(24), even if the imposition of special rights and duties on Indians could be viewed as racial discrimination. (A similar doctrine is applied in American law.)[48]

When the Charter was enacted, the prospect of a conflict between the right to equality and the special rights afforded to the indigenous peoples seemed sufficiently important to warrant the inclusion of an express saving provision, section 25, which provides that the rights guaranteed by the Charter (including the right to equality) do not "abrogate or derogate" from "aboriginal, treaty or other rights" of the indigenous peoples. (Section 25 is subject to section 28, which states that "[n]otwithstanding anything in this Charter, the rights and freedoms referred to it are guaranteed equally to male and female persons.") The Canadian Human Rights Act also contains a saving provision, section 67, that exempts from review "any provision of the Indian Act or any provision made under or pursuant to that Act."[49]

This hierarchy of rights is also apparent in the field of linguistic rights.[50] In a 1990 case, the Supreme Court rejected the idea that section 15 was relevant to the interpretation of the minority-language education rights found in section 23. As Chief Justice Dickson stated, "it would be totally incongruous to invoke in aid of the interpretation of the provision which grants special rights to a select group of individuals, the principle of equality intended to be universally applied to 'every individual.'"[51] He expressed the view that linguistic rights were an "exception" to equality. Lower courts have subsequently considered that equality rights should not be used to supplement or improve on the linguistic rights expressly guaranteed by the Charter. For instance, the Ontario Court of Appeal refused to see a breach of section 15 in the fact that the Ontario government wanted to close the only French hospital of the province.[52] In a similar vein, the Quebec Court of Appeal held that the amalgamation of mainly English-speaking suburban municipalities into the mainly French-speaking City of Montreal did not constitute discrimination against Anglophones.[53]

Ranking rights in a hierarchical fashion, as if minority rights "trumped" the right to equality, is unsatisfactory. It assumes a formal conception of equality, which considers differential treatment as discriminatory even though the law seeks to improve the circumstances of a disadvantaged group.[54] Under that conception, minority rights, like affirmative action, are viewed as a breach of equality. Instead, I have shown in chapter 1 that minority rights further a substantive conception of equality. Under such a conception, judicial review on equality grounds would not have the effect of striking down all legislation concerning minorities. Laws that benefit minorities would be upheld, while laws that impose burdens on minorities or further stereotypes would be invalidated.[55] This highlights the major flaw of the hierarchy-of-rights approach: it exempts from review laws that are unjust or that unacceptably burden certain groups. It does not separate distinctions that are necessary to the implementation of minority rights (and the realisation of substantive equality) from those that simply perpetuate disadvantage or prejudice. The problem is particularly acute with respect to membership criteria, in which distinctions that legitimately define the minority might very well be found alongside discriminatory criteria.

A Substantive Approach? A better approach to the interaction between equality and minority rights can be built upon the recognition in a recent Supreme Court decision that minority rights flow from the requirements of substantive equality.[56] Hence, there is no need to exempt minority rights from judicial review.

Yet in order to give effect to the principle that one portion of the constitution must not be construed as abrogating another, it is necessary to take for granted in the analysis of an alleged breach of equality that the purpose of the minority rights set forth in the constitution is ameliorative. That ameliorative purpose would be a factor tending to show that a particular piece of legislation is compatible with substantive equality. This presumption need not go very far. For instance, where section 91(24) of the Constitution Act, 1867, authorises Parliament to legislate concerning the indigenous peoples, courts must only accept that granting special benefits to those peoples is legitimate, given the historical oppression they have faced and the socio-economic disadvantage they still find themselves in. Nothing would prevent a court from further scrutinising a measure targeted at the indigenous peoples to ensure that it is really beneficial to them.[57]

The suggested approach is similar to the one adopted by the Supreme Court with respect to section 15(2) of the Charter, which states that section 15(1) does not preclude laws or programs that seek to improve the condition of disadvantaged individuals or groups. The Court held that section 15(2) confirms the substantive approach that the Court has taken to section 15(1).[58] Thus, section 15(2) may be viewed as requiring judges to conclude that programs that aim at redressing disadvantage are compatible with substantive equality. But it does not preclude a finding that a program of that kind is discriminatory, for instance if the means adopted are not related to the ameliorative goal.[59]

The suggested approach is also compatible with section 25 of the Charter, which states that the Charter does not abrogate or derogate from the rights of the indigenous peoples. Like section 15(2), section 25 sets up a presumption that laws benefiting the indigenous peoples are compatible with substantive equality. It does not mean, however, that Parliament may discriminate in enacting laws concerning the indigenous peoples. It does not result either in an exemption from Charter review for the decisions of Indian bands or for other indigenous governments. Rather, it is increasingly recognised that the Charter applies to decisions of Indian bands,[60] albeit in a manner that may be sensitive to indigenous culture in appropriate cases.[61]

Nevertheless, a substantive approach to the interaction between equality and minority rights may lead to the invalidation of a minority rights scheme where the legal sources of the right to equality and the minority rights in question do not have the same ranking in the hierarchy of norms. *Waldman* v. *Canada*, a case from the United Nations Human Rights Committee, illustrates this.[62] Jewish parents challenged the Ontario law that, pursuant to section 93 of the Constitution Act, 1867, gave public funds to Protestant and Catholic denominational schools but not to schools of other religious faiths, on the ground that this constituted religious discrimination. They were unsuccessful in the Canadian courts, which held that one provision of the constitution (the right to equality) could not abrogate another (denominational rights of Catholics and Protestants).[63] When the Human Rights Committee decided the case, it noted that the fact that a distinction was mandated by the constitution did not make it *ipso facto* objective and reasonable. Norms of international law prevail over national laws, including constitutions. Thus, Canada could not plead its constitution as a defence against an allegation of discrimination under the International Covenant. The committee therefore looked at the present situation of

Catholics in Ontario and concluded that Catholics were not a minority in need of protection. In the result, the Ontario regime was found discriminatory. The substantive approach adopted by the committee had the advantage of throwing light on the outdated character of denominational rights in the Canadian constitution. Needless to say, the result would most probably have been different had the committee considered the rights of indigenous peoples or of linguistic minorities, since the disadvantaged situation of those groups today is easily demonstrable.

RESPECT FOR INDIVIDUAL RIGHTS

While collective minority rights provide a justification, if not a legal right, for controlling membership in certain minority groups, individual human rights impose limits as to the contents of membership rules. Two particular rights are relevant in this regard: the right to equality, protected by international law and most national constitutions, including section 15 of the Canadian Charter of Rights and Freedoms, as well as cultural rights in their individual dimension, such as the right to enjoy one's own culture in article 27 of the International Covenant on Civil and Political Rights or certain individual aspects of aboriginal or treaty rights guaranteed by section 35 of the Constitution Act, 1982.

An individual who is excluded from a minority group for not meeting the group's membership criteria may institute legal proceedings before a court with the aim of invalidating the group's membership rules, on the basis that those rules are inconsistent with international or constitutional guarantees of equality or cultural rights. The following study of the analytical framework employed by courts to assess compliance with those rights demonstrates that, broadly speaking, they require membership rules to *correspond* to the "actual" identity of group members – status or "identity in law" must reflect "identity in fact" – and that those rules must be *justified* as a reasonable means of achieving a valid objective.

The application of human rights norms to membership control systems certainly has the potential of bringing greater justice to the persons who are excluded from the group on dubious grounds. The judicial enforcement of human rights also has potential shortcomings. In this connection, the problem of access to justice immediately comes to mind. Where the persons who are likely to be

excluded from group membership are disadvantaged and no funding is available to bring public interest lawsuits, it is very difficult
for them to afford the costs of litigation. In addition, relying on
courts to bring membership rules in compliance with human rights
raises well-known issues associated with the adjudicative process,
such as the structural inability of courts to grapple with complex
social problems and the deference courts often show towards the
justifications advanced by government for laws that infringe upon
individual rights.

Most importantly, the application of individual rights in an
intercultural context gives rise to well-known dilemmas. As the discussion of the various conceptions of ethnic identity in chapter 1
made clear, there is not in any given ethnic group a single "identity
in fact" that a judge could accurately "find" by looking hard enough
at the evidence. A judge assessing membership rules will inevitably
be called upon to select among competing conceptions of a group's
identity, on grounds that are not only factual but also normative.
Moreover, and especially where an indigenous group is concerned,
the judge will likely not be a member of the group and will probably be unfamiliar with the group's culture, with the result that a
legally binding decision about group identity will be made by an
outsider. The supposed link between individual rights and Western
culture has led many advocates of minority rights to denounce the
application of charters of rights to minority rules and institutions as
a form of legal imperialism. In particular, several academics have
asserted that the Canadian Charter does not or should not apply to
indigenous governments.[64] On the other hand, feminist critiques of
minority rights insist that compromising individual rights in the
name of culture leaves women vulnerable to oppression. Rather
than forcing one to align with one of those two camps, theorists of
"deliberative democracy" have suggested that individual rights may
inform a political dialogue within the group, which may result in
the evolution of the group's culture in a manner that preserves the
group's distinctiveness while ensuring that women are not
oppressed.[65] In the process, original conceptions of equality may
arise that do not replicate the interpretation given to the right to
equality by the courts but that ensure a substantially equal distribution of power, resources, and respect among group members.[66] In
the remainder of this book, I will assume, in line with the bulk of
trial judgments to this day,[67] that the Charter applies to the deci-

sions made by indigenous governments concerning membership.[68] The fact that such decisions involve cultural considerations may be a factor mandating an increased degree of deference, as we will see below.

The Legal Framework of Equality

Courts that regularly apply the right to equality have devised analytical frameworks in order to constrain reasoning that would otherwise be open-ended. To facilitate the assessment of the framework created by the Supreme Court of Canada, it will be useful to take note of the main findings of comparative research concerning the application of equality guarantees.[69]

Courts tend to focus their assessment of discrimination complaints on two central concepts: comparison and justification. The comparative analysis attempts to determine whether the person or group who alleges discrimination is treated similarly or differently when compared to a person or group "similarly situated." In contrast, the justification analysis evaluates whether the negative impacts that result from the challenged rule are a proportionate means of addressing a valid governmental objective. Yet it has been shown that the comparative analysis cannot be performed in the abstract. It is inevitably premised upon an understanding of the goals of the impugned measure and the goals of equality in general. Hence, comparison and justification are frequently mingled in judicial decisions about equality.[70] This confusion would be harmless were it not for the fact that the burden of proof usually rests with the claimant with respect to comparison and with the state with respect to justification.

Moreover, observers have noted, and some courts have explicitly acknowledged, that equality claims can be reviewed according to a varying degree of intensity or "scrutiny,"[71] not only at the justification stage but also at the comparison stage. The degree of scrutiny applicable in a particular case depends first and foremost on the ground of distinction involved, with particularly "suspect" classifications such as race attracting the most stringent scrutiny, but also, according to recent research, on the type of discrimination involved (whether resulting from state action or state failure to legislate), the personal interest at stake, and the fact that the claim would involve wide-range policy changes.[72]

Canadian Law. There are several protections of equality in Canadian law. Parliament and every provincial legislature have adopted human rights legislation that prohibits discrimination in private activities such as employment, services offered to the public, and so forth (the Canadian Human Rights Act[73] and provincial "human rights codes"). The Canadian Bill of Rights,[74] as well as some provincial codes (such as the Quebec Charter of Human Rights and Freedoms),[75] also provides protection against discrimination flowing from legal rules. But the strongest protection of equality, and the one that will be the main focus of this book, is afforded by section 15 of the Canadian Charter of Rights and Freedoms, which states that "[e]very individual is equal before and under the law and has the right to the equal protection and equal benefit of the law without discrimination and, in particular, without discrimination based on race, national or ethnic origin, colour, religion, sex, age or mental or physical disability." It should be noted that the list of suspect grounds of discrimination is not closed. Courts are left to decide what other grounds might be suspect. A heightened protection is provided in cases of sex discrimination by section 28, which states that "[n]otwithstanding anything in this Charter, the rights and freedoms referred to it are guaranteed equally to male and female persons."

Since the coming into force of section 15 in 1985, the judges of the Supreme Court have advanced deeply conflicting views about how to analyse a claim based on the right to equality. Yet in the recent *Law* v. *Canada* decision,[76] all judges agreed on a common analytical framework that has been used, at least in general terms, in most subsequent cases. Thus, a claimant must demonstrate that (1) he or she has been subjected to a differential treatment (either explicitly or because the law fails to take into account existing social differences), that (2) this differential treatment is based on a ground enumerated in section 15 or on a ground analogous to those, and that (3) this results in the imposition of a burden or in the withholding of benefits in a manner that contradicts the purpose of section 15. Where an infringement of section 15 has been found, the burden of proof shifts to the state, which may rely on section 1 of the Charter to demonstrate that the infringement is justified in a free and democratic society; in the affirmative, there is no violation of the Charter; in the negative, the impugned rule is of no force and effect.

The first inquiry involves the identification of a "distinction" against the person or group complaining about a breach of equality. Direct discrimination occurs where the law itself makes different rules applicable to different persons or categories of persons. Cases of direct discrimination are generally unproblematic in this regard. In contrast, indirect (or "adverse-effect") discrimination takes place where a legal rule that is neutral on its face produces different effects on specific groups or fails to take into account significant factual differences between individuals. For instance, the Supreme Court held that the failure to provide interpretation services for deaf people receiving publicly provided health services constituted indirect discrimination, because the apparently neutral rule that no one would be provided with interpretation services had a distinctly negative impact on a particular group, deaf persons.[77]

The second inquiry is whether the impugned distinction is based on a prohibited ground enumerated in section 15 or an "analogous ground."[78] In fact, at this stage the court is defining the categories of persons who will benefit from equality rights. Contrary to what had been proposed by Justice L'Heureux-Dubé in an earlier case,[79] or to the practice of the United Nations Human Rights Committee, discussed below, the Court will not scrutinise any distinction found in the law but only distinctions based on grounds that raise the suspicion of a tainted decision process. Two general factors underpin the Court's approach to the identification of analogous grounds: the historical oppression or disadvantage suffered by a group and the immutable, or "constructively immutable," nature of the ground of distinction involved.[80]

The Supreme Court's focus on comparison as the basis for a finding of discrimination is problematic in certain respects. It is often possible to manipulate the comparison and to find a person who is treated in the same manner as the complainant, which defeats the equality claim. The Court has asserted that it has discretion to choose a comparator group different from the one proposed by the plaintiff. For instance, in the Hodge case, where the denial of Canada Pension Plan benefits to former common-law spouses was challenged, the Court stated that the appropriate comparators were divorced spouses (who were denied benefits), rather than separated but still legally married spouses (who were admissible).[81] As divorced and former common-law spouses were treated equally, the Court concluded that the law did not draw a distinction based on matrimonial status. That decision has been criticised on the basis that it allows self-serving statements of statutory purpose to determine the choice of a comparator and, in the result, to derail equality challenges.[82] Nevertheless, the Court has been willing to consider cases where negative treatment flowed from a combination of factors, some of which were enumerated or analogous grounds and some of which were not.[83] It has also found discrimination in cases where the adverse treatment was a result of a personal characteristic of a relative of the complainant[84] or where only part of a group identified by an enumerated or analogous ground was affected.[85]

The most contentious issue in the Supreme Court's equality jurisprudence is whether it is sufficient for a plaintiff to prove a distinction based on an enumerated or analogous ground to show that section 15 has been breached or if it is necessary to prove some additional ingredient. In *Andrews*, its first equality case, the Supreme Court rejected the idea that the plaintiff in a section 15 case had to show that the impugned distinction was unreasonable.[86] It was enough that the plaintiff was denied a right or imposed a burden on the basis of an enumerated or analogous ground. The issue of possible justifications could be considered only at the section 1 stage, where the burden of proof rests on the state. Yet in the Court's 1995 equality trilogy, several judges held that the plaintiff had to show that the distinction was not relevant to the purpose of the law.[87] This idea was heavily criticised, as it was reminiscent of the unreasonableness test, added to the plaintiff's burden of proof, and left a wide margin of judicial discretion in judging "relevancy."[88] Most importantly, such an approach takes for granted the validity of the statutory purpose.

In *Law* v. *Canada*, all judges agreed that the presence of a distinction based on enumerated or analogous grounds did not lead to an automatic finding of discrimination. While rejecting the "relevancy" test, the Court added the requirement that the impugned measure must be contrary to the purpose of section 15, identified as the prevention of "the violation of essential human dignity and freedom through the imposition of disadvantage, stereotyping, or political or social prejudice, and [the promotion of] a society in which all persons enjoy equal recognition at law as human beings or as members of Canadian society, equally capable and equally deserving of concern, respect, and consideration."[89]

In order to determine whether a measure contradicts the purpose of section 15 and can thus be said to be substantively discriminatory, several contextual factors must be examined: (1) whether the measure gives effect to or reinforces stereotypes against traditionally subordinated groups, (2) whether the distinction employed relates to the real needs or characteristics of members of the group, (3) whether the measure seeks to improve the condition of a disadvantaged group, and (4) what is the nature and scope of the interest affected by the impugned measure. Critics have lamented the imposition of an additional burden on claimants and highlighted the indeterminacy of the analysis based on human dignity or the fact that it is applied in a manner that puts correspondence before justification.[90] In this regard, an example of the pitfalls of the *Law* v. *Canada* framework is provided by the *Gosselin* case,[91] decided in 2002, which concerned a law that sharply reduced the welfare payments of recipients aged under thirty who did not participate in various training programs. Justice Bastarache, in dissent, concluded that the age distinction was not related to the actual needs or circumstances of welfare recipients aged under thirty: basic shelter and food do not cost less when you are younger.[92] However, Chief Justice McLachlin, writing for the majority, focused on the apparently benevolent purpose of the measure: according to her, the state wanted to "help" unemployed young persons by facilitating their entry into the labour market.[93] In so doing, she returned to the previously discarded relevancy test that scrutinises only the internal coherence of the law and disregards its actual impact on disadvantaged groups.[94] She also failed to assess the validity of the state's proffered purpose or whether the measure was actually benefiting the group targeted. Moreover, in other recent cases, the third contextual factor was applied as an excuse for laws that sought to improve the condition of a disadvantaged group but adopted a restrictive definition of that group.[95] Yet despite these dangers, the *Law* v. *Canada* framework, properly applied, is useful in focusing attention on factors that are relevant to a substantive equality analysis.[96]

Once a breach of section 15 has been established, the analysis moves on to section 1 of the Charter, which provides that the rights contained in that instrument are guaranteed "subject only to such reasonable limits prescribed by law as can be demonstrably justified in a free and democratic society." In its landmark *Oakes* decision,[97] the Supreme Court adopted an analytical framework that governs the review of potential justifications of laws that infringe on guaranteed rights. The state must first demonstrate that the objectives of the challenged rule relate to pressing and substantial concerns. Second, it must be shown that the means chosen are proportional to the purpose. This criterion is subdivided in three inquiries: (1) whether the measure is rationally connected to the purpose of the law, (2) whether the measure minimally impairs the guaranteed right, and (3) whether there is proportionality between the effects of the measure and the importance of the objective. The Court performs this analysis (and in particular the second stage, minimal impairment) according to different levels of intensity. In contrast to other jurisdictions, the criteria employed to set the standard of review are the protection of vulnerable groups and the institutional limits to judicial competence.[98] Under the first heading, the Court has granted the state a margin of appreciation when it enacts laws that protect vulnerable groups (for example, a prohibition on advertising targeted at children under thirteen)[99] or that redistribute or equalise resources (for example, limits on election spending).[100] Moreover, the Court recently adopted a much more relaxed analytical framework for claims that an "ameliorative program" covered by section 15(2) is discriminatory; in those cases, the state need only show that the measures challenged are rationally related to their goals, which amounts to a low degree of scrutiny.[101] Under the second heading, it is acknowledged that governments are in a better position than judges to assess social science evidence, to measure scientifically the harm addressed by the law, and to design complex legislative schemes in a context of uncertainty.[102]

The Canadian framework may now be assessed in the light of comparative research. Comparative and justificative elements are obviously present in the *Law* v. *Canada* framework, even though the test is not explicitly structured around those two ideas. In contrast, however, the Supreme Court does not acknowledge that it performs the section 15 analysis according to varying levels of intensity. Yet the Court's apparently incoherent application of its own framework in recent equality decisions may be explained in terms of lowering the degree of scrutiny where the ground of distinction involved is not inherently suspect and the claim relates to a complex scheme of social benefits.[103] Moreover, three of the four "contextual factors" laid out by the Court in *Law* v. *Canada* are typically more related to the selection of the appropriate degree of

scrutiny than to justfication proper: the historical disadvantage
suffered by the group, the ameliorative purpose of the law (which
suggests a complex issue of social policy), and the nature of the
personal interest at stake.

The purpose of this book is not to suggest a new analytical framework for section 15 of the Charter. For my purposes, it is enough to
say that the analysis of an equality claim involves elements of comparison and justification and that both elements are affected by a
varying degree of scrutiny. Therefore, my analysis of the interaction
of equality and membership control will focus on these three
themes. Before we reach that topic, however, it is necessary to say a
few words about equality in international law.

International Law. The international human rights instruments
comprise the Universal Declaration of Human Rights,[104] a non-
binding resolution of the General Assembly of the United Nations
adopted in 1948, as well as several international treaties signed in
the following decades, which give effect to several aspects of the
Universal Declaration. While Canada was initially dubious about
the Universal Declaration,[105] it has now ratified the International
Covenant on Civil and Political Rights,[106] which guarantees equality rights without distinction based on sex, race, colour, national or
social origin, birth or other status (articles 2, 3, 23(4), and 26), as
well as conventions against racial discrimination[107] and discrimination against women.[108] Canada must provide periodic reports to
United Nations committees concerning compliance with those conventions. Moreover, individuals have the right to complain to those
committees when their rights are infringed, provided that they have
exhausted their recourses before national courts. While they are not
mandatory or binding on domestic courts, the decisions of those
committees with respect to such complaints have a considerable
persuasive value.

Article 26 forbids discrimination in any law or measure of the rati-
fying states. It is not limited to discrimination in the enjoyment of the
other rights guaranteed by the Covenant.[109] As in section 15 of the
Canadian Charter, the list of suspect grounds of classification is not
closed, as it includes "other status." However, to identify the kinds of
distinctions that trigger article 26, the Human Rights Committee,
unlike the Supreme Court of Canada, does not rely on an "analogous

grounds" approach but, rather, adopts a very liberal approach that subjects many kinds of distinctions to further analysis.[110]

One could argue that the interpretation of article 26 should be based on a substantive conception of equality, taking inspiration from the opinion of Judge Tanaka, who admitted in the *South West Africa* case of the International Court of Justice that the separate treatment of ethnic groups might be required in order to combat disadvantage.[111] An additional reason is the fact that other international treaties specifically contemplate the differential treatment of women or racial minorities in order to achieve "*de facto* equality,"[112] thus permitting affirmative action programs. However, the committee does not consistently recognise indirect discrimination or the disparate impact of consistent treatment as a breach of article 26.[113]

When a distinction engages article 26, the committee requires the state concerned to adduce evidence of a reasonable and objective justification for the measure.[114] In a recent decision, the committee clarified its approach and required that the state show that the aims of the challenged measure are legitimate and that the means employed be objective and reasonable.[115] This framework, although it is a very simple articulation of the means-ends proportionality principle, is broadly similar to the one used by Canadian courts under section 1 of the Charter. It has also been shown that the committee frequently relies on comparability as a reason to dismiss a complaint based on article 26: there is no discrimination where the law treats differently two situations that are not comparable.[116] Moreover, the committee has also shown a considerable degree of deference towards legislation of the member states where complex social benefits schemes have been at issue.[117]

Equality Applied to Membership Control

What are the requirements imposed by the right to equality on membership control systems? In other words, how would a court deal with an allegation that the criteria for membership in a particular minority group are discriminatory? Rather than following the complex framework developed by the Supreme Court of Canada, the analysis here will focus on the main elements of equality analysis in comparative law, namely, comparison or correspondence, justification, and degree of scrutiny.

A threshold question, relevant only in cases involving the Canadian Charter, but not the International Covenant, is whether membership rules draw distinctions based on a ground enumerated in
section 15 of the Charter or analogous thereto. It will usually be
easy for a plaintiff to show that membership criteria draw distinctions based on enumerated or analogous grounds. Discrimination
against indigenous peoples is usually considered to be based on
race.[118] Yet one might object that race is not a scientifically valid
concept, which would make its application problematic. Yet in two
recent cases dealing with disability, the Supreme Court insisted that
grounds of discrimination must be viewed subjectively.[119] The fact
that the impugned distinction is not based on an objective reality is
not a defence if the distinction relates to such ground in the eyes of
the person or institution making it. Thus, where a person was
refused employment because of a medical condition that did not
result in any functional limitation, this constituted discrimination
based on a handicap because the employer perceived it in that manner. The same reasoning can be extended to race and to ethnic origin. Even though, as we have seen in the previous chapter, these
concepts have no purely objective meaning, individuals do make
distinctions on those grounds when they identify themselves or others with a particular "race" or ethnic group. Thus, when Parliament decides in the Indian Act who is an Indian and who is not, it is
drawing a distinction on the basis of race or ethnic origin. For their
part, the distinctions drawn by criteria for membership in linguistic
minorities can be viewed in two different ways. First, language can
be said to be an analogous ground according to the factors outlined
above. While languages can be learned, this is a difficult process,
and a mother tongue is immutable. Linguistic minorities have often
been oppressed or disadvantaged. Language is also expressly mentioned as a prohibited ground of discrimination in the Quebec
Charter.[120] Second, distinctions based on language can be linked to
ethnic origin;[121] they would then be based on a ground enumerated
in section 15. Therefore, rules for membership in indigenous
peoples and linguistic minorities will usually attract further scrutiny
under the headings of comparison and justification.

Comparison or Correspondence. The comparative analysis looks at
"correspondence" between membership rules and the social reality
they are supposed to describe. Yet the analysis is not as straightfor-

ward as it might look at first glance, because we need to select which characteristics of individuals are relevant for the purposes of the comparison. To be able to assess whether the classification used in certain membership rules is over-inclusive or under-inclusive, one must have an idea of the class of persons that *should* be granted membership in the group concerned. In turn, who should be a member of a group depends on the purposes of the legal recognition of that group. To use a hypothetical example, if the only purpose of indigenous rights were to foster the development of indigenous languages, it would be logical to define the group of rights-holders in terms of the ability to speak (or, perhaps, the willingness to learn) an indigenous language.

The difficulties in establishing a proper comparison are manifold. As we have seen in the previous chapter, minority rights measures may pursue several objectives. Particular measures may have been adopted in spite of disagreement as to their purpose or philosophical underpinnings. It is not entirely clear in the present state of aboriginal rights jurisprudence in Canada whether aboriginal rights measures aim at redressing a historical injustice, at preserving indigenous culture, or both. Moreover, some membership control systems may have been based on objectives that are no longer acceptable. A policy aimed at preserving the "racial purity" of a particular group would be universally rejected. Reasonable persons disagree as to the rightfulness of constraining individual freedom in order to protect cultures in the long term. Equality analysis does not, and should not, condone rules based on impermissible objectives, unless it is to collapse into a purely formal analysis.

Once a valid purpose is established, the comparative approach invites the jurist to identify the relevant category of persons who are concerned by the measure. In practice, this requires that membership criteria be tested for their correspondence to "real-world" (or sociological) ethnic identity. Again, this is not an easy task, especially as sociological conceptions of identity are constructed rather than pre-existing to the group. The outcome of the analysis will depend on the selection of one conception of the identity of the group concerned. Certain broad purposes of minority rights appear, at first glance, logically linked to one specific conception of identity and might help in that selection. For instance, if one adopts cultural justifications of minority rights, it may seem natural to rely on a conception of identity that is based on the presence of specific cultural traits in individuals (such as in the example of indigenous languages mentioned above). Also, in the negative sense, an analysis of purpose might help in rejecting conceptions of identity that appear related to an improper purpose (for example, a conception based purely on biology). But there are some justifications of minority rights that do not point towards any particular conception of identity. The fact that a group is given particular rights in compensation for an injustice of the distant past does not tell much about the group's identity. Asserting that the state should respect groups that pre-date the establishment of sovereignty gives no clue about how these groups identify their members.

In practice, minority group membership rules rely to a large degree on ancestry. How do these rules fare under a comparative analysis? One is tempted to say that reliance upon genealogy betrays a racial conception of identity, according to which identity is entirely determined at birth. Yet this is not necessarily so. To understand why ancestry may have a legitimate role to play in the definition of indigenous status, it is useful to consider it as a "proxy" for a constitutive element of identity. We have seen in the previous chapter that ancestry may indeed be a proxy for culture, because culture is usually transmitted by parents to their children. Protecting cultural groups is generally considered a legitimate purpose of minority rights.

Yet refining the comparison reveals that the "fit" between ancestry and culture is not perfect. The most obvious case where ancestry has limited predictive value is that of mixed couples: where the two parents of a child come from two different ethnic groups, we cannot deduce, in the absence of additional facts, what culture will be transmitted to the child. There are also a myriad cases where children are not raised by their parents or are raised by only one parent, with or without another person. In these situations, the predictive value of ancestry is obviously limited. Many other factors do influence the acquisition of culture by children, and one might ask, if we are trying to identify people belonging to a particular culture, why use a proxy instead of looking at the real thing? Through external observation or through consulting the people concerned, could the law try to identify the markers that actually define the group's identity and design membership criteria that reflect those markers? Anthropological studies have shown that indigenous peoples in North America conceive of their identity in terms of factors such as ancestry, language, residence, culture, participation in community events, and self-identification.[122] Membership rules would then be compared to those cultural markers. Thus, if it is found that hunting in a particular territory and participating in certain feasts are identity markers of an indigenous group, the law should define the group as the set of persons who engage in those activities.

That method, however, suffers from two major defects. First, it would "freeze" indigenous culture by making a particular activity (for example, hunting on traditional land) an essential element of indigenous identity. It would hamper the evolution of an indigenous culture: individual members would not be free to question the importance of the particular activity to the indigenous culture. One would risk losing indigenous status and all the benefits flowing from it if one decided to engage in other activities or, for example, to hunt only on weekends. Second, that method would require intrusive and possibly recurring inquiries into individual lives. For example, one could imagine the difficulty of sending out inspectors to ensure that indigenous individuals are truly hunting. The problem would only become more acute if the criteria related to very personal beliefs or practices. Ascertaining whether a person actually practices a given religion or actually speaks a particular language at home with his or her children would entail unacceptable invasions of privacy. In fact, the use of cultural factors to identify group members is a regression to the objective (or essentialist) conception of the ethnic group, which has been superseded by a constructivist one.

That illustrates the difficulty of applying the comparative approach where the "real-life" characteristics of the persons involved, to which the criteria employed by the law must correspond, are themselves a social construct lacking any "objective" or "natural" definition. In those circumstances, it is impossible to reach a perfect "fit" or correspondence between membership rules and group identity. In fact, the comparative method may lead to a paradox: the requirement of correspondence may translate into a requirement of allowing several conceptions of identity to coexist. If the social reality is itself blurred, perhaps the right to equality requires legal criteria to be flexible. In practical terms, this means that other factors, such as place of birth, place of schooling, languages learned,[123] and residence on the group's territory, should be used to supplement ancestry.[124] In other words, more than one proxy should be used.

What is important is that these proxies should not have the effect of essentialising the group's culture and making certain cultural practices mandatory. To take the example of language, simply requiring knowledge of an indigenous language would not have an essentialising effect. In contrast, requiring group members to actually speak the group's language at home would "freeze" the group culture and require intrusive inquiries into group members' lives.

Moreover, the above discussion suggests that there is a trade-off between the degree of correspondence and other values, such as efficient decision making and the resulting need to employ criteria that are easily and objectively ascertainable or respect for personal privacy, which in turn allows individuals to make their culture evolve independently of any official definition. Of course, balancing those values is a justificatory exercise, which proves that comparison and justification cannot be neatly separated. The attitude of judges towards the balance struck by particular membership rules will depend in large part upon the degree of scrutiny that is applied. Both issues are canvassed below.

Justification. A lack of correspondence between membership rules and the social reality that they are supposed to reflect brings us to a further stage of the analysis. At that stage, one looks at whether this discrepancy, and its deleterious effects on individuals, is justified by a sufficiently important public purpose. This is usually conceived as a two-pronged test: first, we determine what the objective of the impugned measure is and judge whether it is sufficiently urgent to warrant restrictions upon individual rights, and, second, we decide if the importance of the objective is proportional to its negative effect on individual rights.

We have reviewed, in the first part of this chapter, the kinds of considerations that may justify membership control. Broadly speaking, they can be divided into objectives directly related to the preservation of the group's culture and objectives that are instrumental to the achievement of other objectives. In the first category, we would find membership rules that aim at ensuring the cultural homogeneity of the group. The Supreme Court of Canada validated that kind of objective in the context of Quebec's language laws, accepting that the Quebec legislature could restrict human rights in order to preserve and promote the French language.[125] The second category would comprise measures aimed at the fair allocation of resources (or jurisdiction) destined to improve the condition of specific minorities. The overall validity of "ameliorative" measures is confirmed, in the Canadian context, by section 15(2) of the Charter. Yet when scarce resources are allocated to a group, accountability and fairness in the expense of public funds require that non-members be denied access to those resources. In doing so, it may be impracticable for the law to strive for a perfect definition. As mentioned above, there is a trade-off between "fit" and efficient decision-making. Efficiency may thus ground a justification for membership criteria that do not correspond perfectly to the group's identity. For instance, in the recent *Martin* case,[126] the Court recognised that a provincial legislature could take measures to prevent fraud in the context of a workers' compensation scheme and to ensure that resources are allocated to those who really need them.

Our attention then turns to proportionality. One common manner of assessing the relationship between the challenged measure's objectives and negative impacts is to ask whether there is a less intrusive alternative for achieving the same objective, one that would have less severe impacts on individual rights. This question may be asked with respect to the very existence of membership control. Are there any means of granting rights or benefits to minorities that would not require the law to define the group's identity? Some possibilities may be mentioned here. Where the marginal cost of providing services to additional minority members is small, the exercise of minority rights may be left to individual choice. This is the case for most language rights in Canada: anyone may choose to receive government services in English or French, whatever their mother tongue.[127] Granting territorial autonomy to minorities (such as those in the linguistic regions in Belgium)[128] also avoids membership control: everyone who resides in the minority's territory is subject to its laws, irrespective of their ethnic identity.[129] Yet these policies may not be able to achieve certain kinds of objectives, such as cultural preservation. In particular, it seems very difficult to avoid membership control where the resources granted to group members are significantly different from those available to the rest of the population. The case of the tax exemption granted to status Indians immediately comes to mind in this regard: the absence of membership control would be an invitation to abuse.

The least intrusive means test can also be applied to particular membership rules. One line of inquiry would be to compare the inclusiveness of various possible criteria. Thus, a "one-parent rule" (that is, you are a member of the group if at least one of your parents is a member) would be more inclusive and would constitute a lesser infringement of individual rights than a "two-parent rule" (that is, you are a member only if both your parents are members). Another way to frame the question would be to contrast rigid ancestry-based rules with discretionary admission based on a combination of several factors (language, residence, schooling, and so on). The latter would give individuals a better chance to prove membership and would therefore be less intrusive. Both examples, however, raise the question whether the objectives of membership control (for example, cultural homogeneity) would be achieved to the same degree if the least intrusive alternative were to be chosen. This involves an assessment of the advantages and disadvantages of each option. In this connection, political theorist Avigail Eisenberg suggests that individual interests concerning the accurate reflection of one's identity will usually outweigh group interests, as the admission of one individual is highly significant for the person concerned but has a negligible impact on the group.[130] However, it is precisely with respect to that kind of choice that courts have left legislatures with a wide margin of discretion, or, to use the terminology employed above, that courts have lowered their degree of scrutiny. We will see in the following chapters how this balancing exercise plays out in practice.

Degree of Scrutiny. Under the Canadian Charter, the degree of scrutiny applied to the section 1 justification analysis is said to depend on two main factors: the institutional competence of the court to assess conflicting social science evidence and the fact that the challenged measure aims at protecting vulnerable groups. Other factors, such as the suspect nature of certain grounds of discrimination (such as race), the nature of the individual interest or right at stake, or the type of discrimination involved (related to state action or inaction), may be linked to those two main factors.

It is obvious that the comparative aspect of the equality analysis draws the court into social science concepts of ethnic identity, about which judges usually lack specific training. This may point towards less stringent review. Moreover, where membership rules have been adopted by the group itself, ostensibly to reflect the group's identity, judges are likely to be reluctant to second-guess the group's decision. In this regard, the Supreme Court has said that it would show more deference where a law is based on a disadvantaged group's "own subjective fears and apprehensions of harm."[131] It appears reasonable to extend that holding to the group's own perceptions of its identity. This is consistent with section 25 of the Charter, which, under its most plausible interpretation, requires courts to show sensitivity to indigenous culture when applying the guarantees of the Charter to the decisions made by indigenous governments.[132] (This would not hold, however, where Parliament seeks to define indigenous identity, as most members of Parliament have little inside knowledge of indigenous cultures.)

The vulnerability criterion does not, in contrast, point towards a less stringent analysis. True, minority rights aim, generally speaking, at improving the lot of disadvantaged or vulnerable minorities. However, membership control may, in striving to achieve this general objective, exclude an oppressed subgroup within the minority. Courts must be attentive to such situations, which might go unnoticed if too much deference is shown. In that case, an intersectional approach to substantive equality would require that strict scrutiny be applied to membership criteria that deprive a powerless subgroup within the minority of rights or benefits that other members of the minority are entitled to. As we will see in the next chapter, Canadian law has for a long period held indigenous women in a state of subordination that was distinct from that of indigenous men or non-indigenous women. Thus, gender distinctions in the membership rules of the indigenous peoples are particularly suspect. Another manner of reaching the same result would be to say that race and sex are inherently suspect grounds and that their use in membership criteria automatically attracts greater scrutiny.

The nature and the scope of the rights or interests the access to which depends on membership rules may also point towards a more stringent standard of review. Where a distinction has the effect of withholding a significant material (such as the means of basic subsistence)[133] or symbolic (such as the right to have one's fatherhood recognised)[134] benefit, it is more likely to violate human dignity and constitute discrimination in the substantive sense. In application of that principle, membership rules will more easily attract a finding of discrimination if they constitute the key to an important array of rights that are essential to the well-being of minority individuals than if they only condition the access to a very specific entitlement.

Cultural Rights: the Individual Dimension

When one challenges membership criteria on the basis of a breach of equality, the analysis focuses on the distinctions employed by those criteria, rather than on the substantive rights that are conditioned on those criteria. Yet the centre of attention shifts to those substantive rights when they are themselves guaranteed by the constitution (for example, aboriginal and treaty rights) or an international treaty (for example, the right to enjoy one's own culture). These "cultural" rights are noteworthy because they do not belong to every human being but only to persons belonging to a particular cultural group. Sometimes the constitutional provision that guarantees the substantive rights also contains a precise definition of the rights-holders. Indeed, defining beneficiaries is a crucial dimension of section 23 of the Canadian Charter, the guarantee of minority-language education, which will be studied in chapter 5. But where no definition exists, one may wonder whether admissibility to those rights can be restricted to persons identified by ordinary legislation (such as the rules of Indian status) or, to the contrary, whether the constitutional protection of a right removes from the legislator the power to define who its beneficiaries are.

Consider, for instance, article 27 of the International Covenant on Civil and Political Rights, which guarantees the right of members of linguistic or ethnic minorities to use their language or enjoy their culture in common with other members of their group. This article does not define the category of persons who may benefit from the rights it enshrines. It contains no membership criteria. This does not mean, however, that states have an unbounded liberty to select the persons for whom they will recognise minority rights. The supremacy of international law over national laws requires an independent definition of that category. Imagine, for example, that a state adopted a law that allowed the members of a linguistic minority to communicate in their own language with government officials but that it deemed persons who were university graduates not to be members of the minority, thus requiring them to speak the language of the majority. This law would be inconsistent with article 27, as it would deny the enjoyment of protected rights to some persons who were, in fact, undoubtedly members of the linguistic minority.[135]

However, to reach that conclusion, it would be necessary to compare the national law at issue with "factual" conceptions of ethnic or linguistic identity. This can be illustrated by the case of Sandra Lovelace.[136] As that case is discussed in greater detail in the next chapter, I will focus here on what is essential to the present argument. Under the Indian Act, Sandra Lovelace was deprived of Indian status because she married a non-Indian man. This prevented her, among other things, from legally residing on the reserve where she was born and where the other members of her community lived. The Human Rights Committee found a violation of article 27, because Sandra Lovelace was *in fact* a member of a protected ethnic minority, irrespective of what Canadian law said about the matter, and the loss of her right to reside on her reserve severely impaired the possibility for her to enjoy her culture.

Therefore, international guarantees of substantive minority rights, such as article 27, implicitly set a standard against which the membership criteria found in national laws can be reviewed. This standard is defined by judicial interpretation, based on the judge's conception of the minority's ethnic identity. For instance, the Human Rights Committee relied on the following factors to determine that Sandra Lovelace was entitled to benefit from article 27:

> Persons who are born and brought up on a reserve, who have kept ties with their community and wish to maintain those ties must normally be considered as belonging to that minority within the meaning of the Covenant. Since Sandra Lovelace is ethnically a Maliseet Indian and has only been absent from her home reserve for a few years during the existence of her marriage, she is, in the opinion of the Committee, entitled to be regarded as "belonging" to this minority and to claim the benefits of article 27 of the Covenant.[137]

It is interesting to observe that this kind of analysis conforms to a framework that is broadly similar to the one applying to the right to equality, in that it relies mainly on comparison and justification. In the above-quoted passage, the committee is comparing Sandra Lovelace's "actual" identity to the criteria employed by the Indian Act and has found the latter to be deficient. Moreover, the committee had observed that there was no "reasonable and objective justification" for the exclusion of Sandra Lovelace.[138] In contrast, in the *Kitok* case, the Human Rights Committee held that Kitok's right to engage in reindeer herding activities, which was protected under article 27, had been validly restricted in view of the scarcity of land available for that purpose and of the fact that he was still able to practise other activities that were central to his Sami culture.[139]

The problems associated with review based on the right to equality also occur where a cultural right is at stake. Thus, a court or reviewing body that is foreign to the culture concerned may not have the requisite knowledge to pass judgment on the group's culture or identity. Nothing guarantees that the conception of ethnic identity adopted by the committee approximates the conception that is prevalent among the Maliseet people. It rather looks like a generic conception that could be applied to any minority.

Canadian law also provides an example of the manner in which the guarantee of substantive minority rights allows judges to substitute their own conception of minority identity for statutory membership criteria. Section 35 of the Constitution Act, 1982, guarantees the aboriginal and treaty rights of the indigenous peoples. It does not say, however, which individuals are entitled to benefit from those rights. One would think that entitlement to section 35 rights would be determined by the Indian Act. However, courts have held that someone who does not have Indian status can benefit from aboriginal rights, if he or she has substantial links with an indigenous community.[140] Parliament cannot decide who the holders of constitutional rights are.[141] Again, this line of reasoning requires judges to form their own conceptions of minority ethnic identity (what links are substantial?), which will then displace the membership criteria found in the Indian Act. This line of cases will be discussed in greater detail in chapter 4.

Membership control systems confront the jurist with a particularly difficult situation. A legal assessment of membership criteria necessarily involves the controversies associated with the intercultural application of human rights and requires a grasp of social science conceptions of identity, as well as conceptual clarity concerning the right to equality. In this chapter, we have seen how, through the concepts of self-determination, cultural rights, and equality, the law provides a framework for the reconciliation of individual and group interests with respect to group membership. The concrete balance struck between those interests is the subject of the remainder of this book.

3

Membership Criteria in the Indian Act, 1850–1985

Early colonial legislation did not presume to define membership in the indigenous peoples.[1] It was assumed that indigenous persons could easily be told apart from the white settlers and that any borderline cases could be resolved by the exercise of administrative or judicial discretion. As late as 1845, when it sought to exempt the indigenous peoples from the operation of hunting laws, the legislature simply referred to "the people usually called Indians."[2] In 1850, however, the government felt it necessary to define precisely the category of people entitled to live on Indian reserves and definitions of "Indian" found their way into the statute book. The rules involved crystallised in the 1876 consolidation of the Indian Act and, in their essence, remained in force until the revision of the Act in 1985. For ease of reference I will call those successive statutes the "old Indian Act." This chapter is devoted to their study, in light of the theoretical framework developed in the foregoing chapters.

In general terms, the approach taken by the old Indian Act to the definition of membership in indigenous communities was one of uniform control by the central government. While a more detailed description of those rules will be found in the third section of this chapter, where they are tested for their compatibility with human rights, the following summary will suffice for now. The act established an initial group of Indians, more or less giving legal recognition to administrative enumerations made by government officials at various stages of history, and then provided for the transmission of Indian status from that original group through the male line (that is, through a system of patrilineal *jus sanguini*). One of the most infamous features of the system was a rule to the effect that an

Indian woman who married a non-Indian man thereby lost her Indian status. Through a procedure called "enfranchisement," individual Indians could be deprived of their legal status when they were deemed to be "civilised" enough. With the exception of enfranchisement, the rules of Indian status left no place to individual will or consent: one could not choose to become an Indian, and one could not decide to renounce Indian status.[3] The views of an indigenous community about its own membership were also irrelevant to the determination of Indian status.[4] The highly formal character of the rules of Indian status should not give the impression that they were applied rigorously. In fact, membership issues were not treated consistently and were often left to the discretion of local agents of the federal government, in a manner typical of the general mismanagement of indigenous affairs.[5]

In brief terms, the theoretical framework outlined in chapter 2 requires that, on the one hand, membership control systems respect as much as possible collective indigenous rights, in particular the right of the indigenous peoples to define their own membership rules, and, on the other hand, that membership rules be compatible with individual rights, especially the right to equality and the right to enjoy one's own culture. On both counts the old Indian Act was severely defective. But a more general flaw plagued the Act: its aims were not acceptable purposes of a minority rights scheme. Thus, in this chapter I will show that (a) many of the reasons behind the adoption of a membership control system were objectionable, that (b) the system was developed without consultation of the indigenous peoples and in disregard of their traditional norms, and that (c) several aspects of the Indian Act breached human rights. In the end, it will be seen that this regime was profoundly unjust.

PURPOSES OF MEMBERSHIP CONTROL

Assessing the membership control system put in place by the old Indian Act necessitates a brief review of the policies underlying this piece of legislation. In substance, governmental authorities sought to assimilate the indigenous peoples and, pending the achievement of that ultimate goal, to protect them against the threats that were thought to derive from contact with non-indigenous society.

The initial focus of the old Indian Act was the "Indian reserves." When the government concluded treaties aimed at obtaining a surrender of aboriginal title in order to open land for colonisation, it excepted small tracts of land, called reserves, from the general surrender; they fell under the paternalistic administration of the federal government. In areas not covered by treaties, reserves were created by the administrative allocation of parcels of Crown land.[6] Indigenous peoples were expected to sedentarise on the reserves and to engage in agriculture. Yet it quickly became apparent that white settlers were trying to encroach upon or unlawfully appropriate reserve lands.[7] Statutes were thus enacted to protect the Indian reserves.[8] The indigenous peoples were considered to be unable to defend their own interests and, consequently, to be in need of guardianship. These statutes created a legal link between reserves and the groups of Indians (called "Indian bands") for the benefit of which they were set apart, prohibited non-members of an Indian band from entering the band's reserve without authorisation, and set forth the procedure to be followed when a band wished to sell a part of its reserve.[9]

After the Canadian provinces became a federation in 1867 and the federal Parliament was given jurisdiction over "Indians and lands reserved for the Indians,"[10] this legislation quickly evolved into a complete code, called the "Indian Act,"[11] regulating many aspects of the lives of the indigenous peoples and pushing the "guardianship" ideology to its limits.[12] In the words of Rand J. of the Supreme Court, writing in 1950, the Indian Act was based on "the accepted view that these aborigines are, in effect, wards of the state, whose care and welfare are a political trust of the highest obligation."[13] Hence, elected councils, having certain powers of local self-government on the reserves, were intended to replace the bands' traditional governments.[14] The aim was to familiarise the indigenous peoples with democracy and to prepare them for the exercise of municipal government. However, guardianship carried with it many repressive denials dressed up as necessary for the welfare of the indigenous peoples: for instance, their wills had to be approved by the government,[15] selling alcohol to them was prohibited, and it was an offence for them to be intoxicated.[16] Some disabilities were even imposed on the Indians in the absence of any statutory basis. For instance, for decades officials of the Department of Indian Affairs in the Western provinces operated a system of "passes" whereby an Indian wishing to leave his or her reserve had to ask the local governmental representative for an authorisation to do so.[17] On the other hand, Indians benefited from a tax exemption and an exemption from seizure,[18] apparently in order to protect the integrity of reserve lands.[19]

The guardianship ideology also manifested itself in the fact that during that period, most Indians were denied the right to vote in federal and provincial elections and were thus deprived of political power.[20] Some exceptions, which varied through time, applied to off-reserve Indians, Indians who were war veterans, and Indians who waived their tax exemption. It was only in 1960 that all Indians, male and female, were allowed to vote in federal elections. Most provinces granted Indians the right to vote in provincial elections in the 1950s or 1960s, the last being Quebec 1969. While prohibited from voting at the federal and provincial levels, Indians (initially, only men, and after 1951, both men and women) could vote only in band council elections.

While the government implemented, through the Indian Act and other means, a policy of guardianship, it also pursued a long-term policy of assimilation.[21] That policy, like guardianship, was based on the colonial assumption that indigenous cultures were inferior to Western cultures, that indigenous peoples were unfit to participate in modern society, and that the best thing the government could do for them was to replace indigenous culture with Western culture, or, in more blunt terms, to civilise them. In this connection, Duncan Campbell Scott, a deputy minister of Indian affairs at the beginning of the twentieth century, stated candidly that the aim of the government's policies was to make the Indian problem eventually disappear through the assimilation and integration of the Indians into the general population.[22] Thus, a system of compulsory education of indigenous children in residential schools was put in place, in order to distance the pupils from the presumed "bad influence" of their culture.[23] Certain traditional ceremonies were banned (even when performed on a reserve).[24] The Indian Act also contained a procedure, called "enfranchisement," whereby an Indian, under certain conditions, could renounce his or her legal Indian status and be treated like any other Canadian citizen.[25]

The policies of guardianship and assimilation required measures of membership control. Protecting the Indian reserves against non-Indian squatters entailed defining who the Indians entitled to live there were. Membership control was also required where special disabilities were imposed upon Indians as a result of the guardianship policies: thus the law had to define who was denied the right to vote in federal elections or who was prohibited from drinking alcohol.[26] Then, when the ultimate goal of assimilation was in sight, membership control was again necessary in order to identify those individuals who had become "civilised" enough to stop being considered Indians.

Those objectives, however, do not necessarily *justify* the recourse to measures of membership control. Of course, where the law genuinely aimed at the protection of indigenous interests, membership control would be legitimate. This could arguably be the case for the provisions protecting reserves from encroachment. But membership control also served more questionable goals. It is very difficult to argue, for instance, that the denial of the right to vote or the right to consume alcohol helped in any way to promote indigenous culture, to redress a historical injustice, or to further the substantive equality of the indigenous peoples.[27] As these measures do not advance substantive equality, they discriminate against the indigenous peoples. For instance, in the *Drybones* case,[28] one aspect of the prohibition on drinking alcohol was held to breach the guarantee of equality before the law, without discrimination on the basis of race, found in the Canadian Bill of Rights.[29] Using membership control as a tool to pursue those policies would thus be illegitimate.

Controlling membership in the indigenous peoples also furthered the goal of assimilating those peoples into the population of European origin and the gradual transformation of collectively held reserves into privately owned lands. Starting in 1857,[30] the Indian Act contained provisions concerning what was called "enfranchisement," that is, the fact that a person would be deprived of Indian status upon becoming sufficiently "civilised." That purpose could certainly not be said to be beneficial to the indigenous peoples. In fact, many indigenous peoples viewed the enfranchisement policy as a threat to the integrity of indigenous lands.

When the Indian Act was thoroughly revised in 1951,[31] membership control was retained for similar reasons. While certain of the disabilities imposed on Indians were repealed (such as the prohibition of certain traditional ceremonies), others remained (such as the alcohol provisions). The integration of the indigenous peoples into the general population was still the ultimate aim of the indigenous policy. Moreover, the government was highly concerned with the cost of the programs directed towards the indigenous peoples. The

Department of Indian Affairs's submission to the parliamentary committee that was reviewing the act evinced a clear preoccupation with the size of the Indian population for which public money was appropriated and with the possible abuses that might take place if a liberal definition of membership were adopted.[32] In the end, the report of that committee contained a brief recommendation that a new definition of the Indian be enacted, in order to ensure that public money was spent only for those who were "really entitled to it."[33]

In sum, while certain valid purposes (preserving the integrity of the reserves and controlling the use of public funds) could be invoked to justify the measures of membership control found in the old Indian Act, those measures were also tainted by illegitimate goals, such as the assimilation of the indigenous peoples or the imposition of legal disabilities upon them. Moreover, as we will see in the third section of this chapter, the most objectionable rules from a human rights perspective, the exclusion of women "marrying out" and enfranchisement, were directly related to those inadmissible goals and not to resource protection.

THE DENIAL OF INDIGENOUS
AUTONOMY

In chapter 2, I concluded that membership control systems must respect the collective interests of the indigenous peoples and, in particular, allow for their meaningful participation in the definition of their own membership rules. Yet the rules of the old Indian Act were developed with little or no input from the indigenous peoples. They were simply imposed upon them by the federal bureaucracy. Moreover, they were designed in a manner that ignored the indigenous peoples' traditional norms and political units. But what is most striking is that the federal government excluded several indigenous groups from the ambit of the Indian Act, depriving them of any legally recognised indigenous status.

Absence of Consultation

In formal terms, the rules of Indian status were enacted by the legislature. But beyond the unilateral nature of the legislative process, there is an ongoing controversy among historians as to whether the Indian Act imposed Western racist and sexist stereotypes on the indigenous peoples or, rather, reflected the traditional membership conceptions of the indigenous peoples (or, at least, of certain indigenous groups).

Historians who defend the second thesis rely upon instances where indigenous groups apparently asked the legislature to tighten the rules of Indian status, sometimes invoking the scarcity of reserve land, sometimes invoking their own "customs."[34] There is also evidence that indigenous leaders have used the rules of Indian status to their own advantage. For instance, historian Véronique Rozon demonstrates that in the latter part of the nineteenth century, the traditionalist faction among the Huron of Lorette sought to expel persons of non-indigenous ancestry who had settled on their reserve and mobilised the rules of Indian status to that end.[35]

However, these examples are also compatible with the hypothesis that some indigenous leaders had internalised the racist and sexist assumptions of the old Indian Act or that they strategically used the rules of Indian status where the latter worked to increase their political power.[36] Moreover, in the same period some indigenous peoples protested against offensive features of the Indian Act, such as the exclusion of women who "married out" or the provisions concerning enfranchisement, but their voice was ignored. These particular instances will be studied later in this chapter, but for the moment we can safely state that the indigenous peoples were far from unanimous concerning the statements that are invoked on behalf of the theory that the rules of Indian status reflect indigenous tradition or indigenous demands. It is safer to view those conflicting statements in the context of the ongoing transformation of indigenous societies and the strategic use of colonial institutions and rules by certain indigenous political actors.

The reform of the Indian Act in 1951 sheds some light on the true extent of "consultation." That reform was preceded by hearings of a parliamentary committee to which representatives of the indigenous peoples were invited. However, the government rejected out of hand the main demand of the latter, that Indian bands be allowed to determine their own membership.[37] Moreover, by that time indigenous leaders (who were all male, because the Indian Act then excluded women from band council elections) no longer objected to the exclusion of women who "married out." They had apparently internalised the sexist assumptions of the Indian Act, as well as the idea that indigenous identity was exclusively a matter of descent.

Neither could indigenous groups participate in the individual application of the rules laid down by the Indian Act. In 1887, the act was amended to grant the minister of Indian affairs the power to determine, upon the report of an inquiry officer, who was a member of an Indian band.[38] There was a right of appeal to the federal Cabinet. In the 1951 revision of the Act, the power to settle membership disputes was given to a federal officer called the Indian registrar, with a right of appeal to provincial courts.[39]

Disregard of Traditional Norms and Groupings

The rigid rules found in the old Indian Act sharply contrast with anthropological evidence to the effect that membership in certain pre-contact indigenous groups was flexible. As anthropologist James Smith notes concerning the Prairie Cree, "Membership in the local and regional bands was flexible, varying according to the leaders' abilities, supply of game and other environmental conditions, and family realignments."[40] The emphasis on ancestry was apparently not a feature of traditional indigenous societies. As anthropologist James Clifton says, "no native North American society subscribed to the idea of biological determination of identity or behaviour ... they stressed as criteria of group membership learned aspects of human nature: language, culturally appropriate behaviour, social affiliation, and loyalty."[41] In this regard, Wendat thinker Georges Sioui states that indigenous societies did not classify persons into discrete categories but, rather, recognised the interconnectedness of all human beings.[42]

Moreover, the Indian Act's exclusive focus on patrilineal descent does not reflect the diversity of the traditional kinship systems of the indigenous peoples. Kinship systems are called patrilineal, matrilineal, or bilateral according to whether descent is recognised through the male line, through the female line, or both.[43] Thus, in a matrilineal system, one is related, in family terms, to one's mother but not to one's father. For instance, the Iroquois peoples are well-known for their matrilineal kinship system.[44] Kinship, however, does not necessarily result in rules respecting membership in groups other than the family or the clan, such as present-day village communities. The difference between kinship and group membership is illustrated by the fact that many aboriginal peoples adopted persons of European origin, either as prisoners of war[45] or as marriage partners in the trade context.[46] Clan identity was not based exclusively on descent.[47] Recent research shows that in the Canadian West, indigenous individuals moved between local communities, so that the latter often included persons of different ethnic backgrounds.[48]

The Indian Act also divided the country's indigenous population into discrete units called "Indian bands," which do not correspond to pre-colonial indigenous groups.[49] An Indian band generally corresponds to a local collectivity or an indigenous village. It is legally defined as a group of Indians who collectively own reserve lands.[50] As reserve lands are attributed only through governmental intervention,[51] the government effectively decided which groups of indigenous persons constitute a band. The recognition of pre-colonial indigenous groups has never been the aim of the process of reserve creation and band recognition. For instance, it is well known that the Huron, Mohawk, and Abenaki bands of southern Quebec were initially composed of refugees seeking to avoid war or religious conflict in their traditional homelands located elsewhere.[52] In the Prairie provinces, the government once adopted the practice of allocating a reserve to any group of one hundred Indians or more who were willing to enter into a treaty and to adopt a sedentary way of life.[53] Indigenous groups have also evolved in response to trading patterns: many indigenous persons settled in the vicinity of trading posts or religious missions, and bands moved and merged as posts moved and closed.[54] Moreover, several indigenous groups were forgotten during the treaty process. Some of these omissions have been corrected through subsequent adhesion to treaties and the creation of new bands, but several groups remain unrecognised to this day.[55] Thus the present-day Indian bands reflect the accidents of the process of sedentarisation rather than the contours of the pre-colonial indigenous groups. While those groupings may have become internalised over time, it would be a mistake to seek congruent entities in pre-contact times.

Group Exclusions

The definition of "Indian" in the Indian Act did not encompass all persons who considered themselves as indigenous or who had some degree of indigenous ancestry. The Métis, the Inuit, and the indigenous peoples of Newfoundland were excluded as a result of conscious decisions of the federal government, which wanted to terminate its special responsibilities towards those groups or to avoid them altogether. At various times, the federal government argued that those groups were not "Indians" contemplated by section 91(24) of the Constitution Act, 1867, and were thus not within its jurisdiction. This was consistent with its policy of assimilation: those groups, who were considered "less indigenous" than status Indians, or more promising candidates for assimilation, would have a better chance of integrating into mainstream Canadian society if no special rights were granted to them and if they were not segregated on reserves.

It is difficult to escape the conclusion that this disparate treatment was discriminatory. It was based on stereotypes about certain cultures being less indigenous than others, not on a fair evaluation of the cultural differences of the groups concerned. There is no rational basis for treating the Inuit differently from their Cree neighbours or the Newfoundland Mi'kmaq differently from the Nova Scotia Mi'kmaq, nor for holding that these groups have different needs. Moreover, as the ultimate purpose of the exclusion was the assimilation of the groups concerned, the distinction cannot be justified by any ameliorative purpose or by the quest for substantive equality.

The federal government has been unable to maintain the total exclusion of those groups from the rights recognised for the indigenous peoples. In various ways, their indigenous identity is now recognised by the law, and certain rights are granted to them. We will see in the next chapter to what extent the persistence of disparate treatment today is contrary to the right to equality. In the following pages, I simply describe how these exclusions were first implemented and how the government was forced to retreat from them.

The Métis. "Métis" is a French word meaning a person with mixed ancestry. Taken literally, it would apply to a large number of indigenous individuals who can trace at least one non-indigenous ancestor. For instance, the daughter of an Indian father and a non-Indian mother could be called a Métis, although she would be entitled to Indian status. However, "Métis" has acquired more specific connotations in Canada.[56] First, the term has become the label under which particular groups of people of mixed ancestry self-identify. Métis, then, is an ethnic category of its own, separate and distinct from Indian, that has come into existence as a result of a process called "ethnogenesis."[57] Second, many individuals of indigenous descent who do not qualify for Indian status may call themselves Métis or "non-status Indians." Those persons may or may not have links with a particular Indian band or Métis community. In that second sense, Métis and non-status Indians are residual categories used by indigenous persons whose identity is not recognised by the law to describe themselves.

The largest and best-known group of Métis, often known as the Métis Nation, stems from marriages between French or English traders, or *coureurs des bois,* and indigenous women in the Canadian West in the eighteenth century.[58] Many descendants of such unions settled in the Red River valley, in Manitoba (around present-day Winnipeg), where they formed a distinct community. When the Hudson's Bay Company relinquished control over the territory in favour of Canada, the Métis of Red River formed a provisional government under the leadership of Louis Riel, which negotiated the terms of the creation of Manitoba as a new province in 1870. Those terms included Métis land rights under a policy that differed markedly from that followed by the government vis-à-vis Indian tribes. The government's response to their claims was expressed in terms of individual rather than collective entitlements. It did not sign treaties with Métis communities, nor did it grant them reserves. Rather, Métis families would receive a certificate (called "scrip") entitling them to receive a fixed amount of land in private property, in satisfaction of claims based on aboriginal title.[59] In fact, many scrip certificates were acquired by speculators, and little land was actually left to the Métis. The system has been characterised as a total failure.[60] One of the major terms of the 1870 compromise had been breached.

In order to manage the scrip system, a distinction had to be drawn between Indians, with whom the Crown would sign a treaty, and Métis, to whom lands would be granted individually. As the definitions of "Indian" in force in the 1870s, when treaties were signed in that region, included persons with mixed ancestry, there was no sharp line separating the Indians from the Métis. In practice, persons with mixed ancestry who lived among Indian bands were allowed to choose between "taking treaty" and "taking scrip."[61] In the former case, they would become Indians governed by the Indian Act and members of an Indian band, and they would be entitled to receive treaty annuities and to live on reserves. In the latter case, they would receive Métis land and were otherwise treated as non-indigenous citizens. The definition of "Indian" in the 1876 Indian Act was adjusted in consequence. By virtue of section 3(3)(e), "no half-breed in Manitoba who has shared in the distribution of half-breed lands shall be accounted an Indian." Moreover, Métis heads of families were not to be accounted Indians unless they had already been admitted into a treaty or in exceptional circumstances, at the discretion of the government. Three years later, the Act was amended to allow Métis who had "taken treaty" to withdraw therefrom upon reimbursing the annuities received.[62] After the 1885 rebellion, the government induced many persons of mixed ancestry to leave Indian bands and receive scrip and the associated financial compensation.[63] The boundary between "Indian" and "Métis" was thus left imprecisely defined and depended to a large extent on individual self-identification and governmental discretion.[64]

While a legal distinction was maintained between the Indians and the Métis, the latter were assimilated into the population of European origin for all legal purposes once they had received scrip. Their existence as a separate people went unrecognised. They did not form a legal category of their own. With one exception,[65] they had no special rights. This explains why Métis identity was not legally defined, and largely remains so today. In fact, the federal government has always contended that the Métis are not "Indians" covered by section 91(24) of the Constitution Act, 1867, but rather ordinary citizens falling under provincial responsibility. So far, the Supreme Court has accepted that proposition with respect to a constitutional provision other than section 91(24),[66] but there is little doubt that its reasons would apply as well to the latter provision. Nevertheless, the Métis did achieve considerable success in 1982, when section 35(2) of the Constitution Act, 1982, included them among the indigenous peoples of Canada and protected their aboriginal rights on an equal footing with those of the other indigenous peoples.[67] Of course, the recognition of special rights begs the question of membership. Contemporary efforts to define the Métis are reviewed in the next chapter.

The Inuit. The Inuit are the indigenous people who occupy the northern shores of Canada and the islands of the Arctic Archipelago. As they have a unique language and particular genetic characteristics, they are believed to have come to America through a later wave of migration than the other indigenous peoples.[68] Often the enemies of other peoples inhabiting territories more to the south, they were for a long time known under the name "Eskimo," a derogatory Cree term. Government representatives had little contact with them until the early twentieth century. At that time, government officials came to the conclusion that it was not useful to bring the Inuit under the Indian Act system, because Inuit were perceived as racially and culturally different from Indians and more able than Indians to be educated in the ways of Western civilisation.[69] Contrary to the Métis, who had at least agreed to the 1870 compromise, there is no evidence that the Inuit were ever consulted on the matter.

In the 1930s, the economic situation of the Inuit of northern Quebec required the State to provide them with urgent assistance. The cost of that assistance became the subject of a dispute between the federal and Quebec governments. Quebec argued that the Inuit were Indians falling under federal jurisdiction according to section 91(24) of the Constitution Act, 1867, making the federal government responsible for their well-being. Conversely, Ottawa argued that the Inuit had always been considered distinct from Indians, so that in law they were ordinary citizens having no special rights to whom the province had to provide the necessary social assistance. The matter was resolved by a reference to the Supreme Court, which held that the Inuit came within the constitutional category of "Indians" under the responsibility of the federal government.[70] Although it had been presented with a wealth of anthropological evidence highlighting the similarities and differences between the Inuit and other indigenous groups,[71] the Court based its decision on the narrow ground that the drafters of the constitution probably understood the term "Indian" as encompassing the Inuit. Several official documents, dictionaries and books published in the period immediately prior to the enactment of the constitution in 1867 were cited in support of the latter proposition. The Court thus avoided giving a comprehensive definition of the term "Indian" and ignored the anthropological evidence.

Although the federal government was forced to admit that the Inuit were indigenous peoples under its financial responsibility, it chose not to bring them under the Indian Act. In fact, the Inuit were expressly excluded from the purview of the 1951 revision of the act, through section 4(1). One of the consequences of this exclusion is that they do not benefit from the tax exemption set forth in the act.

However, the courts have recognised that the Inuit have the same aboriginal rights as other indigenous peoples.[72] Section 35(2) of the Constitution Act, 1982, now recognises that the Inuit are among the indigenous peoples of Canada.

The Indian Act is of no assistance in determining who is an Inuk.[73] There is no official "Inuit status." Nevertheless, beginning in the 1940s the federal government attempted to identify administratively the Inuit with the aid of medals bearing a serial number for each individual. In the 1970s this system was discontinued and the Inuit were induced to adopt family names. It was only when the Inuit entered into land claims agreements in 1975, 1984, 1993, and 2005 that a formal legal system was created for their identification. This system will be studied in the following chapter.

The Indigenous Peoples of Newfoundland. Newfoundland remained a colony separate from Canada until 1949. After the disappearance of the Beothuk, largely as a result of persecution by British settlers in the late eighteenth and early nineteenth century,[74] the indigenous population of the colony was comprised of Mi'kmaq, Innu, Métis, and Inuit. During the colonial era, Newfoundland did not enact legislation similar to the Indian Act. Despite the presence of an indigenous population, Canada and Newfoundland agreed that no citizen of Newfoundland would be considered an "Indian" under the Canadian Indian Act upon Newfoundland joining the federation.[75] It was believed that the indigenous people of Newfoundland were already enfranchised when the province joined Canada, because there was no special legislation enacted for them. It was also the view of the federal government that bringing indigenous Newfoundlanders under the Indian Act would not be consistent with the long-term goal of assimilating the indigenous peoples. This, in effect, amounted to a complete denial of the identity of indigenous Newfoundlanders. Again, there is no evidence that the latter were consulted.

This policy was partly reversed in 1984, when the federal government constituted one of the Mi'kmaq communities as the Miawpukek Band.[76] Two Innu communities were also constituted as bands in 2003.[77] A "modern treaty" was also signed in 2005 with the Inuit of the province, recognising their indigenous identity and their power to define their own membership criteria.[78] A recent agreement between the Federation of Newfoundland Indians, representing the province's Mi'kmaq communities, and the government of Canada provides for the creation of the Qalipu Mi'kmaq Band, a band under the Indian Act that will encompass all the indigenous inhabitants of the Island of Newfoundland.[79]

INDIAN STATUS AND INDIVIDUAL RIGHTS

Needless to say, the legislation of that period showed no concern for the human rights of the persons who were subject to it. As we shall see below, it contained a definition of indigenous identity that was rigid and uniform, that gave expression to racist and sexist prejudice then prevalent in Western thought, rather than to indigenous conceptions of identity, and that was developed in disregard of the specific objections voiced by the indigenous peoples. Many of the rules of the Indian Act would be found discriminatory under today's standards. Only in the 1960s, after the adoption of the Canadian Bill of Rights,[80] which included a statutory protection of the right to "equality before the law," would Canadian jurists begin to realise that the Indian Act was, in many respects, inconsistent with the principle of equality.

In order to demonstrate those violations of individual rights, I will, for each major aspect of the rules, give a short account of its substance, indicate the conception of indigenous identity that underlies it, and describe how it conflicts with the right to equality or the right to enjoy one's own culture. With the exception of the *Lavell* and *Lovelace* cases, which dealt with the exclusion of women "marrying out," this discussion will remain theoretical, as there are no decided cases and the rules have now been repealed. However, this exploration of the old rules is still useful in that it highlights the human rights problems that are inevitably associated with rigid racial conceptions of identity.

The Rule of Patrilineal Descent

From the outset, the Indian Act employed descent as the main criterion of transmission of Indian status. Nevertheless, descent was used in a flexible manner in the statutes enacted in the mid-nineteenth century. In the 1850 statute applying to Lower Canada, a person was considered an Indian if he or she was descended on either side from Indians.[81] Thus, the children of an indigenous mother and a non-indigenous father would fall under the definition. The rule was gender-neutral.

However, when the existing patchwork of legislation was consolidated into the Indian Act in 1876,[82] patrilineal descent alone conferred Indian status. The definition of "Indian" in the act read:

> The term "Indian" means
> *First*. Any male person of Indian blood reputed to belong to a particular band;
> *Secondly*. Any child of such person;
> *Thirdly*. Any woman who is or was lawfully married to such person.

The same principle was embodied in the 1951 revised *Indian Act*.[83] Section 11 of that act, after describing the initial group of Indians in paragraphs (*a*) and (*b*), defined the rules of transmission of Indian status as follows:

> 11. Subject to section twelve, a person is entitled to be registered if that person ...
>   (*c*) is a male person who is a direct descendant in the male line of a male person described in paragraph (*a*) or (*b*),
>   (*d*) is the legitimate child of
>   (i) a male person described in paragraph (*a*) or (*b*), or
>   (ii) a person described in paragraph (*c*) ...
>   (*f*) is the wife or widow of a person who is entitled to be registered by virtue of paragraph (*a*), (*b*), (*c*), (*d*) or (*e*).

As we can see from the 1876 rule, Indian men transmitted their status not only to their children but also to their wives.[84] The legislative history of that rule illustrates the prejudices that informed the Indian Act and sheds light on the concerns, common to the government and at least some indigenous groups, that underlay the definition of Indian status. In the 1850 legislation, "persons intermarried with Indians," irrespective of gender, were themselves considered to be Indians.[85] Thus, a white man marrying an indigenous woman would gain Indian status and the right to live on the woman's reserve. This rule immediately drew protests from certain indigenous peoples of Lower Canada.[86] The council of the Abenakis of St

François (composed exclusively of male chiefs) petitioned the governor saying that the new definition would facilitate intermarriage and lead to the enlargement of the tribe's membership, with the result that there would be less land available for each individual. The Mohawks of Kahnawake (also represented by male chiefs) made the additional point that the statute was contrary to their customary laws. According to Mohawk tradition, they argued, an Indian woman marrying a non-Indian man lost tribal membership, while this was not true of an Indian man marrying a non-Indian woman. (That statement appears doubtful, as the Mohawks were traditionally a matrilineal people.)[87] A year later, the 1850 act was amended so that only women could acquire Indian status through marriage.[88]

This appears to be the only instance where the views of the indigenous peoples were taken into account in the definition of the rules of Indian status. However, it must be realised that the views expressed in the letters that have been kept in the archives were compatible with the commonly held stereotypes of that period, according to which the man was the directing mind of the household. By way of example, the Civil Code that had been adopted in Lower Canada in 1866 denied married women the capacity to enter into contracts or to appear alone in judicial proceedings.[89] The father alone exercised paternal authority over the children of the marriage.[90] The rule that children took the family name of their father, not that of their mother, appeared so obvious that the drafters of the code did not find it necessary to state it expressly.[91] Be that as it may, the rule that non-Indian women acquired Indian status when they married an Indian man was carried over into the 1876 and 1951 Indian Acts.[92]

Therefore, the old Indian Act gave effect to a racist and sexist conception of indigenous identity. The supposed intellectual, cultural, or behaviourial inferiority attached to indigenous status was presumed to be acquired at birth and then to be unchangeable. Gender was the decisive factor in cases of interracial unions. There is no indication that genealogy was used as a proxy for culture, as the rules were rigid.

The rule of patrilineal descent has never been tested in the courts for its compatibility with the right to equality. (The *Lovelace* case, studied below, dealt with a different aspect of the rules of Indian status, the exclusion of women "marrying out.") However, a cursory inquiry into the factors of correspondence and justification reveals little reason for upholding the validity of the rule. First, it is difficult to argue that patrilineal descent corresponds to actual indigenous identity. To argue that it did would be to assume a difference in the role of each gender in the transmission of culture. For instance, if mothers played a greater role than fathers in educating their children and in inculcating the values of their indigenous community, one could argue that indigenous status should follow the female line. The relevance of gender in the transmission of culture, of course, seems difficult to prove and the courts have shown reluctance to accept arguments of that nature in the context of discriminatory citizenship rules.[93] Moreover, such arguments can be valid only with respect to a particular indigenous culture and cannot justify a rule that is uniform throughout the country.

Yet even assuming strongly differentiated roles in a given culture, this difference is not likely to hold where a person of that culture marries a person of another culture in which the roles are reversed or not strongly differentiated. In the end, it is highly probable that parents in mixed marriages will not follow any gender patterns of cultural transmission that may exist in the culture of one of them. Therefore, there is no correspondence between the transmission of Indian status through the male line and indigenous identity. Second, it is difficult to find a valid public purpose for maintaining racist and sexist rules, especially as the overall aim of the old Indian Act was the assimilation of the indigenous peoples. "Mirroring the tradition" is not particularly persuasive where the purported tradition is racist or sexist.[94] Moreover, respect for "tradition" is less compelling where the alleged tradition is shown to be the result of Western influence. Recognising minority rights does not forestall the criticism of certain aspects of the minority's culture, especially if they violate human rights.[95]

Several accessory aspects of the rule of transmission of Indian status deserve closer scrutiny. The early legislation made no distinction between legitimate and illegitimate children. However, section 3(3)(a) of the 1876 Indian Act allowed the Department of Indian Affairs to exclude illegitimate children from Indian status. The 1951 act adopted a more complex approach. Section 11(e) governed the fate of illegitimate children (either sons or daughters) of Indian *women* through a presumption that the father was an Indian (in which case the child was entitled to be Indian) unless proven otherwise (in which case the Indian status of the mother would not be transmitted to the child). No express provision was made concerning illegitimate children of Indian *men*. In *Martin v. Chapman*,[96] the Supreme Court of Canada held that illegitimate *sons* of Indian *men* were entitled to Indian status under a literal reading of paragraph (*c*) of section 11. This left the illegitimate *daughters* of Indian men without status, as paragraph (*c*) is restricted to male persons and paragraph (*d*) to legitimate children.

That case was exclusively based on the formalistic interpretation of the Indian Act. No human rights arguments were raised. Yet the special treatment imposed on illegitimate children would certainly be found discriminatory in today's context. Legitimacy is a highly suspect ground of distinction that was held to be analogous to those enumerated in section 15 of the Charter.[97] There is no correspondence between distinctions based on legitimacy and actual indigenous identity. In addition, the disparate treatment of illegitimate sons and daughters, underscored by the *Martin v. Chapman* case, is entirely irrational and was probably not intended by Parliament. Illegitimate children form a group that has historically been a victim of prejudice. Thus, the rules concerning illegitimate children infringe human dignity and are discriminatory. Moreover, they also replicate the sexual distinctions inherent in a male-transmitted status, which are discriminatory for the reasons developed above.

The treatment of adoption reveals a similar fluctuation over time. The 1850 Lower Canada statute included an explicit provision whereby a person adopted in infancy by Indians would be considered an Indian.[98] No restriction was made on the basis of the biological ancestry of the child. Curiously, the 1876 Indian Act remained silent about adoption. The 1951 Indian Act, for its part, defined "child," in section 2(*b*), as including a legally adopted *Indian* child. Thus, the adoption of a non-Indian child by Indian parents did not confer Indian status on the child, as section 2(*b*) is limited to Indian children.[99] The emphasis on "legal" adoption meant that (contrary to marriage) "customary" adoptions, performed in accordance with an indigenous people's customs but without complying with the formalities of provincial adoption laws were not recognised.[100] This rule was entirely unsatisfactory and would never survive a human rights challenge. The only purpose of excluding adoptees who have no biological indigenous ancestry would be to ensure a form of "racial purity" of the group. *This is an entirely illegitimate purpose*. Neither is there any correspondence between the exclusion of those children and actual indigenous identity, as there is no reason to think that indigenous parents would not transmit their culture to their adopted children. Human dignity is therefore violated.

This point can be illustrated by the case of Peter Jacobs, who was born of non-indigenous parents, was adopted at a very young age by Kahnawake Mohawks, and was raised in Kahnawake. He identified as a Mohawk and was considered as such by other members of the community. Yet, the Indian Act (in its 1951 version) deprived him of Indian status, as his biological parents were not Indians. The Mohawk Council of Kahnawake refused to provide him with services offered to other band members. Jacobs alleged that this refusal was contrary to the Canadian Human Rights Act,[101] which prohibits discrimination in the provision of public services. The Canadian Human Rights Tribunal agreed and characterised the denial as discrimination on the basis of race.[102]

Patrilineal descent and its accessory rules were thus fundamentally flawed, as they reflected a racist and sexist conception of indigenous identity, likely originating in Western culture, rather than in pre-contact indigenous tradition. They discriminated on the basis of gender, and gender equality must take precedence over the preservation of any purported tradition to the contrary. The rules concerning illegitimacy and adoption were also discriminatory, in the latter case on racial grounds. The whole construction of Indian status in the old Indian Act would surely have collapsed if Parliament had attempted to keep it in force after the advent of the Canadian Charter of Rights and Freedoms.

Exclusions from Indian Status

In spite of the principle of patrilineal descent, children of Indian men were not always considered Indian. The Indian Act excluded certain persons of indigenous ancestry for reasons that had nothing to do with cultural identity but that reflected the stereotypes of the day and furthered the government's policy of gradual assimilation. Those exclusions breached modern conceptions of human rights. Indeed, the most prominent challenge to provisions of the old Indian Act was targeted at the infamous exclusion of women who "married out." That rule will be studied first, after which I will turn to the procedure of enfranchisement, the so-called "double-mother" rule and exclusions based on residence.

Women "Marrying Out." Indian women who married non-Indian men were deprived of their Indian status and, consequently, of the right to reside or to inherit land on the reserve where they were born. While there are indications that government policy was to that effect as early as 1818,[103] the rule was first formally enacted in 1869,[104] and was carried over into the 1876 Indian Act[105] and into the 1951 revision to the act.[106] This is in sharp contrast with the treatment afforded to Indian men: not only would an Indian man keep his status upon marrying a non-indigenous woman, but he would also transmit it to her. Woman followed man, in both directions. This clear instance of gender discrimination would remain in force for more than a century and would be repealed only in 1985.

A controversy still rages concerning the purpose of that exclusion. As purpose is critical in assessing the justification of a rule that infringes human rights, a close review of that issue is in order. A widely held theory, echoed in twentieth-century judicial decisions, is that the government wanted to ensure the "control of Indian lands by male Indians."[107] While the sexist focus is clearly questionable, this theory appeals to a legitimate goal of minority rights, protecting Indian reserves from encroachment by white settlers, which appears to have been a significant concern of certain bands in that period.[108] From that perspective, the rule would be consistent with the demands of certain Indian bands, made in 1850, that white men who married indigenous women not be granted Indian status. The rule's focus on indigenous women marrying white men might be explained by the fact that in the nineteenth century that form of mixed union was far more common than that of indigenous men marrying non-indigenous women.[109] The fact that the possession of reserve lands was usually attributed to men rather than women might also explain a greater concern with women, rather than men, "marrying out."

However, this interpretation is problematic. While it cannot be assumed that the policies of the time were fully coherent, the "male control" thesis is contradicted by several important pieces of historical evidence. In 1869, the "control of Indian lands by male Indians" was already secured by the fact that non-indigenous men could not acquire Indian status through marriage. Hence, they could not acquire a right to live on the reserve or to vote in band council elections. Depriving women who "married out" of Indian status was not necessary to achieve that goal. This interpretation is also contradicted by a careful reading of the debates in the House of Commons when the rule was initially adopted in 1869. In response to a question from the opposition, Minister Langevin stated that the government had no intent of expelling from reserves non-Indian men married to Indian women unless they behaved improperly, for instance by selling alcohol or stealing the Indians' property.[110] He added that the government did not want to discourage mixed marriages. This suggests that the government was not intent on applying the rule systematically.

Neither was Parliament attempting to mirror the traditional rules of the indigenous peoples. These rules would not have been uniform throughout the country. Moreover, the rule that an indigenous woman would lose her status upon marrying a stranger would make no sense for a matrilineal people. In fact, there is evidence that the indigenous peoples actually protested against the exclusion of women "marrying out." In 1872, the General Council of Ontario and Quebec Indians asked that the exclusionary provisions of the 1869 Act be repealed, so that Indian women might be free to marry whomever they wished without risking exclusion from their band.[111] Three years later, the Joint Council of the Garden River and Batchewana Bands also demanded the repeal of those provisions and insisted that Indian women who "married out" could remain members of the band.[112]

The fact that those protests were disregarded shows that the most plausible purpose of the rule was the gradual assimilation of the indigenous peoples and the reduction of their numbers (and, consequently, the allocation of smaller reserves).[113] Indeed, the rule was first found in a statute that mainly sought to facilitate enfranchisement. Basing itself upon the sexist assumption that the white husband would "civilise" his indigenous wife, the government simply wanted to exclude from the indigenous population, and from the presumed bad influence of their community, those women who had a "chance" to be induced to follow the Western way of life. This objective is clearly detrimental to the indigenous peoples; it cannot be linked to any attempt to protect their lands or to promote their substantive equality. It is not an ameliorative purpose that might explain why the law makes certain suspect distinctions.

What is particularly striking is that in the parliamentary committee hearings that led to the 1951 revision of the Indian Act, the indigenous organisations did not raise any objection to the rules whereby Indian status flowed through the male line and women who "married out" lost Indian status.[114] This shows that these rules had been, over the seventy years after their adoption, internalised by the indigenous leadership, who now viewed them as unproblematic.[115] The fact that women and off-reserve Indians were not entitled to vote in band council elections[116] also explains why those councils were not concerned with the fate of the excluded women. Yet concerns began to emerge about the concrete effects of the exclusion in cases of marriage breakdown. Some indigenous organisations mentioned that they would like Indian bands to have the power to readmit women who "married out" but subsequently became widowed or deserted.[117]

The discriminatory effects of the exclusion became only more apparent in the late 1960s, with the liberalisation of divorce law.[118] Upon divorce, women who had "married out" did not regain Indian status and were left in a legal limbo, as the cause of their loss of status had disappeared. In practical terms, they could not legally return to their reserve of origin or inherit their parents' property.

Then in the early 1970s, several women's groups embarked on a campaign to convince Parliament to repeal section 12(1)(b) of the Indian Act, the provision that deprived of Indian status "a woman who is married to a person who is not an Indian."[119] At the same time, two indigenous women challenged the validity of section 12(1)(b) before the Canadian courts, on the grounds that it discriminated on the basis of sex and infringed the right to equality before the law guaranteed by the Canadian Bill of Rights,[120] a statute of Parliament enacted in 1960 that declared a list of fundamental rights and sought to make them paramount over other federal statutes. Jeannette Lavell appealed the federal government's decision to strike her name off the Indian register on the basis that she had married a non-indigenous man.[121] Yvonne Bédard, for her part, had married a non-Indian, then divorced and returned to her reserve, where she lived in a house legally attributed to her brother. When the band council threatened to remove her from the reserve, alleging that she had no right to live there, she applied to the court for an injunction restraining the band from doing so. Both cases were joined for hearing before the Supreme Court of Canada.[122]

These cases raised the dilemma described in chapter 2: the reconciliation of equality and minority rights. The only case where the issue had been considered at that time was *Drybones*,[123] in which the Supreme Court had struck down a provision of the Indian Act that made it an offence for an Indian to be drunk outside a reserve, even though no such offence existed for non-Indians. As the indigenous population was not treated consistently with the non-indigenous population, this was held to be racial discrimination and the provision was thus invalid. However, the Court in *Drybones* did not articulate a coherent conception of equality, nor did it explain how the existence of a special statute governing persons of a certain "race" was consistent with equality. Hence, in the following years, many people who viewed equality mainly in formal terms believed that the *Drybones* interpretation of the Canadian Bill of Rights would lead to the wholesale invalidation of the Indian Act.

This dilemma was particularly acute for the indigenous leadership, who considered the Indian Act, despite its colonial origins, as the only legal protection of indigenous lands, culture, and identity.[124] Thus, the potential application of the right to equality before the law to strike down certain provisions of the Indian Act became a matter of great concern to them. They feared that the ideas of the white paper, a federal policy statement that advocated the assimilation of the indigenous peoples and that was retracted as a result of stark indigenous opposition, would be imposed by the courts.[125] In the result, several indigenous associations representing Indian bands intervened before the Supreme Court in *Lavell* to defend the validity of the act. Maintaining the protective legislation was considered more important than removing discrimination against women. (Of course, those views may be explained in part by the fact that the indigenous leadership was almost entirely male, as women could not vote in band council elections until 1951.) Certain indigenous leaders were also apprehensive about the cultural changes that might result from a non-discriminatory rule: at least one leader mentioned that he was reluctant to see "white men" come to the reserves.[126] At the end of the day, only certain women's organisations (indigenous and non-indigenous) intervened in support of Lavell and Bédard.

In a divided judgement, the Supreme Court dismissed the challenge to section 12(1)(*b*). The judges forming the majority gave priority to minority rights over equality in their reasoning: they strove to uphold the Indian Act and to maintain Parliament's power to legislate concerning Indians, which flowed from section 91(24) of the Constitution Act, 1867. They apparently failed to consider a substantive conception of equality that would be sensitive to the concrete effects of legislative distinctions. Their assumption seems to have been that any distinction based on race in the Indian Act was inconsistent with equality. This, of course, presumes a purely formal conception of equality. Therefore, the majority judges had to find reasons to exempt the Indian Act from judicial review for consistency with the right to equality. Justice Ritchie, for one, said that it was implicit in section 91(24) that Parliament had the power to define who is an Indian and that the Canadian Bill of Rights could not affect that constitutional provision.[127] He also affirmed that the Indian Act, as "special" legislation, could not be presumed to have been implicitly repealed by the "general" provisions of the Canadian Bill of Rights.[128] Justice Ritchie went even further: contrary to his own previous holding in *Drybones*, he denied that the right to "equality before the law" had anything to do with the substance of legislation, which judges were not empowered to review; rather, it referred to equality in the administration of the law.[129] In this, he was joined by Justice Pigeon, who wrote a brief concurring judgment stating that the Bill of Rights did not authorise the judicial review of legislation and could not be construed so as to suppress all legislation concerning Indians.[130] Thus, the majority seemed to consider the indigenous peoples according to the popular conception of "race" described in chapter 1, based on strict transmission by descent, which would explain their perplexity at having to reconcile the special treatment of a "race" mandated by the constitution and the prohibition of racial discrimination.

Justice Laskin, in dissent, rebutted those arguments. He criticised the idea that an exemption from the prohibition on discrimination was an implied consequence of the constitutional provision authorising Parliament to legislate concerning Indians: "[d]iscriminatory treatment on the basis of race or colour or sex does not inhere in that grant of legislative power."[131] Moreover, he insisted that the Court, in *Drybones*, had accepted that the Canadian Bill of Rights mandated the judicial review of the contents of legislation.[132] He then referred to certain factors that are typical of a substantive equality analysis. He highlighted the benefits that flowed from Indian status and that were denied to women who had "married out," such as the possibility of living on a reserve and participating in the administration of its affairs through the band council, or the availability of government assistance.[133] He held that discrimination had been proven in this case, as section 12(1)(*b*) of the Indian Act was a "legal instrument of separation of an Indian women from her native society and from her kin"[134] and imposed disabilities and disqualifications on female persons. He also considered, and rejected, possible justifications of the distinction. There was no biological or physiological rationale for it. Arguments based on tradition were not supported by the facts, at least not when the legislation was considered on a nation-wide basis.[135] Thus, Justice Laskin was closer to a cultural conception of indigenous identity, in which rigid racial and gender considerations were not relevant.

Yet Justice Laskin did not touch on the broader implications of his holding. He did not adopt a general framework for the analysis of alleged breaches of the right to equality, nor did he say whether he considered the other provisions governing Indian status to be discriminatory. His judgment could thus be understood as standing for the other horn of the equality/minority rights dilemma: that the right to equality must apply without restriction to minority rights legislation.

The *Lavell* judgment is unsatisfactory, first and foremost in its outcome, as a blatantly discriminatory provision was upheld. But the reasons given by both the majority and the dissent are also problematic. They contain no indication of what the legitimate purposes of membership control measures might be. For instance, the interest that the indigenous peoples themselves have in controlling their own membership was entirely ignored. Moreover, the case does not provide guidelines for applying equality rights in a manner that would not jeopardise the very existence of special legislation concerning the indigenous peoples.

Yet the Supreme Court did not have the final word on the matter. In 1976, Canada ratified the International Covenant on Civil and Political Rights, as well as its additional protocol authorising individual complaints to the United Nations Human Rights Committee. Sandra Lovelace, an Indian woman who had married a non-Indian man and subsequently divorced, brought a complaint before the committee, alleging that the provisions of the Indian Act depriving her of Indian status were contrary to several rights guaranteed by the Covenant, including equality rights, the right to choose one's residence, the right to marry and the right, enshrined in article 27, of persons belonging to ethnic minorities to enjoy their culture in common with other members of their group. The Canadian government, in reply, agreed that section 12(1)(b) of the Indian Act was flawed but still sought to justify it by a blend of concerns related to the protection of reserve lands, the autonomy of the indigenous peoples, and the preservation of the status quo. First, according to the government, there had to be a definition of Indian status in view of the rights that were afforded to Indians, such as the right to reside on reserves. Second, it argued that Canadian law historically used patrilineal criteria in order to deal with indigenous claims. Third, the government sought to rely on the theory that non-Indian men posed a more specific threat than non-Indian women to the integrity of the reserves.[136] Fourth, it was reluctant to amend the act without the agreement of the Indian organisations, and those organisations were divided on the issue.

While the application of many Covenant rights had been argued on Lovelace's behalf, the committee chose to deal with the case solely on the basis of the rights of members of minorities guaranteed by article 27. The aspect of the case that most concerned the committee was the fact that Lovelace had lost the right to reside on her native community's reserve: while article 27 does not expressly provide a right to reside on an Indian reserve, the committee concluded that it implicitly did so, because there was no other place where Lovelace could live among other members of her community and enjoy the culture of the group. Therefore, article 27, and not the anti-discrimination provision, was the "most directly applicable" to the situation. Yet, the analysis bears close resemblance to that employed in equality cases, in that it focuses on correspondence and justification.

With respect to the first prong of the inquiry, correspondence, the Committee refused to defer to the indicia of indigenous identity contained in Canadian legislation. To the contrary, it made its own assessment of Sandra Lovelace's ethnic identity and came to the conclusion that she was a member of an ethnic minority protected by article 27. It based its conclusion on a combination of factors:

Persons who are born and brought up on a reserve, who have kept ties with their community and wish to maintain those ties must normally be considered as belonging to that minority within the meaning of the Covenant. Since Sandra Lovelace is ethnically a Maliseet Indian and has only been absent from her home reserve for a few years during the existence of her marriage, she is, in the opinion of the Committee, entitled to be regarded as "belonging" to this minority and to claim the benefits of article 27 of the Covenant.[137]

Both objective and subjective factors were considered: the place where one is born and brought up, as well as one's "ethnicity" (presumably a reference to indigenous ancestry), are traits that one cannot change. Conversely, the fact that one maintains ties with one's community and wishes to continue to do so depends upon one's individual will. However, the opinion of the committee does not indicate how these factors are combined and which ones are more important. Yet it is important to underline the fact that the committee did not refer to any element that may be linked to a racial conception of indigenous identity. The committee considered that one's ethnicity is determined by the place where one was born and raised, rather than one's ancestry. However, it is unclear from the committee's reasons whether it received any evidence about how the Maliseet themselves view their own identity. Hence, even though it must be commended for rejecting racial conceptions of identity, the committee's assessment was that of an outsider.

The committee then turned to the second prong of its analysis: whether denying rights to a person prima facie covered by article 27 was objective and reasonable. In general terms, it recognised "the need to define the category of persons entitled to live on a reserve, for such purposes as those explained by the Government regarding protection of its resources and preservation of the identity of its people."[138] Thus, the legitimacy of membership control was acknowledged in principle, for reasons broadly compatible with those studied in chapter 2. This did not conclude the matter, however, as the rule's effects must be proportional to its objective. The committee's reasons in this regard were very much fact-specific. It emphasized that Lovelace's case had to be considered in the light of the breakdown of her marriage, after which her "main cultural attachment" was to her band. In those circumstances, "Whatever may be the merits of the Indian Act in other respects, it does not seem to the Committee that to deny Sandra Lovelace the right to reside on the reserve is reasonable or necessary to preserve the identity of the tribe."[139] Article 27 was thus violated.

The committee's decision was useful in that, at last, it provided indigenous women with an official recognition of the justice of their struggle to have section 12(1)(b) of the Indian Act repealed. Yet its reasons provided only very general guidance for further analysis. As they were explicitly limited to the case of a woman who had divorced, nothing was said about the validity of the exclusion of an Indian woman who remains married to a non-Indian man. The committee does not make clear either whether a system of Indian status based on descent would be compatible with Covenant rights. Moreover, the Committee's reasoning was not based on the notion of discrimination, which would decrease its precedential value in cases where only the right to equality woud be invoked.[140] Yet *Lovelace* caused considerable embarrassment to the Canadian government, which by then was posing as a champion of human rights. It spurred the 1985 reform to the membership provisions of the Indian Act, which will be studied in the following chapter.

Enfranchisement. Under the old Indian Act, in addition to "marrying out," a person could also lose Indian status upon becoming "enfranchised." As the reason offered for the separate legal treatment of the indigenous peoples was their "inferiority," it followed that such special treatment should be terminated when an indigenous person had acquired "superior" skills, knowledge, or character. Therefore, starting in 1857, the law set out a procedure whereby an Indian who was considered to have acquired the qualities of a good citizen could be deprived of his Indian status, so as to be thereafter legally treated for all purposes as a non-Indian.[141] That person would then lose all the benefits associated with Indian status and be absolved from all the disabilities attached to it. As one of those disabilities was the denial of the right to vote, the whole procedure was called "enfranchisement." To induce Indians to become enfranchised, the Indian Act provided that, upon enfranchisement, an Indian would receive, in individual property, a portion of his band's reserve lands. When an Indian was enfranchised, his wife and children were automatically enfranchised as well. The government's enfranchisement policy was never successful or popular among the indigenous peoples.[142] When the government sought to pursue it more aggressively, it quickly drew protests from indigenous leaders.[143]

From the perspective of the Indian bands, enfranchisement meant the loss of parts of the collectively held reserves, which largely explains their opposition to the procedure.[144] Initially, enfranchisement did not depend on the consent of the person's band. However, this was changed in 1876, but consent could again be dispensed with under an 1884 amendment.[145] A compromise was reached in the 1951 act: the consent of the band was not required for enfranchisement as such but remained necessary for the attribution of a part of the reserve to the person concerned.

A persistent question was whether a person could be enfranchised without his or her consent. It quickly became obvious to the government that very few Indians wished to lose their distinct status or to renounce their identity. In order to increase the enfranchisement rates, the Indian Act made individual consent unnecessary from 1869 to 1876, from 1920 to 1922,[146] and from 1933 to 1951.[147] Yet the protests of the indigenous peoples, especially in 1920,[148] forced Parliament to withdraw those aggressive provisions.

A remarkable feature of the 1876 Indian Act was section 86(1), which automatically enfranchised Indians who became doctors or lawyers, obtained a university degree, or became ministers of the Gospel: these persons were irrefutably presumed to have become "civilised." Four years later the operation of that extraordinary provision was made conditional on the person concerned making an application to that effect, so that no one could be enfranchised against his will on that basis alone.[149]

The provisions of the Indian Act concerning enfranchisement somehow depart from the rigid racist and sexist conception of indigenous identity that permeates the rules of Indian status, according to which identity is solely a function of descent. Even though indigenous status was determined by birth and marriage, the law admitted that individuals could change their culture and reflected this by the deprivation of Indian status. In this case, indigenous status appears based upon culture rather than "race." This apparent lack of coherence may nevertheless be explained by the fact that financial, rather than philosophical, considerations seem to be the main reason for the adoption of the procedure.

Enfranchisement has never been challenged as a breach of human rights. Yet it is quite clear that involuntary enfranchisement violates the right to culture guaranteed by article 27 of the International Covenant on Civil and Political Rights. Persons who are enfranchised lose all the special rights guaranteed to the indigenous peoples at common law, under the treaties and pursuant to the Indian Act. Like Sandra Lovelace, they face severe restrictions if they want to live in community with other persons who share their culture. There does not appear to be a plausible "objective and reasonable" justification for enfranchisement. The actual purpose of those provisions was the assimilation of the indigenous population. Forced assimilation is not a purpose consistent with article 27. As such, it can never ground a reasonable justification under that article.

Rules providing for involuntary enfranchisement also draw a distinction based upon race or ethnic origin, as only indigenous persons are subject to the prospect of being legally cut off from their identity and culture. Again, this would most certainly be considered as substantively discriminatory under the *Law* v. *Canada* framework, as it imposes burdens on a group that is already disadvantaged and as no ameliorative purpose compatible with minority rights theory can be identified.

Voluntary enfranchisement raises slightly different issues. One might argue that the law should not ascribe a particular ethnic identity against someone's wishes. Voluntary enfranchisement, in that perspective, would simply give effect to individual choices. In practice, however, it is difficult to assess whether such instances of enfranchisement were truly voluntary. Historical studies have shown that the prospect of receiving a sizeable lump sum of money was a strong inducement for individual Indians to apply.[150] Moreover, there is no way to reverse enfranchisement: one cannot reapply to regain Indian status. In that sense, the enfranchisement provisions curtailed individual freedom. The fact that enfranchisement was a one-way street shows that it was based on a hierarchy of cultures, which may in and of itself violate the right to equality.

The "Double-Mother" Rule. Another exclusion was introduced by the 1951 revision of the Indian Act: the so-called "double-mother" rule, contained in section 12(1)(a)(iv), which provided that an Indian who reached adult age would lose Indian status if his or her mother and paternal grandmother were not Indians by birth (that is, if they had acquired Indian status only through marriage). This reflected a new preoccupation of the 1951 legislation with blood quantum. Under the former Indian Act, Indian men could marry non-Indian women for several generations without losing their status, although this would result in the latter generations having a low percentage of Indian blood. The government considered, however, that it was undesirable that persons with one-quarter Indian blood or less be allowed to live on reserves or receive benefits reserved for Indians.[151]

Yet the correlation between blood quantum and the double-mother rule is far from perfect because the rule applied only to children of marriages entered into after 1951 and persons who had Indian status by then could have much-diluted Indian blood. Thus, it seems that the purpose of the rule was to reduce the Indian population and the public expenses in its favour, rather than to preserve, to a certain degree, the integrity of the indigenous communities. The rule favoured the government, not the indigenous peoples. If the government's aim had been to enable the indigenous communities to maintain a form of cultural homogeneity or a common identity, the logical thing to do would have been to accede to the demands of many Indian bands, demands expressed in the parliamentary committee hearings that preceded the revision of the Indian Act, to have the power to control their own membership.

The double-mother rule clearly evinces a racial conception of indigenous identity, even though it implements it in a quite irrational manner, especially because it applies only prospectively. Courts have never had the opportunity to test its compatibility with the right to equality, but the problems related to correspondence and justification can be summarily stated. The rule employs distinctions based on race and gender that do not seem to correspond to any defensible conception of indigenous identity. The protection of scarce resources against a large number of potential claimants, the likely aim of the 1951 legislation, might be a valid objective, but it is hardly proportional to employ irrational racial and sexist distinctions to further it. More will be said about the validity of the use of blood quantum in definitions of indigenous status in the following chapter.

Another discriminatory feature of the double-mother rule flowed from a curious drafting oversight: because it referred to children of "marriages," it was held to apply only to legitimate children.[152] Thus, illegitimate children were not liable to lose their status if they lacked the requisite ancestry. Although this distinction had the effect of favouring a disadvantaged group (illegitimate children) that had been the victim of stereotypes, it impinged upon human dignity, as it was not designed to improve the lot of that group and relied on a characteristic – legitimacy – that could hardly be rationally related to any valid legislative purpose.

Exclusion of Non-residents from the Right to Vote. An additional layer of exclusion resulted from the fact that the right to vote in band council elections was denied to certain categories of Indians.[153] First, only *male* band members resident on a band's reserve had the right to vote. Women who lived on their band's reserve were given that right only in 1951. (In contrast, non-indigenous women were given the right to vote in federal elections in 1917.) In those conditions, it is not surprising that the indigenous leadership has been predominantly male. Second, band members residing *outside the reserve*, irrespective of their gender, were also deprived of the right to vote in band council elections, perhaps reflecting an assumption that they were not interested in the affairs of their band. As a result, band councils rarely responded to the interests of off-reserve band members, who were thus left to create their own political associations in the absence of any recognised statutory structure.

The latter exclusion lasted until 1999, when the Supreme Court struck it down, in the *Corbiere* case,[154] as inconsistent with section 15 of the Charter. While all the judges concurred in the result, their reasons were based on divergent perspectives about the right to equality. The majority judgment, co-authored by Justices McLachlin and Bastarache, offered a relatively simple and abstract analysis. The first main issue was to determine whether the exclusion of non-resident band members from voting was based on a ground enumerated in section 15 or an analogous ground. The majority insisted that analogous grounds must be established on a permanent basis: if a ground is analogous in one case, it will be so in all others. The common feature of analogous grounds was said to be their link with characteristics of the person that are immutable (such as place of birth) or "constructively immutable" (such as religion). Hence, the focus is on the ground of distinction, rather than on the vulnerable group delineated by that ground. Applying that framework, the majority had no difficulty in finding that the Indian Act drew a distinction based on "aboriginality-residence" (the fact that an Indian lives on or off a reserve) and that this was an analogous ground. That characteristic of the individual was seen as constructively immutable, because, owing to a shortage of housing on the reserves, "off-reserve Aboriginal band members can change their status to on-reserve band members only at great cost, if at all."[155]

The majority then had to decide whether that distinction was substantively discriminatory. The factor that seemed the most important was the fact that the act furthered the stereotype to the effect that off-reserve band members were less interested in the affairs of their band. Therefore, the distinction infringed upon their human dignity and was discriminatory.[156] And it was not saved by section 1, which allows for restrictions to human rights that are justified in a free and democratic society: even assuming that some restrictions on the off-reserve members' voting rights were necessary to protect the interests of on-reserve members, the response adopted by the act, complete denial of the right to vote, was not shown to be proportional. Other, less intrusive restrictions (such as two-tier councils, reserved seats for off-reserve members) could be imagined.[157]

Justice L'Heureux-Dubé, in her concurring judgment, adopted a more contextual approach focusing on the protection of groups and on the intersectional nature of the discrimination in this case. For her, the common thread of the analogous grounds is that they refer to fundamental personal choices. As the decision to live on or off a reserve is fundamental to one's identity,[158] off-reserve band members were considered to be a protected group. An additional reason was that off-reserve band members had historically been victims of prejudice. Then Justice L'Heureux-Dubé found the denial of the right to vote to be substantively discriminatory. She focused on the particular forms of prejudice suffered by off-reserve band members and noticed that women who had left the reserve and lost their status upon "marrying out" were doubly disadvantaged.[159] She also found that the challenged rule could not be saved by section 1, for reasons similar to those of the majority. In the end, her analysis has a greater potential to identify substantive discrimination. It is not limited by the formal notion of fixed analogous grounds but, rather, focuses on the actual circumstances of the group affected. The intersectional nature of the discrimination that flowed from the Indian Act makes such a contextual analysis all the more necessary.

This chapter must have left the reader with a dim view of the manner in which the Canadian state ascribed an official status to its indigenous population. The rules of the Indian Act were ridden with sexist and racist prejudice and were geared towards the ultimate goal of assimilation. Several groups were excluded altogether from Indian status. The indigenous peoples were deprived of the power to control their own membership. It was only in the 1970s that the discriminatory provisions of the Indian Act attracted public scrutiny. Following the realisation that the old rules were incompatible with human rights, gender distinctions in the transmission of Indian status were finally eliminated, after a struggle that lasted more than fifteen years, by legislation that is the subject of the next chapter. Yet as Justice L'Heureux-Dubé's judgment in *Corbiere* shows, the injustice suffered by several sub-groups (notably women) within the indigenous population has been complex and enduring and resists simple analysis. As we will see in the following chapter, some aspects of this injustice still persist today.

4

Modern Definitions of Indigenous Identity

In the previous chapter, the rules of Indian status found in the "old" Indian Act were shown to be deficient with respect to the two main requirements developed in chapter 2: respect for the autonomy of the indigenous peoples in defining their own membership and respect for individual rights, especially the right to equality and the right to culture. Indeed, those rules were developed without consultation and without regard for the autonomy of the indigenous communities. They also discriminated in many ways, especially against women. Moreover, their purposes (assimilation of the indigenous population and their paternalistic protection) could not be reconciled with any modern notion of minority rights.

During the second half of the twentieth century, these orientations of the Indian Act came under attack, as they were incompatible with the notions of human rights and self-determination that were gaining in popularity. Cultural assimilation became discredited, and a 1969 federal policy paper advocating the termination of Indian status and the integration of the indigenous peoples into mainstream Canadian society was withdrawn in the face of vigorous indigenous opposition.[1] At the same time, a Supreme Court decision forced the government to admit that aboriginal rights had not been extinguished by colonisation and the passage of time. The fundamental shift from a policy of guardianship and assimilation towards a policy of recognising and valuing indigenous difference is highlighted by the inclusion in the 1982 Constitution of a provision (section 35) stating that "the existing aboriginal and treaty rights" of the indigenous peoples, including Indians, Inuit, and Métis, were "recognised and affirmed."[2] In the following years, the Supreme

Court construed this provision as mandating judicial review of federal or provincial legislation that infringed upon aboriginal and treaty rights.[3] According to the Court, those rights include the right to hunt and fish for food,[4] to harvest wood for domestic use,[5] and in certain circumstances, to engage in commercial fishing.[6] The extent of the aboriginal rights protected by section 35 is still uncertain. Most important is whether self-government is included. The Supreme Court has not yet decided this issue,[7] but the federal government has recognised that self-determination is an aboriginal right protected by the constitution and has declared itself ready to negotiate its implementation with the indigenous peoples.[8]

The transition from assimilation and guardianship to the promotion of indigenous difference is also evident with respect to legislation and administrative practice. The Indian Act is still in force and remains criticised for its colonialist foundations, but it has been stripped of its most paternalistic aspects. For instance, the prohibitions on the consumption of alcohol and on indigenous traditional ceremonies have been repealed. The Indian Act can now be conceived mainly as a statute regulating the use and possession of Indian reserves and the government of Indian bands. Thus its nature has evolved from a statute imposing disabilities on members of a "race" deemed to be inferior to a statute conferring benefits on members of a disadvantaged ethnic group. The main benefits conferred by the act on individuals are the possession of land within an Indian reserve (section 20) and the tax and seizure exemptions (sections 87 and 89). ·

Quite apart from the Indian Act, the federal government also confers benefits on indigenous persons, including the reimbursement of university tuition fees or the free provision of certain medical services that are not insured by provincial health regimes. Moreover, the federal government funds heavily the construction of houses and other infrastructure on Indian reserves, as well as the operating expenses of Indian bands. This is not to say that those benefits fully correct historical injustices imposed on the indigenous peoples or remedy their present disadvantaged situation in Canadian society. In this regard, the United Nations Committees on the Elimination of Racial Discrimination and on Economic, Social and Cultural Rights have criticised Canada's treatment of its indigenous peoples and expressed deep concern with the indigenous peoples' economic marginalisation, endemic mass unemployment, high rate

of suicide and high rate of incarceration, as well as with the shortage of adequate housing and the frequent lack of safe drinking
water in the indigenous communities.[9] If the United Nations Human
Development Index were to be calculated for the indigenous peoples
of Canada alone, they would rank 79th among 170 countries, close
to countries such as Brazil or Peru,[10] while Canada as a whole
stands at the very top of the list.

In this context, the increasing importance of individual human
rights induced a growing recognition of the unacceptability of gender or other types of discrimination in the rules of Indian status.
The membership control system of the old Indian Act was crum-
bling under the injustices it generated. Nevertheless, the nature of
the rights of the indigenous peoples made it impossible to simply do
away with membership control systems. In this connection, legal
historian Paul McHugh states that "[g]roups receiving considerable
resources, as from settlements, government servicing, or (as in the
on-reserve casino industry in the United States) administration of
lucrative enterprises, had to have in place the means of determining
who could or could not participate in the benefits. Whereas once
identification of membership through enrolment was regarded as a
precondition to the dismantling of the tribal asset base, this now
became a precondition to its rehabilitation."[11]

In Canada, the impetus for reform of the rules of Indian status
came from the *Lovelace* decision of the United Nations Human
Rights Committee in 1981 and the enactment of the Canadian
Charter of Rights and Freedoms in 1982. In 1985, after difficult
negotiations between the federal government and indigenous political associations, Parliament enacted Bill C–31, which effected a
thorough reform of the rules of Indian status found in the Indian
Act. However, while Parliament retained control over Indian status,
it also allowed Indian bands to enact their own membership codes.
Indian status now determines only the eligibility to benefits conferred by the federal government directly to indigenous individuals
(for example, the tax exemption). In contrast, access to band
resources (for example, the right to reside on a reserve) depends
upon band membership. In parallel to those developments, certain
indigenous peoples signed "modern treaties" with the government.
Those treaties contain definitions of membership that replace, for
most purposes, Indian status and that remedy the problems created
by the old Indian Act. Another interesting case of membership defi-

nition is provided by the Métis, who are presently attempting to create their own membership control system, without the intervention of the federal government.

These new systems of membership control afford different degrees of autonomy to the indigenous peoples. In the first part of this chapter, those systems are described in ascending order of autonomy. In the second part, I analyse whether those regimes comply with individual rights. An important point that will emerge from this discussion is that the autonomy of the indigenous peoples does not necessarily lead to violations of individual rights.

INDIGENOUS AUTONOMY IN THE DEFINITION OF STATUS

The Indian Act and Bill c–31: State Control of Indian Status

When considering how to respond to the *Lovelace* decision, the federal government was faced with two different indigenous lobbies advancing claims related to individual rights or autonomy.[12] On one side were the indigenous women's groups, most importantly the Native Women's Association of Canada (NWAC), which came into being during the *Lavell* controversy. They had the support of non-indigenous women's groups and of the Canadian Human Rights Commission. They asked for the immediate repeal of section 12(1)(*b*) of the Indian Act (the provision that excluded women who had "married out") and for the reinstatement of women who had lost their status through the operation of that rule.[13]

On the other side were the Indian bands and their national association, the Assembly of First Nations (AFN). They insisted that gender discrimination was but a part of the colonial and discriminatory scheme of the Indian Act. Thus, what was required was the replacement of the act with a new system based on the recognition of the indigenous peoples' right to self-government.[14] Under such a system, Indian bands would have the power to determine their own membership, and the federal government would not regulate Indian status at all. However, the AFN was opposed to a piecemeal reform of the Indian Act that would address only the issue of gender discrimination. It effectively used the issue as a lever to obtain a broader reform.

Moreover, the AFN also expressed concerns with the reinstatement of excluded women. It was anticipated that a large number of
women (as well as their children) would claim Indian status and
attempt to establish their residence on the reserves. The already
insufficient housing available on the reserves could not accommo-
date such an influx of new members. This led some bands to conclude that the federal government was trying to have them bear the
costs of a problem that it had created.[15] Certain Indian bands also
feared that the return of reinstated women, who had lived for some
time outside the reserves, would jeopardise indigenous culture and
bring Western influences into the indigenous communities. For
instance, a group of Alberta Indian bands argued that the reintegration of those women would lead to a dramatic enlargement of the
population of the reserves, through the addition of persons who
were thought to have adopted an "individualistic lifestyle" incompatible with the collective values of the band members who had
always resided on the reserve.[16] This antipathy towards excluded
women is also apparent from the fact that when the federal government offered to use its power to suspend certain provisions of the
act to make the exclusion of women "marrying out" and
the double-mother rule inapplicable to bands who requested it,
many more bands asked for a suspension of the double-mother rule
(which excluded men as well as women) than for a suspension of
section 12(1)(b).[17]

Needless to say, NWAC and its supporters disagreed with the AFN's
approach and felt that it subordinated women's concerns to the
more general goal of self-government. They pressured for an immediate reform. The diverging views of the AFN and NWAC led many
people to conceive the debate in terms of whether the right to self-
government should trump the right to gender equality or vice versa.
Women's groups often came to the conclusion that the mainly male
leadership of the AFN could not be trusted to adequately represent
indigenous women.

The new rules that were eventually enacted in 1985, commonly
known as Bill C–31,[18] attempted to give some degree of autonomy
to the Indian bands in the determination of their own membership, while giving priority to the elimination of discrimination.
The new legislation reflected some of the principles of an agreement between the AFN and NWAC.[19] That agreement, however,
proved to be fragile, as several bands from Alberta quickly dis-

sented from it and later events showed the reluctance of many bands to implement it.[20]

Full autonomy of the Indian bands with respect to Indian status, as claimed by the AFN, was unacceptable to the federal government. Under such a system, an Indian band could decide who would benefit from a tax exemption and who would be entitled to the reimbursement of university tuition fees or non-insured medical services, and the government would have to bear the cost of those benefits without being able to control the size of the class of beneficiaries. The solution was to separate Indian status from band membership. Indian status is still determined by the rules of the Indian Act but is now relevant only to the eligibility to benefits provided directly by the federal government. Under section 10 of the act, bands have been granted the power to adopt membership codes that are wider or narrower than the rules of Indian status. Band membership conditions admissibility to rights related to the collective resources of the band. For instance, only band members (whether they are status Indians or not) can hold land on a reserve or vote in band council elections. Thus, if a band chooses to enlarge its membership, it must draw on its existing resources to provide new members with land, housing, and so on. Under that system, the enlargement of a band's membership has no impact on the financial obligations of the federal government.

Having decided to retain control of Indian status, Parliament had to purge it of gender discrimination. Under Bill C–31, Indian status is now transmitted by descent, without any distinction based on gender. In fact, the principle of descent is now subject to fewer exceptions than in the previous law. Section 12(1)(*b*), which disentitled women who "married out," was repealed. The possibility of enfranchisement was eliminated. Hence, Indian status cannot be lost or voluntarily renounced. The rule whereby a non-Indian woman marrying an Indian man acquired Indian status was also repealed. Adopted non-Indian children may now inherit their adoptive parents' status. In the result, a person's status is entirely determined at birth (or adoption) and cannot be changed afterwards. Men do not have a better right to transmit Indian status than women. However, to reflect the financial concerns of the government, Indian status is lost after two generations of intermarriage with non-Indians (sections 6(1)(*f*) and 6(2), also known as the "second-generation cut-off rule").

Under sections 6(1)(c), 6(1)(d), and 6(1)(e) of the new act, women who had lost their status by marrying a non-Indian, persons who had lost their status by application of the "double-mother" rule (both their mother and paternal grandmother were not Indians), and persons who had been enfranchised regained Indian status (in the technical parlance, they were "reinstated"). The children of those persons were also reinstated. By section 6(3)(b), the reinstatement provisions could be deemed to apply to dead persons, in order for their living descendants to regain status accordingly. For instance, if a woman lost status by "marrying out" but died before the coming into force of the new rules, her children would be entitled to status, as their mother would now be deemed to have been an Indian. It is estimated that in the years 1985–2000, about 115,000 persons regained Indian status through the operation of the new provisions and that approximately 60,000 children born after 1985 owe their Indian status to Bill C–31's new rules.[21]

It is obvious that retaining the concept of Indian status in the Indian Act does not result in any autonomy for the indigenous peoples. Nevertheless, federal control over Indian status is justified by the benefits granted directly to indigenous individuals by the federal government. The autonomy granted to the Indian bands by Bill C–31 flows from their new power to adopt membership codes. Yet, as we will see later, even this power is subject to important constraints. Before studying those codes, however, I turn to the rules contained in the modern treaties which in most cases recognise only a slightly higher degree of autonomy.

Modern Treaties: Autonomy by Agreement

While conflict and controversy characterised the reform of Indian status, the consensual changes brought about by the "modern treaties" signed during the last thirty years were less noticeable but equally important. "Modern treaties," also known as comprehensive land claims agreements, have been entered into with certain indigenous groups since 1975. Typically, those agreements extinguish the aboriginal land rights of the indigenous party over the whole of its traditional territory, in exchange for specific rights in respect of smaller areas of land and a significant amount of money. More recent agreements employ formulae, such as an "exhaustive definition of rights," that avoid the increasingly discredited concept of "extinguishment." Indigenous peoples are also given a voice in certain decision-making processes concerning the use of the territory, such as environmental-assessment procedures. "Modern treaties" also contain various provisions relating to self-government. In some cases, this translates into the creation of indigenous bodies entrusted with the delivery of public services, such as health and education, to the indigenous population. In other cases, the agreement creates local and regional bodies with extensive powers of self-government. The first "modern treaty" was the James Bay Agreement, signed in 1975 with the Crees and Inuit of Northern Quebec.[22] Other treaties were signed in the Northwest Territories in 1984,[23] 1992,[24] 1993,[25] and 2003,[26] in the Yukon starting in 1993,[27] in the new Nunavut territory in 1993,[28] in British Columbia in 1998,[29] and in Newfoundland in 2005.[30]

All "modern treaties" contain a definition of the group of persons who constitute the indigenous party to the agreement and may benefit from its provisions (the "beneficiaries" or "participants"). Where the signatory group was previously governed by the Indian Act, those definitions supersede Indian status for most purposes. For Inuit groups who had never been brought under the act, the rules contained in the agreement amount to a first official definition of their identity. However, in the James Bay and the Yukon Agreements, the concept of Indian status was retained in parallel to that of beneficiary of the agreement.[31] The only significant remaining purpose of Indian status is to determine who benefits from the exemption from tax and seizure.[32] This underlines the importance of the tax exemption in motivating the federal government to retain control of Indian status.

Most agreements do not allow the indigenous party to amend the membership rules without the consent of the federal government. Therefore, the federal government keeps control over the substance of membership criteria, even though their application is delegated to indigenous bodies. In the Yukon and Nisga'a agreements, the self-government powers of the indigenous nations involved include the power to define their own "citizenship"; however, this power is subject to the proviso that any person who is a participant in the land claims agreement has an automatic right to citizenship.[33] In practice, this means that the self-government powers regarding membership have been severely curtailed and can be exercised in a meaningful way only with the concurrence of the federal government.

The modern treaties concluded with the Inuit stand in contrast to all other modern treaties in that they recognise the full autonomy of the Inuit in the definition of their own membership. Under the Nunavut Agreement, which pioneered this approach, an Inuk is defined as someone who is an Inuk according to Inuit customs and who self-identifies as an Inuk and who has links with a Nunavut community or the Nunavut region.[34] This definition has a continuing effect, as it does not provide for transmission of status through descent from an initial group. Hence, the agreement refers entirely to the Inuit legal system (or "customs") for the determination of Inuit identity. In so doing, the agreement uses the method of self-identification by the individual and recognition by the group. No reference is made in the agreement to indigenous ancestry. These rules are applied by local enrolment committees composed of community members.[35] A dissatisfied individual may also bring the committee's decision before an appeals committee.[36] Most recently, the Inuit of Labrador and Quebec also negotiated a similar system, whereby Inuit status is defined by reference to Inuit customs and traditions.[37]

With the exception of the agreements with the Inuit, however, modern treaties grant only a limited autonomy to their indigenous signatories. The basic policies are determined by the federal government. While the indigenous peoples participated in the drafting of the membership provisions of the treaties and agreed to them, they have a very limited margin of manoeuvre to adapt or modify those definitions in the future.

Band Membership Codes:
Limited Autonomy

As we have seen earlier in this chapter, Bill C–31 included a delegation of power to the Indian bands concerning the determination of their membership. Studying the resulting "membership codes" from the perspective of the autonomy of the indigenous peoples entails two questions: who exercises that autonomy and what are the limits of that autonomy? In both cases, the actual controversy focuses on the same group: the women who "married out," lost Indian status, and were subsequently reinstated by Bill C–31. To make the reinstatement policy effective, the federal government had to ensure that those women would regain not only Indian status but also band membership, because band membership now controls access to a wider range of benefits than Indian status. Yet this move was perceived by many Indian bands as a breach of their autonomy.

Adoption Process and Participation. In order to ensure the most extensive participation in the adoption of membership rules, section 10 of the Indian Act requires a band that wishes to control its membership to give notice to that effect to its existing members and to have the rules approved by a majority of its electors.[38] This minimises the risk that membership criteria would be designed by a ruling élite to exclude political opponents or persons who do not adhere to its view of indigenous culture.

As reinstated women automatically regained membership in their former bands upon the coming into force of Bill c–31, they theoretically formed part of the existing band membership that had to be consulted and that had the right to vote upon any proposed membership code. Even though these women had an automatic right to band membership that a subsequent code could not negate, they had a very important interest in the process, as their children's right to membership was directly affected (as discussed below) and as they could bring a different perspective on the factors that constitute indigenous identity. Yet gaps in section 10 of the act and administrative difficulties, coupled with the negative attitude of many bands towards reinstatement, prevented the full participation of those women in most cases. Section 10 requires the approval of a majority of the band's *electors.* Section 2 defines an elector as a person who is *actually registered* on a band list. Persons who are entitled to membership but not registered are not electors. Because of the larger than expected number of applicants for reinstatement, the Department of Indian Affairs took many years to process their applications and to register eligible persons. As a result, many women who had a right to be reinstated were not actually registered on their band lists and were not electors when their bands adopted a membership code.[39] That provided a legal excuse for the bands not to give them a voice in the process. Moreover, at that time it was thought that band members who did not reside on the band's reserve were not electors.[40] Because very few reinstated women succeeded in returning to live on their reserves, band councils could argue that they were not electors entitled to vote on a membership code. Studies have shown that the actual participation of reinstated women in the development of membership codes was minimal.[41]

Another characteristic of a democratic process is the publication of its outcome. Yet the Indian Act does not require that membership codes be made public; it does not even say that band members have a right to consult them. In 1987, in order to resolve the doubts about the issue, the government adopted an order-in-council expressly exempting those codes from the requirement of publication in the *Canada Gazette*.[42] In the result, it may be difficult to obtain the membership code of a particular band.[43]

Reinstated Members and Acquired Rights. In the process leading to the enactment of Bill c–31, Parliament became sufficiently wary of the fate that Indian bands would reserve for reinstated women to enact specific guarantees of their status as band members. Obviously, if Indian bands were granted complete liberty to define their own membership, they could simply choose to reverse the government's reinstatement policy. To prevent this from happening, the new Indian Act gives limited priority to reinstatement over the self-definition of membership and limits the autonomy of the Indian bands accordingly.

Thus, under section 11(1) of the new act, women who had lost their status upon "marrying out," as well as persons to whom the "double-mother" rule had been applied, were automatically granted membership in their former bands. Then, sections 10(4) and 10(5), the acquired-rights provisions, made clear that bands could not deny membership to those persons. Yet children of reinstated women were not covered by this mechanism. The new Indian Act, in section 11(2), delayed their acquisition of band membership by a two-year transitional period (1985–87). Thus, during that period the acquired-rights provisions did not apply to them and bands could adopt membership codes that excluded them.

Section 10(7) allows the minister of Indian affairs to refuse to transfer control of a membership list to a band if the band's membership code does not comply with the requirements of section 10, in particular the acquired-rights provision of section 10(4). Thus, where a band attempts to disregard the rights of reinstated women, the affected individuals do not need to take action: the minister will not bring the membership code into effect. In fact, the minister has refused certain membership codes that were deficient in this respect.[44] Almost all membership codes that have been approved appear to comply with section 10(4). However, certain bands have attempted to impose additional conditions for the readmission of reinstated women, such as residence on the reserve or demonstration of a commitment to the traditions and customs of the band.[45] In a recent decision involving the Sawridge Band, the Federal Court of Appeal decided that a band could not impose additional requirements of that kind and that section 10(4) granted an automatic right to band membership.[46]

Reinstatement met with widespread opposition from Indian bands.[47] Reinstated women often became the object of prejudice and faced discrimination when they returned to their reserves.[48] As the acquired-rights provisions forced Indian bands to grant them membership, one strategy of recalcitrant bands was to adopt policies that treated reinstated women less favourably than other members. Certain court cases have shown that this strategy constitutes discrimination. Bands are not in a good position to put forward arguments based on their autonomy, as that autonomy is specifically restricted by the acquired-rights provisions of the Indian Act. For instance, the Mashteuiatsh Innu Band Council adopted a "moratorium" concerning the rights of reinstated women, effectively denying them the right to reside on the reserve, the right to hunt, the right to have their children admitted to the reserve school, and the possibility of obtaining employment with the band council.[49] Moreover, the band council attempted to exclude them from participation in a committee mandated to draft a membership code, in order to ensure the "objectivity" of committee members. Only reserve residents were given the right to vote in the referendum concerning the membership code. In that case, the Canadian Human Rights Tribunal upheld several complaints of discrimination made on the part of reinstated women. The tribunal noted that the band council had no power to enact a "moratorium" suspending, in reality, the operation of the Indian Act with respect to the band.

Another example is provided by the Sakimay Indian Band, who denied reinstated women the right to vote in band council elections.[50] When that policy was challenged in the Federal Court as constituting a breach of the Indian Act, of the band's membership code, and of section 15 of the Charter, the band argued that it had acted pursuant to its custom, which denied membership to women who married out, unless they applied to the band to regain membership. The judge overruled the band's defence, noting that reinstated women were band members according to the band's own membership code, so that they had the right to vote in band council elections according to the provisions of the Indian Act. The judge also dismissed the band's argument that its custom was protected and made paramount over ordinary legislation by section 35 of the Constitution Act, 1982. According to him, the band had not proven its custom and had admitted, in its membership code, that women who had "married out" could be members.

In contrast to the latter cases, the reinstatement policy was directly confronted in a constitutional challenge against Bill c–31 brought before the Federal Court by the Sawridge Band, allegedly the richest Indian band in Canada. That band possesses important oil and gas resources, is composed of less than forty members, and has been involved in continuous efforts to restrict its membership. To resist the application of Bill c–31, the band argued that it has an aboriginal right, protected by section 35 of the Constitution Act, 1982, to define its own membership rules. In particular, the band sought to prove that its custom provided that men who married non-member women brought them into the band, while women who "married out" left the band. Hence, according to the band, Bill c–31 infringed its right to self-government, because Parliament had imposed a gender-neutral rule that deviated from the band's alleged custom. A decision was rendered by the Federal Court in 1995 dismissing the band's claims.[51] However, in an unusual move, the Court of Appeal reversed this decision and ordered a new trial, on the basis of the apparent partiality of the trial judge, a trial that has not yet reached a conclusion.[52]

The trial judgment nevertheless deserves analysis. Basing himself on expert testimony, the judge found that the indigenous peoples of the region in pre-contact times did not control their membership. According to the judge, those peoples were constituted of small groups under the informal leadership of respected hunters, groups that anyone could join or leave at will. Hence, there could be no aboriginal right to define membership criteria, as aboriginal rights must reflect the practices of the indigenous peoples prior to their contact with European colonists. Moreover, the trial judge held that section 35(4) of the Constitution Act, 1982, which provides that "Notwithstanding any other provision of this Act, the aboriginal and treaty rights ... are guaranteed equally to male and female persons," precluded the recognition of any constitutional right to adopt sexually discriminatory membership rules, which was what the Sawridge Band was seeking to do. The latter argument is the most convincing: as we have seen in the previous chapter, it is very difficult to see how gender distinctions are relevant to ethnic identity and why such a distinction, if it exists in a given culture, should be respected by the legal system. Section 35(4) adequately reflects this principle by giving priority to gender equality over aboriginal rights.

In the end, unless the judgment in *Sawridge* is ultimately reversed, Indian bands' autonomy in adopting their membership rules is subject to important constraints imposed by Parliament to ensure conformity with human rights and compliance with the basic policies underlying Bill c–31, in particular the reinstatement of formerly excluded women.

The Métis: Room for Autonomy?

Section 35(1) of the Constitution Act, 1982, guarantees the aboriginal and treaty rights of the indigenous peoples of Canada. Section 35(2) adds the clarification that the latter peoples include the Indians, the Inuit, and the Métis. The addition of that subsection was a victory for the Métis, whose indigenous identity was at last recognised and whose rights were (in principle) guaranteed on the same footing as those of the Indians and the Inuit.

However, the practical implementation of those rights ran into a serious difficulty: there were no accepted legal criteria to identify the Métis population, both from a collective and from an individual perspective. The constitution granted rights to the Métis without defining who they were. There was no federal legislation, similar to the Indian Act, delineating Métis groups (this is the collective dimension) and regulating membership in them (this is the individual dimension). No official registry existed that would confirm the Métis identity of any given person. In fact, estimates of the Métis population varied widely. Governments have often mentioned the uncertainty as to who the Métis were as a reason to postpone the recognition of their constitutional rights.[53]

The basic hurdle in the way of the autonomy of the Métis to define their own membership is the logical priority of the collective recognition of groups over the definition of those groups' membership.[54] Given the collective nature of aboriginal rights in Canadian

law, one must know who the Métis groups are before one can determine if an individual belongs to such a group. The recognition of
indigenous groups may derive from negotiated agreements between
the state and the groups concerned, from unilateral legislation, or
from court decisions. As recognition is a relationship between the
state and the indigenous peoples, the latter never have full autonomy in this regard. Currently, the federal and provincial governments do very little in terms of official recognition and leave it to
the Métis to organise themselves politically.[55] Métis associations
may come into existence, split, merge, or disappear for reasons
entirely unrelated to changes in Métis identity.[56] The federal government recognises, for funding purposes only, two national associations representing the non-status indigenous population: the Métis
National Council (the MNC), which represents the historic Métis
Nation of the Canadian West, and the Congress of Aboriginal Peoples (the CAP, formerly the Native Council of Canada, or the NCC),
which federates various groups of indigenous peoples not living on
Indian reserves, including Métis communities other than the Métis
Nation, Indians living in urban centres, "non-status Indians," and
so on.[57] However, governments do not recognise those associations,
or their provincial chapters, as representatives of indigenous *peoples* possessing constitutional rights. Thus, in practice courts have
assumed the task of identifying which groups constitute Métis
communities or peoples.

Once a particular group is recognised, membership in that group
can be determined autonomously by the group, by state legislation,
or by the courts. In theory, legislation could recognise a particular
community as a Métis group and leave it to the rule-making bodies
of that community to enact membership criteria. This would lead to
autonomy, provided (and this is an important qualification) that the
group that is recognised is a true representative of the people concerned. In other words, if the wrong group is recognised, there can
be no meaningful autonomy in defining membership.

Currently, certain Métis organisations are making efforts at
defining their own membership in an autonomous fashion. However, given that these organisations are not officially recognised as
the bearers of collective rights, it is interesting to observe how
Canadian courts are constructing their own definitions of Métis
identity in parallel – partly in tune, partly in dissonance – with the
Métis' own efforts.

Métis Organisations' Membership Rules. In the last decade, the MNC and its provincial affiliates have attempted to develop membership control systems in order to bolster their credibility as representatives of Métis groups. The culmination of those efforts is found in a resolution adopted in 2002 by the General Assembly of the MNC stating that "Métis means a person who self-identifies as Métis, is of historic Métis Nation ancestry, is distinct from other Aboriginal peoples and is accepted by the Métis Nation."[58] This definition is meant to be implemented by the MNC's provincial affiliates, whose constitutions indicate who may apply for membership.[59] Two restrictive features of this definition are to be noted.[60] First, the reference to "historic Métis Nation ancestry" sets the Métis Nation apart from other groups of persons of mixed ancestry who call themselves Métis. The historic Métis Nation is defined by reference to its homeland in west central North America. Thus, Métis groups in Eastern Canada are not covered by the MNC definition.[61] Second, the reference to a distinction from other indigenous peoples excludes persons who hold Indian status. Hence, according to the MNC, an individual cannot be both Métis and Indian. In addition, the MNC definition requires "acceptance" by the Métis Nation. However, the precise meaning of this condition is not clear. When the constitutions of the MNC affiliates are examined, it seems that such acceptance is to be given by local community officials who must approve individual application forms before membership cards are issued.

In contrast, reaching a definition of Métis or aboriginal identity has not been a priority of the CAP. Its affiliated provincial organisations usually admit as members anyone who has indigenous ancestry and who is not an Indian living on a reserve.[62] As such, Indian status is not a bar to membership in the CAP affiliates provided that one lives off reserve. (In fact, about half of status Indians do not live on reserves.) Hence, the definitions employed by the CAP affiliates are much wider than the one put forward by the MNC.

Judicial Definition of Métis Identity. The first case in which the Supreme Court dealt with Métis identity is *Powley,*[63] where two Métis individuals were accused of hunting moose without a permit but argued in defence that they were exercising their aboriginal rights protected by the constitution. In its judgment, rendererd in 2003, the Court set out principles for the identification of Métis communities who hold rights under section 35 of the Constitution Act, 1982, and for the definition of membership in those communities. While the Court recognised that the process must take into account "the value of community self-definition,"[64] the framework it suggested imposes subtle limits on the autonomy of the Métis with respect to membership, in particular through "indicating the important components of a future definition."[65] (The reference to the future seems somewhat ironic, as the MNC had adopted a definition of Métis identity the year before.) Those limits on autonomy seem to be motivated by concerns related to potential abuse (only "true" Métis must be able to exercise Métis rights), to fairness (persons must not be excluded for irrelevant reasons), and to ease of application (government officials must be able to know readily whether someone is a Métis).

The Court began by giving a comprehensive definition of the term "Métis," focusing on its collective dimensions, or, in other words, on the recognition of Métis communities: "The term "Métis" in s. 35 does not encompass all individuals with mixed Indian and European heritage; rather, it refers to distinctive peoples who, in addition to their mixed ancestry, developed their own customs, way of life, and recognizable group identity separate from their Indian or Inuit and European forebears ... A Métis community can be defined as a group of Métis with a distinctive collective identity, living together in the same geographic area and sharing a common way of life."[66] Hence, not just any set of persons of mixed ancestry can declare itself a Métis community. Courts are called upon to decide whether a given community shows a sufficiently coherent group identity defined in terms of the ancestry and way of life of its members and whether that community has a sufficient historic continuity. For instance, a trial court has refused to recognise a non-profit association of individuals of indigenous ancestry residing in various communities as a Métis group possessed of section 35 rights, describing it, rather, as a "pressure group."[67] The autonomy of Métis groups in defining their own identity is curtailed by this process, where identity is judged from the outside, although the judicial process does allow for a measure of community input.

Another restriction on autonomy results from the guidelines set forth by the Supreme Court in *Powley* with respect to individual membership in Métis communities: Métis identity is based on self-identification, ancestral connection, and community acceptance.[68]

While on the surface it seems that the Court adopted the main elements of the 2002 MNC definition, it gave a particluar twist to some of the relevant criteria that have the effect of limiting group autonomy in the definition of identity. Let us review the criteria adopted by the Court in detail.[69]

By relying on self-identification, the Court ensures that no one is ascribed Métis identity against his or her will. But this factor has another function : the prevention of abuse. The Court requires that a person must have identified with a Métis community over a long period of time in order to qualify. Thus, persons who assert Métis identity only to benefit from constitutionally protected rights and who do not otherwise participate in a Métis community or in Métis culture would be excluded. Self-identification must be genuine and consistent, as shown by the person's participation in the group's culture, customs, and traditions.

The fact that the Court views indigenous rights mainly in historical terms explains why it insists on the ancestral connection of the claimant. As Powley's Métis ancestry was not in dispute, the Court gave only general indications as to what degree of ancestry was sufficient to meet the test. A specific degree of "Indian blood" would not be required. Proof that one's ancestors were Métis "by birth, by adoption or otherwise" would suffice. Yet, it remains to be seen whether remote indigenous ancestry satisfies the requirement. Trial court decisions have denied section 35 rights to persons who could identify only one distant indigenous ancestor in the seventeenth century,[70] while one ancestor in the mid-nineteenth century would be sufficient.[71] Moreover, the Court in *Powley* insisted that the ancestry condition cannot be dispensed with. A Métis group could not adopt membership rules that conferred Métis status on persons with no indigenous ancestry, or, at least, this would be ineffective in conferring section 35 rights upon them. Here again we see the concern that constitutional rights over scarce resources could potentially be abused if Métis communities were allowed to admit anyone without external control.

The third condition, community acceptance, derives from the collective nature of indigenous rights.[72] The concept of community acceptance suggests that Métis communities would have the power to enact and apply membership rules in an autonomous fashion. In other words, the community would be able to decide which individuals would exercise its collective rights. Yet the conception of community acceptance put forward by the Supreme Court departs from the complete autonomy of Métis groups. The Court indicated that membership in a Métis political association (such as the MNC affiliates or the CAP affiliates) is not conclusive proof of community acceptance unless there is appropriate evidence concerning the association's membership rules and role in the community.[73] In other words, courts will scrutinise the representativity of those associations and evaluate their membership rules in light of the Supreme Court's framework before giving weight to their decisions.

In this regard, problems may arise if the rights-bearing community identified by the court does not correspond to a Métis organisation that has developed membership rules. For instance, the *Powley* decision has been criticised for identifying the relevant community as being the "Sault Ste Marie Métis."[74] That community does not have a membership registry; the Métis Nation of Ontario and the Ontario Métis and Aboriginal Association do. Membership in those associations, however, does not relate specifically to the "Sault Ste Marie Métis" community and would be of little assistance to Métis individuals if they bore the burden of proving their links with such a local community. As long as the courts have difficulty in identifying Métis communities and their representative associations, it will be difficult to recognise the Métis' autonomy with respect to membership.

The Court went further and outlined a conception of community acceptance based mainly on persistent self-identification and participation on the part of the individual: "The core of community acceptance is past and ongoing participation in a shared culture, in the customs and traditions that constitute a Métis community's identity and distinguish it from other groups. This is what the community membership criterion is all about. Other indicia of community acceptance might include evidence of participation in community activities and testimony from other members about the claimant's connection to the community and its culture."[75]

Hence, community acceptance is taken out of the hands of the community, so to speak, and becomes an objective reality that depends on individual conduct, such as participating in community ceremonies or festivals[76] or even hunting and fishing.[77] In the result, Métis identity would be a function of ancestry and individual participation in the Métis culture. The role of the community would be simply to give official recognition to this participation, but it could not refuse to recognise someone who met the objective test. If the community attempted to do so, courts would then disregard its decision and recognise that the individual may exercise Métis rights. In so modifying the community acceptance criterion, the Supreme Court was probably concerned with the potential for injustice that would arise if Métis groups had the power to deny membership to individuals for arbitrary reasons. In other words, it would be alarming if the exercise of constitutional rights should depend on the discretion of local elected officials purporting to grant or withhold "community acceptance."

In sum, the case of the Métis shows how state inaction led to subtle limits being imposed by the courts on the autonomy of the Métis in defining their own membership. In the absence of federal or provincial legislation or of an agreement between all the parties concerned, the Supreme Court in *Powley* assumed the power to recognise specific Métis communities and to assess whether an individual may legitimately claim membership in them. Nevertheless, the framework adopted by the Court reproduces in large part the definition of Métis identity adopted by the MNC, with the exception of the criterion of community acceptance, to which the Court gave more objective content. This framework has an interesting potential to foster the autonomy of the Métis in membership matters, provided that the courts show a willingness to understand the representativity of Métis organisations and to defer to their membership decisions.

INDIGENOUS STATUS AND INDIVIDUAL RIGHTS

Having ascertained the degree of autonomy afforded to the indigenous peoples by each of the current membership control systems, I can now turn to the compatibility of those systems with individual rights. I discuss them again in ascending order of autonomy. This ordering will highlight the absence of correlation between indigenous autonomy and violations of individual rights.

The Indian Act and Bill c–31: Residual Discrimination

It would be overly optimistic to think that Bill c–31 entirely eliminated discrimination from the rules of Indian status.[78] Most of the remaining problems are related to a rule whereby Indian status is lost after two generations of marriages with non-Indians. That rule, aimed at limiting the public expense in favour of persons who have a slight proportion of indigenous ancestry, is remarkably similar to the "double-mother" rule[79] in force from 1951 to 1985, but without the gender distinctions of the latter. Studies have shown that it may, in the long term, lead to a sharp decline in the status Indian population if the current rates of marriage with non-Indians persist.[80] To understand how this leads to discrimination, it is necessary to review in some detail the technical working of the rule. I will then show how the rule, when combined with the way in which reinstatement was effected in 1985, results in what is often called "residual discrimination" on the basis of gender. I will also show that the rule is discriminatory when considered alone.

Under the new Indian Act, Indians can be entitled to status under section 6(1) or 6(2); they are colloquially referred to respectively as "6(1) Indians" and "6(2) Indians." In simple terms, "6(1) Indians" have a full right to transmit their status to their children, while "6(2) Indians" have only a limited right. (There is no other difference between the rights of 6(1) and 6(2) Indians.) The provisions implementing this principle are the following. Section 6(1)(f) states that a person is entitled to be registered if both of his or her parents have a right to be registered under section 6 (either subsection (1) or (2)). Section 6(2) states that a person is entitled to be registered if one of his or her parents has a right to be registered under section 6(1) only (and not section 6(2)). Therefore, where two Indians marry (whether they have status under section 6(1) or 6(2) is irrelevant), their children will have 6(1) status. Where a "6(1) Indian" marries a non-Indian, their children will have 6(2) status. Where a "6(2) Indian" marries a non-Indian, their children are not entitled to Indian status. The net effect of those rules is that Indian status is lost after two generations of marriages with non-Indians. (Another way of summarising the rule is to say that in order to be an Indian, a person must have at least two Indian grandparents.) Hence, in practical terms section 6(2) and the "double-mother" rule are very similar, but for the gender distinctions.

The operation of these rules may be illustrated in the first set of diagrams.

The combination of those rules over two generations is depicted in diagram 2 showing the operation of the "second-generation cut-off" rule.

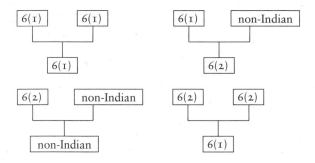

Diagram 1

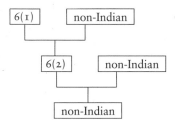

Diagram 2

This rule must be analysed in light of the reinstatement provisions of Bill c–31. In framing Bill c–31, the government decided to respect the "acquired rights" of women who gained Indian status upon marriage to an Indian man. Thus, according to section 6(1)(*a*) of the new act, non-Indian women who had married an Indian man prior to 1985 kept the Indian status that they had acquired upon marriage. (No one lost Indian status upon Bill c–31 coming into force.) However, respecting "acquired rights" of those women had the effect of treating children of mixed marriages differently, according to the sex of their Indian parent. Thus, children of an Indian man and a non-Indian woman (married before 1985) are considered as "6(1) Indians." If they were born after 1985, this flows from the fact that both their parents are Indians (section 6(1)(*f*)), as their mother would have acquired Indian status upon marriage. If they were born before 1985, they were already Indians when Bill c–31 came into force, so they obtained 6(1) status. In contrast, children of an Indian woman and a non-Indian man are granted only 6(2) status, as only one of their parents is Indian. The difference in status depends exclusively on the gender of the Indian parent. The differential treatment is only exacerbated if we consider the next generation. Assuming the children of the first couple marry non-Indians, the grandchildren will still be Indians, but with 6(2) status. In contrast, if the children of the second couple do the same, the grandchildren will not be Indians at all. Therefore, the rules of descent in the new Indian Act, coupled with the provisions concerning reinstatement, still result in discrimination against women.

Residual discrimination may be illustrated in diagram 3, with the example of an Indian brother and an sister who both "married out" before 1985:

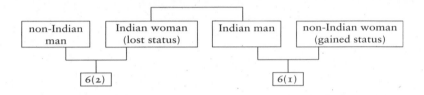

Diagram 3

Another layer of discrimination against women results from the presumption that an undeclared father is not Indian.[81] This often forces indigenous women to choose between keeping the identity of the father secret, possibly for valid reasons, and ensuring that their children have Indian status.[82] In certain regions of the country, the paternity of as many as 30 percent of indigenous children remains unstated, so the problem cannot be dismissed as insignificant.

Hence, there are two distinct ways in which the new rules of Indian status employ suspect distinctions: through residual discrimination against women and through the very fact that the rules draw distinctions based on the degree of Indian ancestry, through the second-generation cut-off rule. The significance of the latter issue cannot be overestimated: if ancestry requirements were deemed invalid, the whole edifice put in place by Parliament to keep the size of the Indian population under control would collapse. To analyse these crucial issues, it is useful to return to the categories of correspondence and justification relevant for addressing claims based on the right to equality. As residual discrimination was the subject of a recent trial decision, I will deal with it first, addressing the wider issue of the second-generation cut-off rule afterwards.

As we have seen above, "residual discrimination" results from the manner in which the transition from the old to the new rules was implemented. This particular aspect was the focus of the recent *McIvor* decision of the British Columbia Supreme Court,[83] in which the trial judge held that section 6 discriminated on the basis of sex and marital status; in particular, she underlined that there was no correspondence between sexual distinctions and the actual characteristics of the persons involved.[84] In fact, a recurrent theme in the judgment is the gap between the indigenous identity of the plaintiffs and the rules of Indian status in the Indian Act, which deprived the plaintiffs of an official recognition of their identity.[85] With respect to justification, the trial judge had difficulties finding a valid objective for the rules that resulted in residual discrimination. Respecting acquired rights would be discriminatory in itself if those rights were acquired according to discriminatory rules.[86] Moreover, it would have been possible to allow non-indigenous women to retain their Indian status gained through marriage while adjusting the status of their children to reflect the fact that only one of their parents had status or by deeming children of reinstated women to have two Indian parents, which would give them 6(1) status, like their cousins. Hence, respecting acquired rights does not necessarily entail the kind of distinctions employed by the Indian Act,[87] and section 6 was invalidated in this respect.

On a more general level, the distinctions drawn by section 6 of the Indian Act appear to correspond very poorly to actual indigenous identity. One manner of revealing this gap is to show that the rules of the act do not correlate with the degree of indigenous ancestry (or "Indian blood") of the persons concerned. Thus, a woman with no indigenous ancestry at all would have Indian status if she married an Indian man before 1985, whereas the above illustrations show that persons with 25 percent "Indian blood" could be deprived of status. Another example involves two persons with 50 percent indigenous ancestry. The first is born to a "6(1) Indian" and a non-Indian: he or she has 6(2) status. The second is born to two "6(2) Indian" parents: he or she has 6(1) status. It is difficult to understand the logic behind those erratic results. However, these comparisons are based on proportions of indigenous ancestry alone, which appear to be the sole focus of the act. This leads to another, more fundamental level of criticism: the rules of Indian status do not take into account any other indicator of identity.

Any conception of identity based exclusively on ancestry assumes
that culture and identity are transmitted genetically. This is a racial
conception of indigeneity that cannot, as we saw in chapter 1,
ground public policy. For instance, in the *McIvor* case, the trial
judge noted that there was absolutely no evidence in support of the
government's assertion that "people who are two generations away
from the reserve … would not likely have much contact with their
Indian culture."[88]

Can the federal government justify the use of distinctions that
poorly reflect indigenous identity and that have racial overtones?
The aim that is most likely to be invoked to sustain section 6 of the
Indian Act is the need to restrict the category of persons who enjoy
the benefits associated with Indian status. As we saw earlier, ensuring the fair allocation of scarce resources is a valid reason for the
enactment of a membership control system. In principle, public
funds destined to benefit the indigenous peoples should not be
diverted towards non-indigenous persons. Yet the federal government is increasingly extending the benefit of its programs to indigenous peoples not covered by the Indian Act. For instance, job
training programs have been made available to non-status indigenous persons.[89] This tends to show that it is not necessary to resort
to rigid ancestry criteria to ensure the fair allocation of benefits.

In fact, the most significant benefits allocated according to Indian
status appear to be the tax exemptions provided by section 87 of
the Indian Act and the reimbursement of certain health services that
are not insured by provincial regimes.[90] One can understand that
the federal government does not want to enlarge the category of
persons who are exempted from paying taxes. On the other hand, it
seems that the continuing existence of that single benefit, the tax
exemption, the soundness of which is questionable in terms of public policy,[91] has deleterious effects on the issue of indigenous status
because it induces the federal government to take a hard stance on
the definition of status. Another reason that might lead to the conclusion that section 6 of the Indian Act cannot be justified lies in its
forecasted long-term effects on the size of the status population.
Given the current rate of intermarriage between status and non-status persons (including non-indigenous persons and indigenous persons without status), demographers forecast that the status
population will start to decline within fifty years.[92] It appears
unreasonable to jeopardise the long-term existence of a recognised

indigenous population in order to control the present distribution of benefits.

Moreover, the imposition of arbitrary criteria to distinguish Indians and non-Indians has been the cause of divisions and conflicts among First Nations.[93] Individuals who do not have status are often forced to leave the community, or if they stay, they may face discrimination. Traditional clan relationships are disregarded by the rules of Indian status. Individuals within one family may have different status. Pressure is also felt to declare the parternity of a child in order to ensure the recognition of the child's Indian status, or even to choose a partner who has Indian status. Such hardships call for a very convincing justification.

The only justification of the rigid use of ancestry in the Indian Act appears to be the impracticability of a more flexible system whereby federal bureaucrats would assess a combination of several markers of identity (for example, place of birth, residence, knowledge of the group's culture and history) to reach a decision about the status of each indigenous person. While, as we will see later in this chapter, several Indian bands have adopted such a system in their membership codes, they at least have the cultural and social knowledge that enables informed decision-making. The federal bureaucracy would be utterly lacking in such particular knowledge.

On balance, the validity of section 6 of the Indian Act appears doubtful. The justifications that can be advanced in its support are tenuous when compared to the arbitrariness of the classifications it creates. The outcome of a court challenge is likely to be a function of the degree of deference that a court will be willing to extend to Parliament. On the surface, it might be tempting to say that a high degree of deference is mandated because the government would be in a better position than the courts to assess social science evidence concerning indigenous identity. Yet section 6 is based not on the findings of social science but on (doubtful) assumptions about the links between ancestry, culture, and identity. It cannot be defended as a "proxy for culture," especially on a nationwide basis. Moreover, classifications related to race usually attract strict scrutiny. In *McIvor*, the trial judge rejected the government's claims to deference because Indian status concerns only the relationships between individuals and the state and does not affect indigenous communities as such, and the judge also rejected arguments based on financial considerations or the need to draw lines.[94] While the *McIvor* trial decision is an encouraging start, only time will tell if the right to equality enshrined in the Charter will be effective in eradicating discrimination in the rules of Indian status.

In this connection, one may be surprised that it took more than twenty years after the enactment of Bill c–31 for a trial court to issue a first ruling concerning the constitutional validity of some of its main provisions. That demonstrates the limited effectiveness of litigation in protecting individual human rights. In a previous case, a woman brought a legal challenge to the constitutional validity of section 6, but, given the federal government's last-minute factual concessions, which made her eligible for Indian status, the court did not pronounce on the Charter challenge.[95] In another case, a motion for certification of a class action was dismissed on the basis that it was not the preferred procedure,[96] which had the effect of disentitling the complainant to funding available for class actions. The recent termination by the federal government of the court challenges program, which funded test cases based on the right to equality, closed another door to those in search of funding for mounting a challenge to the Indian Act rules.

Modern Treaties

With respect to membership, modern treaties may be divided into two categories: the "First Nations model," which resorts to the usual basic method for defining membership in indigenous peoples – transmission of status through descent – and the "Inuit model," which refers to Inuit customs to define membership.

Much of the human rights problems associated with the old Indian Act have been avoided by the parties to the First Nation treaties. The membership rules are gender-neutral. They do not require a minimal degree of indigenous ancestry: a person is eligible if one of his or her parents is indigenous.[97] This means that all descendants of a member are themselves members, regardless of the degree of subsequent intermarriage. There is no exclusion similar to the "double-mother" rule. Adopted children are included as well, irrespective of their biological origins. Thus, the problems associated with requiring a specific degree of indigenous ancestry do not arise. In one case, non-indigenous persons married to members may also be admitted.[98] In fact, the First Nation treaties evince a cultural conception of identity whereby genealogy is used in a flexible manner, as a proxy for culture.

The definition of the initial group of members is usually cast in wide terms, ensuring that persons who have been deprived of Indian status may be enrolled if they have sufficient indigenous ancestry. For instance, the initial Cree beneficiaries of the James Bay Agreement included members of the Cree bands formerly governed by the Indian Act, persons of Cree ancestry residing in the territory covered by the agreement (which would include women who had "married out"), persons of Cree or Indian ancestry recognised as members by a Cree community, and persons adopted by persons falling into the first three categories (irrespective of the status of their biological parents).[99]

Those features of the membership rules of the modern treaties correspond to the policies of gender equality and reinstatement pursued by the federal government in Bill c–31. What is striking is that they were adopted without difficulty, at the time of the *Lavell* and *Lovelace* controversy about the rules of the old Indian Act. An explanation lies in the fact that those agreements relate to remote or isolated regions where the non-indigenous population remains small. Many concerns underlying membership issues, such as the effects of repeated intermarriage with non-indigenous peoples, affect the parties to those treaties significantly less than they affect other indigenous peoples who live in the southern parts of Canada.

Other features enhance those membership rules' consistency with human rights. First, in the most recent agreements, registration as a beneficiary or a participant is dependent upon the individual's will. Hence, no one can be a member against his or her wishes, and one can renounce membership at any time.[100] These agreements thus provide a "right of exit," which bolsters the legitimacy of the minority rights regime they contain. Second, all agreements also contain detailed provisions concerning the registration procedure. The power to decide upon a person's enrolment is devolved to registration committees composed of community members. Individuals are granted rights to appeal decisions concerning their status,[101] thus ensuring a high degree of procedural justice.

The Inuit treaties employ a very different method of membership control. The agreements themselves do not purport to define an Inuk, and they do not set out rules of transmission by descent.

Rather, they refer to Inuit custom for the definition of an Inuk. Local committees are set up to make decisions concerning membership. This system adopts a relational conception of identity, as it asks the groups concerned, through the local committees, to apply their own criteria to membership issues, rather than imposing those criteria from the outside. The fact that the Inuit have never been governed by the Indian Act and have had no prior experience of excluding women who "married out" may explain why it has been possible to recognise their total autonomy in membership matters.

The actual outcome of this new process is difficult to assess and more research is needed. Two of the agreements (the Labrador Inuit Agreement and the amendment to the James Bay and Northern Quebec Agreement) are very recent, and the membership committees are only in the early phases of their implementation. The system in Nunavut has been in place for about ten years, but only limited information about its functioning is available. According to certain local committee members,[102] a person is an Inuk if one of his or her parents is Inuit. There is no minimal blood quantum. Marriage does not confer Inuit status.[103] There are no circumstances under which a person can cease to be an Inuk, although an Inuk may ask to be removed from the enrolment list. However, an independent review of the implementation of the Nunavut Agreement has indicated that the Inuit find it challenging to implement this new system, especially as there seems to be confusion between the respective roles of community acceptance and Inuit blood or ancestry. Moreover, the report mentions that there are disparities in the criteria applied by each community.[104] In Nunavik, Makivik Corporation has issued guidelines that would grant membership to children born to one Inuit parent and resident in Nunavik and in other cases has emphasized a set of factors such as respect for the land and animals, knowledge of Inuit traditions and language, residence, family connections, and so on. These guidelines, however, do not purport to be binding. A more thorough analysis of decisions rendered by the local membership committees in specific cases would be needed to reach an informed assessment.

In both Nunavik and Labrador, the rules also provide for the suspension of rights when a beneficiary resides for a long period outside the "territory" covered by the land claims agreement.[105] For example, an Inuit beneficiary of the James Bay and Northern Quebec Agreement who resides in Montreal for more than ten years cannot avail himself of the special hunting rights or of the reimbursement of tuition fees provided under the agreement. These rules resort to a relational conception of identity, whereby residence in a group's territory is an indication of identification with the group. Residence is used in a flexible manner, as one may resume the enjoyment of beneficiary rights upon reestablishing residence in the territory.

Band Membership Codes

The compatibility of band membership codes with individual rights is a complex and controversial subject. Apart from the sheer number of codes involved (about 250 throughout the country), several hurdles face the researcher. Bands do not have an obligation to make their codes available to the public, and it may be very difficult to obtain information about decisions made in specific cases. While there have been ongoing allegations of widespread discrimination against women by Indian bands, discrimination is more likely to be the result of a band official's decision to deny certain rights or services than of a denial of band membership resulting from the provisions of the band's code.[106] There is only a handful of cases where the validity of membership codes was challenged on the basis of a violation of the Charter or of the enabling provisions of the Indian Act. Hence, the following remarks will be based only on the publicly available information, as well as on a review of the codes, about fifty in number, adopted by Ontario bands.

The now familiar criteria of correspondence and justification will be used to identify potential breaches of the right to equality. Three specific issues will be reviewed: requirements of indigenous ancestry, discretionary admission, and conduct-based exclusions. While the application of the correspondence criterion will be discussed with respect to each issue, justification can be dealt with at the outset. Two general categories of objectives may justify membership measures: the protection of the group's scarce resources against a potentially large number of claimants and the protection of the group's culture and identity against too intense contact with nonmembers. In particular, it is obvious that a large majority of membership codes were adopted to prevent the massive arrival of new band members that was expected to result from Bill c–31, in the context where bands felt that the federal government would not provide sufficient resources to resolve the housing crisis that plagues many indigenous communities. Indeed, most membership codes were adopted in May and June 1987, close to the end of the two-year transitional period after which the children of reinstated women would gain an automatic right to band membership.

Requirements of Indigenous Ancestry. The central provision of a membership code is the one that regulates the transmission of status from one generation to the next.[107] The manner in which ancestry is used reveals the conception of identity that underpins the code in question. Certain codes grant membership as long as a person has at least one member parent: they require indigenous ancestry but do not specify the degree of that ancestry.[108] (This is called a "one-parent" rule.) Such a flexible use of ancestry indicates a cultural, rather than a racial, conception of indigenous identity. That does not give rise to any human rights problems, as it can fairly be assumed that a person is not sufficiently connected with a band if his or her parents were not members of that band. From the perspective of equality, the rule satisfies the requirement of correspondence: every person who can conceivably claim indigenous identity is included.

However, most codes require a specified degree of indigenous ancestry, although they do so in different ways. The most stringent form of this requirement is to say that a person is a band member only if both parents are themselves members.[109] (This is called a "two-parent" rule.) In theory, this amounts to a norm of 100 percent indigenous ancestry, but it may amount to less in practice if the persons who are members when such a rule comes into force already have some mixed ancestry. The two-parent rule sends the bold message that children of mixed marriages cannot be members of the band. It is difficult to escape the conclusion that such codes are based on racial assumptions; a cultural conception of identity seems to be excluded, because the two-parent rule implies that any degree of non-indigenous blood would, so to speak, "corrupt the culture." Between those two extremes, one can find many variations that aim at ensuring a certain degree of indigenous ancestry without automatically excluding the children of mixed marriages. Some frequently employed rules include a requirement of Indian blood quantum[110] (typically 50 percent); a requirement that members must have Indian status[111] (that is, a "one-parent" rule plus

Indian status); and a requirement that a person must have at least two grandparents who were members of the band or status Indians.[112] Another compromise, discussed below, is to adopt a two-parent rule for automatic membership but to allow persons who have only one band-member parent to apply for membership through a process that evaluates their links to the band.[113] Most of those rules are vulnerable to a challenge of racial discrimination, as they resort to ancestry-based criteria and their correspondence with actual indigenous identity seems to be questionable. The decisive issue is likely to be whether the infringement of individual rights resulting from a lack of correspondence between status and identity is proportional to the aims sought to be achieved. In this regard, two cases dealing with adoption, *Jacobs*[114] and *Grismer*,[115] are instructive.

The *Jacobs* case concerned the Mohawks of Kahnawake, who live in a small reserve just outside Montreal. They adopted particularly restrictive membership criteria that had the effect of depriving the plaintiff, Peter Jacobs, from band membership essentially because he had no Indian blood.[116] However, as he had been adopted in infancy by Kahnawake Mohawks, the Canadian Human Rights Tribunal found that the membership code discriminated against him on the basis of race. The band council sought to justify its code by the fact that no land was available to cope with the massive influx of new members that would result from more relaxed membership rules and that the presence of many non-indigenous persons on the reserve would impede the efforts of the community towards cultural revival. The tribunal accepted that the aims invoked by the band were valid, especially in view of the fact that Kahnawake was surrounded by a very large non-indigenous population.[117] However, it reached the conclusion that the exclusion of the Jacobs family was not necessary to achieve those aims, especially as there were very few non-indigenous persons adopted by Mohawk parents and their inclusion would likely not jeopardise the band's resources or culture.

The *Grismer* case involved two persons who, after reaching the age of majority, were adopted by a member of the Squamish First Nation, in the vicinity of Vancouver. The Squamish code granted membership to persons having one *biological* parent who was a member of the band. The Grismers were the *adopted* children of a member, so they could not avail themselves of that rule. The membership code allowed children under eighteen years of age to apply for membership if they had been adopted by *two* band members. The Grismers' other parent was not a band member, and they were over eighteen when adopted. The Federal Court held that the provisions of the Squamish code discriminated between biological and adopted children, thus infringing section 15 of the Charter, but that they were "saved" by section 1. Their objective, the preservation of Squamish culture and aboriginal identity, was a valid reason for restricting individual rights. Moreover, according to the judge: "Restricting membership to persons who have a bloodline connection to the Squamish Nation is [a] rational way of preserving and protecting the unique Squamish culture and identity."[118]

The Squamish also argued that recourse to ancestry to define their identity was a traditional practice. The proportionality of the code with respect to its objective of preserving the group's culture flowed from the fact that the band reached a compromise in providing for the admission of adopted children, but on terms somewhat more stringent than for biological children. As the judge noted, "Considerable deference should be accorded to the Squamish in making this policy decision, particularly since it concerns questions of citizenship, Band custom and lineage."[119] The calibration of the degree of scrutiny appears to have played a critical role in the decision. The Squamish First Nation's focus on culture to explain its membership rules, rendered more plausible by the flexible manner in which ancestry was employed, proved to be a successful strategy, as the judge evidently felt uncomfortable at making decisions about Squamish culture and identity. This may be contrasted to the *Jacobs* case, where the rigidity of the exclusion of someone who was raised in Kahnawake as a Mohawk appeared to have racial overtones and led the Human Rights Tribunal to require a more convincing demonstration of proportionality, which, in the end, was lacking.

Even though they dealt with adoption, which increases the contrast between racial and cultural conceptions of identity, the *Jacobs* and *Grismer* cases give a hint at the tensions that will necessarily arise when the ancestry-based rules of a membership code are confronted with the goal of equality. On the one hand, classifications based on ancestry are usually considered suspect. The history of discrimination in the rules of Indian status only reinforces the negative perception towards rules that appear to have racial underpinnings. On the other hand, courts are quite aware that there are, in principle, valid justifications for controlling membership in indigenous groups. The outcome of a particular case is likely to be a function of the severity of the threats facing the culture or the resources of the group (which will be greater where an indigenous community is in close proximity to a large non-indigenous population, as in *Jacobs* and *Grismer*) and the efforts made by the group to consider alternative ways of proving a person's identity (which were apparent in *Grismer* but seemingly lacking in *Jacobs*). In other words, membership rules that may be reconciled with a cultural (or even a relational) conception of identity are more likely to survive an equality challenge than are rules that evoke a racial conception.

Before leaving this topic, I should add that it is not surprising in the context of the *Lovelace* case and Bill c–31 that the codes I have reviewed do not use gender distinctions in the forumlation of ancestry requirements. Some of them even contain provisions guaranteeing gender equality.[120] But this does not mean that discrimination has not occurred in fact. Some cases have already been mentioned. For instance, the Sawridge band sought to subject women who had regained Indian status to a complex process designed to assess their knowledge of the band's culture. The Federal Court of Appeal invalidated those provisions of the Sawridge membership code, as they were contrary to section 10(4) of the Indian Act, the acquired-rights provision.[121] The Sakimay band, for its part, denied the right to vote to reinstated women, even though they were members of the band according to the latter's membership code. The Federal Court quashed the band's policy, as it was in breach of section 15 of the Charter.[122]

Discretionary Admission. In addition to criteria based on descent, certain membership codes allow individuals to apply for membership in a band. The decision is usually made by the governing body of the band or a "membership committee" appointed for that purpose, which must consider several factors. No single criterion is decisive, but the decision-making body has to reach a conclusion after balancing all the relevant factors. In some cases, this procedure is open to anyone who wishes to join the band. In others, only persons who have a particular link to the band but do not meet the specified ancestry requirements are allowed to apply (for example, children of only one band member where a two-parent rule is in force, members of other bands who marry a band member, and so forth).

At first sight, discretionary admission seems to be squarely based on a cultural or relational conception of identity and thus clearly preferable to rigid rules based on indigenous ancestry. The flexibility of this procedure would allow for a finer appreciation of all the factors that contribute to the formation of one's ethnicity. Hence, the correspondence between legal criteria and social reality would be maximised, defusing any challenge based on individual rights. In the *Grismer* case,[123] for instance, the combination of descent-based rules with the discretionary admission of adopted children went a long way towards convincing the judge that the rules were justified. By analogy, courts have tended not to find discrimination where decision-making processes are based on the evaluation by a neutral and specialised body of individual situations according to factors that can be shown to be relevant to the decision. For instance, the Supreme Court of Canada held that there was no violation of section 15 of the Charter where an independent committee was set up by statute to determine if mentally disabled pupils would be integrated into a normal classroom or segregated in a special group.[124] Justice Sopinka noted that the actual personal characteristics of disabled persons had to be taken into account in order to avoid discrimination and that a process aimed at reaching a decision based on the best interests of the disabled pupil complied with that requirement. Similarly, if article 27 of the International Covenant is considered, as in *Lovelace,* a review of several factors is the method used to determine whether an individual is a member of a minority protected by that article.[125]

However, a closer examination reveals certain potential problems. The factors employed in the process must be demonstrably relevant to the determination of a person's cultural links with the group. In this regard, the criteria set out in the membership code of the Chapleau Cree Band, which has been published, are fairly representative of those of other codes:

a) whether the applicant is knowledgeable of the way of life culture, laws and history of the Chapleau Cree Band;
b) whether the applicant follows a way of life consistent with the common good of the Chapleau Cree Band;
c) the extent to which the applicant is prepared and able to support himself and his dependants, if any, in the Chapleau Cree Band community;

d) the social, cultural and family ties of the applicant to the Chapleau Cree Band;

e) how long the applicant has lived among the Chapleau Cree Band;

f) the availability of suitable land, housing and ancillary services which will be required to support the applicant and his family in the Chapleau Cree Band community;

g) any other consideration that in the opinion of the Chief and Council is relevant to the application or to the health, safety, good order and advancement of the Chapleau Cree Band.[126]

These criteria show both the advantages and the pitfalls of the method. The criteria in paragraphs (a), (d), and (e) are clearly related to a person's indigenous identity. A decision based on them would correspond to the actual circumstances of a person and would therefore not offend human dignity. However, the criteria in paragraphs (b), (c), and (f) relate not to indigenous identity but rather to a person's behaviour and to the strain that the person would put on the band's resources. What is apparently sought is the exclusion of persons who adopt criminal behaviour or who have no income. These distinctions do not correspond to actual indigenous identity; instead, they are linked to other goals, such as the prevention of crime or the protection of the band's resources. Does their use result in discrimination? The basic principle is that the separate treatment of the indigenous peoples is justified by cultural difference. When the identification of the persons subjected to that separate treatment is based on factors that are relevant to cultural affiliation, the differentiation corresponds to the actual characteristics of the individual concerned. However, if irrelevant factors are used in the decision-making process, correspondence vanishes, and there is discrimination.

The caveat, of course, is that a system of discretionary admission that looks good on paper may be applied in a manner that discriminates. The *L'Hirondelle* case,[127] although decided on the basis of a violation of the acquired-rights provisions of section 10 of the Indian Act, illustrates an abuse of discretionary admission. The Sawridge band, in its membership code, sought to make the readmission of reinstated women conditional upon an application where the person involved would have to show that he or she "has a significant commitment to, and knowledge of, the history, customs, traditions, culture and communal life of the Band and a character and lifestyle that would not cause his or her admission to membership in the Band to be detrimental to the future welfare or advancement of the Band." According to the trial judge, "the process ... requires the completion of an application form some 43 pages in length and calling upon the applicant to write several essays as well as to submit to interviews." Political scientist Caroline Dick has criticised the fact that the band does not appear concerned at all with the cultural knowledge of band members who can show the required ancestry, so that the process is truly a way of excluding reinstated women and has nothing to do with a genuine concern for culture.[128]

A different kind of abuse would occur if cultural knowledge criteria (such as those in paragraph (b) of the Chapleau Cree code) were construed as a requirement of cultural conformity: adopting a dissenting view of the band's culture could be said not to be consistent with the common good of the band, and membership could be refused on that basis. As we have seen in chapter 1, preserving a form of cultural orthodoxy is not a valid purpose of minority rights. An even clearer case of discrimination would arise if "way of life" were interpreted so as to include religious beliefs.

Hence, a judgment about a discretionary system of admission must necessarily take into account how the system is applied in practice. Grounding legal decisions on an individual's cultural attributes may give effect to inclusionary or exclusionary attitudes.

Conduct-Based Exclusions. Certain membership codes contain provisions that make membership conditional on a person's behaviour or conduct. A first case is where a person can be deprived of band membership for reasons related to the person's criminal behaviour. For instance, the membership code of the Chapleau Cree Band provides for the expulsion of a member who "has been convicted of a serious personal injury offence or a pattern of property offences and constitutes a threat to the life, safety or physical or mental well-being of other persons resident on the reserve."[129] The expulsion is decided by a vote of the members of the band. This, however, seems to be a bad substitute for (or addition to) a criminal conviction. There is no link between cultural affiliation and criminal activity. The fact that one commits a crime does not entail that one has adopted a different culture or has become a member of a different ethnic group. The person deprived of membership through the application of those provisions might have an otherwise very good claim to be a member of the indigenous group concerned. There is no correspondence between such an exclusion and a person's ethnic identity. Moreover, the rule seems very difficult to justify. By way of comparison, Canadians who commit criminal offences are not deprived of their citizenship. The Supreme Court has also held that inmates serving a prison term of two years or more could not be deprived of the right to vote.[130] While the objective of preserving the safety of community members is certainly valid, band councils may regulate residence on the band's reserve[131] and may also enter into housing contracts that provide for the expulsion of residents who engage in criminal activities.[132] Those means may ensure community safety without entailing the denial of status.

Another membership code provides that the band council may revoke the membership of a person who does not live on the reserve and who "does not have a significant commitment to the history, customs, traditions, culture and communal life of the Band."[133] That rule may be vulnerable to a challenge based on article 27 of the International Covenant. It is one thing to admit a person after a discretionary evaluation of cultural affiliation but quite another to expel someone based on a perceived lack of cultural commitment. In the latter case, a person who is legally recognised as a member and who may subjectively identify with the band is deprived of his or her rights on the basis of a cultural judgment made by band officials. There is a great risk that such a process will be used to enforce a particular vision of the band's culture or to silence dissent. This is contrary to the purposes of minority rights.

The membership code of the Mohawks of Kahnawake contains a very singular provision: any member who marries a non-Indian automatically loses membership in the band.[134] This rule applies equally to men and women. In the *Jacobs* case, the Canadian Human Rights Tribunal held that this rule constituted discrimination on the basis of family status and that it was not a reasonable way of achieving Kahnawake's objectives of cultural preservation. It is indeed very hard, if at all possible, to justify rules that deprive a person of indigenous status on the sole basis of marriage to a non-member. In addition to the right to equality, those rules constitute a severe infringement of several other individual rights. They constitute an indirect attempt to regulate one of a person's most intimate decisions, the choice of a spouse, by attaching severe consequences to a choice that the community disapproves of. The right to marry the person of one's choice is enshrined in many international instruments[135] and is perhaps an implicit guarantee of the Canadian constitution.[136] It is interesting to note that article 9 of the Convention on the Elimination of All Forms of Discrimination Against Women[137] prevents states from depriving a woman of her citizenship on the sole basis that she married a stranger. While membership in an indigenous people is not expressly covered by article 9, the principle behind that provision can easily be transposed to our case. Those rules are also likely to infringe upon the right to enjoy one's culture, guaranteed in article 27 of the International Covenant on Civil and Political Rights, as illustrated by the *Lovelace* case.[138] Given that they severely limit basic human rights, rules depriving a person of indigenous status upon marriage to a non-indigenous person would require very strong justification.

The Métis

The membership rules adopted by the various Métis organisations, such as the Métis National Council and its affiliates, do not employ gender distinctions or requirements of a specified degree of indigenous ancestry, thereby eschewing the human rights concerns resulting from those rules. Thus, the MNC defines the Métis as persons who self-identify as Métis, are of historic Métis Nation ancestry, are distinct from other aboriginal peoples, and are accepted by the Métis Nation. This is not to say, however, that the attempt to identify the Métis does not give rise to tensions between legal status and actual identity. Let us review some of those conflictual issues.

Link to a Historic Community. As we have seen above, the MNC views the Métis Nation of the Canadian West as the only Métis group recognised under section 35 of the Constitution Act, 1982. At the individual level, this translates into a requirement to show a genealogical connection to a historic community of people at a certain date in the past. How that historic community is defined remains unclear; Métis law professor Paul Chartrand underlines the circular nature of those definitions.[139] Certain Métis organisations refer to persons who in 1870 were eligible to receive scrip under the Manitoba Act.[140] As scrip was not offered to Ontario residents, the Métis Nation of Ontario resorts to a different method: an applicant must be able to trace his or her ancestry to a specified group of families or local communities that are recognised by the organisation's registrar as forming the historic Ontario Métis community.[141] Persons who have indigenous ancestry but who are unable to trace their ancestry to those historic communities would not be accepted. For instance, a person whose ancestors have lost Indian status and is unable to qualify under Bill c–31 would be considered a non-status Indian, but not a Métis.

The strict application of such a system pursues a strategic aim: ensuring that membership in the relevant Métis organisation will be taken by the courts as serious, if not conclusive, evidence of one's Métis identity. Moreover, it seeks to draw a clear distinction between "Métis," who are recognized by the constitution, and "non-status Indians," who are not.[142] Métis organisations understandably want to be as rigorous as the courts with respect to genealogy. However, the chronic underfunding of the various Métis registries and the difficulty of identifying the members of the historic community, coupled with the habitual difficulties associated with genealogical research, have produced significant backlogs in the processing of applications. As a result, many persons who self-identify as Métis could be deprived of official recognition of their identity. Ironically, they could become "non-status Métis."[143]

Discretionary Admission? Another feature of the MNC definition is the requirement that a person be "accepted by the Métis Nation." This might be construed simply as a requirement of obtaining the administrative verification of the other criteria (especially ancestry) or as an additional, discretionary element to be proven. The Métis Nation of Ontario takes the former view and admits anyone who supplies an adequate genealogy, without any inquiry into the individual's participation in community activities.[144] Moreover, the MNO's registrar is independent of the organisation's political leaders and of the local communities. However, the constitution of other provincial Métis organisations delegates to local community Métis associations the power to decide upon membership applications and remains unclear about any residual discretion to admit persons on the basis of the "community acceptance" criterion.[145] The comments made earlier about the advantages and dangers of discretionary admission into Indian bands also apply to Métis groups, if that is what is really meant by "community acceptance."

To avoid the pitfalls associated with unbounded discretion, the Supreme Court, in the *Powley* case, put forward a conception of community acceptance that relies more on objective criteria that reflect the applicant's conduct than on the subjective views of community leaders: "The core of community acceptance is past and ongoing participation in a shared culture, in the customs and traditions that constitute a Métis community's identity and distinguish it from other groups."[146] In other words, community acceptance should flow from genuine and continuous self-identification as a Métis. Subsequent lower court decisions have considered participation in community activities as a presumption of community acceptance.[147] Membership rules that employ a narrower conception of community acceptance risk being set aside or ignored by the courts.

The Indian/Métis Boundary. Another salient feature of the MNC definition is the exclusion of other indigenous peoples. One cannot be a Métis if one is already Indian or Inuit. This criterion makes sense at the group level, as the Métis Nation perceives itself to be distinct from the indigenous peoples governed by the Indian Act. When applied at the individual level, however, it may lead to some difficulties. For instance, where a child has a Métis father and a status Indian mother, the child may have Indian status. This would deny him or her access to Métis status, regardless of whether he or she has more ties with Métis culture. The problem is exacerbated by the fact that Indian status is not a matter of choice: in the foregoing example, the child could not renounce Indian status in order to gain Métis status. Moreover, many persons who did not qualify for Indian status and considered themselves as Métis recovered Indian status in 1985 through the provisions of Bill C–31. According to the MNC definition, they would be ineligible for Métis status.

The validity of a similar exclusion was at the core of a recent case dealing with the Métis Settlements Act,[148] an Alberta statute that grants a land base and a measure of local self-government to certain Métis "settlements" of the province. Membership in those settlements is regulated by the provincial legislation in a manner that excludes, subject to narrow exceptions, any person who holds Indian status. Judy Willier, who describes herself as a Métis, gained Indian status by marrying an Indian man before 1985. She subsequently divorced but could not waive her Indian status, so that her membership in the Métis settlement where she spent most of her life was put into question. The Métis Settlements Appeal Tribunal, which has jurisdiction over membership issues, decided that the exclusion of Indians from Métis status breached section 15 of the Charter and was not saved by section 1.[149] According to the Tribunal, Ms Willier was "discriminated against based on her legally imposed ethnicity." With respect to justification, the tribunal noted that preserving a land base for the Métis was a valid objective but that the exclusion of Ms Willier was not rationally tied to that objective, as she was excluded even though she was in fact a member of the community.

In 2004 the Métis Settlements Act was amended to empower the Métis Settlements General Council to make exceptions to the prohibition on holding both Indian and Métis status (which they had not done so far). The validity of the revised membership scheme was again challenged, this time in the Alberta Court of Queen's Bench.[150] The Court recognized that Indian status is an "analogous" ground of discrimination.[151] The judge, however, observed that Métis Settlements have received the power to define, at least in part, their own membership. Moreover, the Métis Settlements Act was described as a "partnered initiative" aimed at securing benefits for the Métis. Therefore, in the judge's view the distinction between Indians and Métis corresponded to the actual situation of the persons involved and did not violate the human dignity of the Indians and was not discriminatory.[152]

The decision of the Alberta Court of Queen's Bench does not seem to give due weight to the fact that, while it is true that the Métis have a group identity separate from that of the Indians, the boundary between the two groups has always been porous and could be crossed by individuals. For instance, when treaties were concluded in the Prairies in the late nineteenth century, individuals with mixed ancestry were given the choice to "take treaty" and be considered Indians or receive a land grant intended for the Métis.[153] The *Powley* case also provides an example of Métis individuals living on an Indian reserve for a period of time and acquiring Indian status.[154] Hence, it is doubtful that the exclusion of persons who hold Indian status corresponds to actual Métis identity, which would suggest that it is discriminatory.

It is true that other membership control regimes provide that one cannot be a member of two indigenous groups at the same time. For instance, a given individual cannot be a beneficiary of more than one modern treaty[155] or a member of two Indian bands whose membership is governed by the Indian Act.[156] However, in those cases an individual who has the required ancestral connections to two such groups is allowed to choose to become a member of either one. Discrimination is then avoided, because the individual is allowed to choose the status that corresponds the most to his or her identity. In contrast, a person who has Indian and Métis ancestry has no choice: he or she will have Indian status and will not be eligible for Métis status under the MNC definition. The inflexibility of the rules of Indian status was a decisive factor in the Métis Settlements Appeal Tribunal's decision.

The Supreme Court held in *Powley* that the fact that a Métis acquired Indian status or received treaty benefits does not, as such, negate Métis identity.[157] The descendants of such persons can properly claim constitutional Métis rights. In so doing, the Court distanced itself somewhat from the definition of Métis adopted by the MNC. Under the *Powley* framework, courts may therefore recognise that a person who self-identifies as a Métis may exercise Métis constitutional rights, even though he or she also holds Indian status. Consequently, if the MNC and its affiliated organisations wished their definition of Métis to be accepted by the courts, they would have to provide a mechanism whereby an Indian may apply for Métis status if that better reflects his or her identity. Another solution would be for Parliament to amend the Indian Act so as to authorise individuals to renounce Indian status in order to satisfy the requirements for membership in a Métis organisation.

This chapter was organised around the themes of autonomy and individual rights. The existing systems of membership control were ranked according to the degree of autonomy they give to the indigenous peoples in defining their own membership rules. At one end of the spectrum, Indian status is governed by the rules of the Indian Act, which leave no autonomy to the indigenous peoples but, as we have seen, still have important discriminatory effects. Modern treaties do not afford much more autonomy, but they avoid most human rights problems. Autonomy was granted to the Indian bands, under some important constraints, to define their own membership. While their conformity with individual rights can be assessed only on a case-by-case basis, we have seen several examples of problematic provisions. Then at the other end of the spectrum, we find the Métis, who are developing a legal definition of their identity in an autonomous fashion. The latter definition presents only minor human rights problems, mainly related to its coexistence with Indian status. Yet, this autonomy is not total, as the Supreme Court set out guidelines in the *Powley* case that Métis membership criteria must comply with if they are to be recognised by the courts. This comparison demonstrates that the autonomy of the indigenous peoples does not necessarily lead to violations of individual rights. Rather, the continuing human rights problems in the current membership control systems are mostly related to the past discrimination against women who "married out" and the attempts to remedy it. Moreover, we saw that most problematic rules relied on a racial conception of identity, one that uses ancestry in a rigid fashion. In contrast, definitions that aim at tracing cultural belonging, often through alternative manners of proving one's attachment to the group, raise less difficult human rights problems.

5

Access to Minority-Language
Education

From the earliest times of Confederation, the Canadian legal system
has ascribed a special status to the indigenous peoples. Until
recently, it had not done so for the members of the French-speaking
minority. The protection of the interests of Francophones was
implicit and indirect: it derived from federalism and from provincial boundaries that ensured that Francophones would form a large
majority in Quebec and would effectively control the government
of that province. Contrary to Indian status, there was no legally
ascribed "French status" that would govern entitlement to a broad
array of rights. Linguistic identity was not legally captured.

However, in the last thirty years the situation has evolved, and it
has become necessary, in certain cases, to make the freedom to
choose the language of education of one's children dependent on
identification with a linguistic community. In Quebec until the
1970s, a large majority of immigrants were sending their children
to English schools. Thus, as Quebec became more and more
dependent on immigration to maintain its demographic balance,
increasing concerns were expressed by Quebec nationalists with
respect to the eventual marginalisation of Francophones in Canada
and even in Quebec itself. The solution adopted in 1977 in "Bill
101" was to reserve the English schools for the members of the
Anglophone minority. Francophones and immigrants were required
to send their children to French schools. Immigrants were, so to
speak, integrated into the Francophone community. Obviously, to
implement that policy, it was necessary to "legislate identity," so
that one's linguistic affiliation was not only a matter of choice but
also of meeting certain objective criteria set out by law.

In contrast, during the same period the federal government, concerned with the bleak situation of French education in the English-speaking provinces and animated by an ideal of individual autonomy, sought to integrate language rights into the country's constitution. It wanted to grant Canadians, irrespective of their linguistic affiliation and province of residence, the choice of the language of education (English or French) of their children. However, political realities allowed only for the protection of the rights of the official-language minority of each province (Anglophones in Quebec, Francophones elsewhere). Thus, Quebec remained free to require Francophones and immigrants to have their children instructed in French, but the 1982 constitution specifically defined, in section 23, the categories of persons who would be entitled to English schooling in that province. The compromise between the two policies thus hinged around a question of membership control: the identity of the members of Quebec's English-speaking minority.

At first blush, one might wonder what the link is between Indian status or the other membership regimes studied in the foregoing chapter and access to minority-language schools. After all, the law does not define a "linguistic status" that follows the individual in various contexts of social interaction. Yet the close scrutiny of the criteria governing access to minority-language schools, as well as the history of their adoption, shows that the intent was to condition admission to such schools on membership in a linguistic community. Hence, even though the law contains no explicit mention of linguistic groups or linguistic identity, it does amount to a form of membership control.

One might also wonder whether linguistic minorities, in the Canadian context, can properly be characterized as ethnic groups. Many French-speaking Quebeckers or Franco-Ontarians may dispute the use of the label "ethnic" to describe themselves. However, one cannot deny that the process of group formation and individual identification with the group conforms with the social science model of ethnicity. Using that concept makes it possible to compare membership control in indigenous peoples and linguistic minorities. Simply put, the markers that define that ethnic identity are different in each case. With respect to Quebeckers, for instance, the importance of markers such as religion and ancestral links to New France has decreased, leaving language a central defining feature of their group.[1] In that sense, linguistic identity may be understood as conforming to a cultural conception of ethnicity, language being a central element of culture. Hence, rather than testing the law's correspondence to factors such as indigenous culture or community belonging, I will be analyzing how legal distinctions relate to language and linguistic identity.

After setting out the historical context, the first part of this chapter analyzes the emergence of the regulation of the choice of language of education. I show how the Canadian constitution restricts Quebec's autonomy in an otherwise provincial jurisdiction by imposing threshold membership criteria and how provincial legislation restricts the autonomy of the Francophone minorities in other provinces. Although the restrictions on autonomy flowing from section 23 have generated more controversies than human rights issues per se, it is also useful to analyse whether the present regime results in discrimination or a breach of the right to culture. This is the subject of the second part of this chapter.

It should be emphasised at the outset that the relationships between the two official-language groups in Canada developed largely on the premise that the indigenous peoples were irrelevant to the equation. Indeed, for many years the government's policy was to eradicate native languages and to induce indigenous children to learn English or French, especially through the infamous residential school system. As a result of the marginalisation of the indigenous languages, the language debate in Canada has been framed in terms of the English-French duality, and only those two languages received official status at the federal level, to the exclusion of indigenous languages. Only recently have some public efforts been made to ensure the survival of the latter languages. This chapter focuses on the rights afforded to speakers of French and English in Canada.

THE LANGUAGE OF EDUCATION AND MEMBERSHIP CONTROL

The language of education debate must be situated in the larger context of Canadian federalism and its relationship with the protection of linguistic minorities. In 1867, when Canadian political leaders sought to frame a new political system, the need to protect the Francophone minority led to the choice of a federal system rather than a unitary state. As the Supreme Court recently noted, "the social and demographic reality of Quebec ... was one of the essential reasons for establishing a federal structure for the Canadian union in 1867."[2] Under a federal system, French Canadians would control the government of the province of Quebec (the new name for Lower Canada), where they formed a large majority. As that government was to have jurisdiction over education and civil law, among other matters, it could ensure the long-term survival of the French Canadian society, with its linguistic, legal, and religious specificity.[3] Hence, federalism was a tool of minority protection. Through a delimitation of the territories of the provinces that roughly paralleled linguistic boundaries, it ensured that the French-speaking minority would have its own political institutions. In fact, for many French Canadian writers and politicians, the federal constitution was the legal expression of a moral compact between English and French Canadians, considered as the "two founding peoples," the essential requirement of which was that the federal system, and especially the creation of Quebec as a distinctly French-speaking province, would further the preservation of the French language and culture in Canada and allow French Canadians to maintain their distinctive identity.[4] (Note, again, how the indigenous peoples were absent from that compact.)

Federalism, however, provides only an indirect method for protecting minorities, especially where, as in Canada, the various provinces are not totally homogeneous in linguistic (or religious or other) terms. Where a provincial government disregards the interests of a minority within the province, federalism as such provides no remedy. It may thus be necessary to supplement federalism with explicit minority rights. However, the 1867 constitution scarcely refers to language. Its only language-rights provision, section 133, is of limited scope and simply requires the federal Parliament and the Quebec legislature to enact laws in English and French and to allow both languages to be used in their debates; it also permits the use of both languages in federal and Quebec courts. No mention is made of the language of education. Religion, though, was the object of closer attention. While section 93 attributes jurisdiction over education to the provinces, it also sets out the right of religious minorities to establish their own separate schools. In Quebec, where almost all Protestants speak English, section 93 operated in fact as a guarantee that Anglophones would have their own school system.[5] This is not true, however, in the other provinces, where there are many English-speaking Catholics, so that the Catholic school system was not entirely, or even mainly, French.

The inadequacy of section 93 as a guarantee of the right of Francophones outside Quebec to receive education in French is dramatically illustrated by the controversies of the first half-century of federal Canada.[6] In the 1890s, Manitoba made English its only official language and united its school system, which was previously divided into Catholic and Protestant sections. The validity of Manitoba's legislation was upheld by the Privy Council,[7] but the intervention of the federal government led to a compromise whereby Catholic and French instruction was tolerated in schools attended by Francophones. In 1916, the provincial authorities reneged on that compromise and French ceased, at least officially, to be a language of instruction in Manitoba.[8] In Ontario, where a significant French-speaking population had settled over the years, bilingual schools were tolerated until 1912, when the infamous "Regulation 17" sought to forbid the use of French after third grade. Again, the validity of that rule was tested in the courts, but the Privy Council concluded that the choice of the language of instruction was not among the rights protected by section 93; the constitution, reasoned the Privy Council, protected religion and not language.[9] French was reintroduced in Ontario schools in 1927 after persistent political pressure by Francophone leaders.[10]

In the result, until the 1960s French was marginalised in the educational systems of all the provinces except Quebec, the situation being somewhat better in Ontario and New Brunswick. In most cases where its use was allowed, the intent was to introduce French-speaking pupils gradually to the use of English, so that they would have the capacity to continue their secondary instruction entirely in English. The purpose was assimilation, rather than the development of the French-speaking communities.[11]

The situation of the English-speaking minority in Quebec was entirely different. Because of its economic and political strength, that minority always had its separate school system, including three universities, as well as a separate network of hospitals and other institutions. With respect to the elementary and secondary schools, this flowed in any event from section 93 of the Constitution Act, 1867, which guaranteed the existence of Protestant school boards. In practice, this guarantee translated into essentially English school boards. But as there were also English-speaking Catholics, the

Catholic school boards, at least in Montreal, also offered instruction in English. As a result, parents in Quebec could have their children educated in either language. Members of the English-speaking minority could receive their entire instruction in their own language, without being much exposed to French. In reality, as Quebec Anglophones also formed part of the linguistic majority of Canada, the term "minority" did not adequately render the complexity of their situation.[12] While that group may have been vulnerable to the decisions of the provincial government in the latter's spheres of jurisdiction (such as education or health services), it remained in a (relatively) dominant position in the business sector and could count on the federal government to defend its interests.

That situation seemed to have been generally uncontroversial until the 1960s. The parallel existence of two school systems was well accepted in Quebec. In the other provinces, while certain measures restricting the use of French had been bitterly resisted, the lack of political weight of French-speaking minorities allowed the provincial authorities to impose English as the main, if not the exclusive, language of instruction.

Quebec's Language Laws

Until the 1960s, parents in Quebec were free to send their children to either French or English schools. There was no verification of the parents' membership in the relevant linguistic community. However, in the context of the rise of Quebec nationalism in the 1960s, one particular issue, the integration of immigrants, generated a demand to curtail that freedom of choice.[13] Thus, through a series of statutes the Francophone community in Quebec exercised its autonomy to define its own identity by highlighting one fundamental defining characteristic, the French language, and by requiring Quebeckers to be schooled in that language. At that time, Quebec's autonomy in this regard was unrestricted, as provinces have jurisdiction over education, including the language of schooling, and the religious guarantees of section 93 (which limit provincial autonomy) did not extend to language matters.[14] However, Quebec excepted Anglophones from the obligation to send their children to French school. In doing so, the Quebec legislature, dominated by Francophones, assumed the power to define the Anglophone community and did so in a manner that generated much controversy, which, in the end, induced the federal government and the other provinces to include in the 1982 Canadian constitution a restriction on Quebec's autonomy with respect to language of education.

The problem at the root of this struggle was that for many years a large proportion, in some cases as high as 85 percent, of the immigrants who settled in Quebec had been sending their children to English schools instead of French schools. While the traditionally high birth rate of the Francophone community had been viewed as guaranteeing its long-term growth, its future became less certain as the birth rate fell sharply. The government soon realised that unless immigrants were induced to send their children to French school and to integrate into Francophone society, the Francophone population would eventually decline. Certain Francophone school authorities considered that situation to be "abnormal" and a risk to the relative weight and political power of Francophones in Quebec. Nationalists began to advocate the integration of immigrant children into the French school system. In 1968, the controversy turned into a crisis when the school board in Saint-Léonard, a suburb of Montreal, abolished the bilingual (French-English) classes mainly attended by children of Italian immigrants and required them to be instructed in French only.

The response of Quebec's National Assembly was to enact a statute commonly known as Bill 63 that recognised the right of all parents to send their children to English schools and required school boards to provide education in English if so requested.[15] As a concession to nationalists, Bill 63 stated that English-speaking pupils had to acquire a working knowledge of French. Thus, the provincial government, even though in the hands of the conservative-nationalist Union Nationale party, was not ready to depart from the long-standing tradition of bilingualism and freedom of choice. Bill 63 only instructed the minister of immigration to take measures so that immigrants could learn French and send their children to French school, but this goal was not to be achieved by compulsion. Calls for stricter regulation of language, however, led to the mandating of a public inquiry (the Gendron Commission) into the status of the French language and linguistic rights in Quebec.

The adoption of Bill 63 did not reverse the existing trend: immigrants continued to send their children in large numbers to English schools. The Gendron Commission, reporting in 1972, adopted a cautious approach.[16] It recommended the adoption of legislation making French the language of work, of business, and of public administration, hoping that this would be sufficient to improve the status of French and to reverse the existing trends. With respect to the language of education, it advocated the status quo for a period of three to five years, after which the government could consider restricting the linguistic choices of immigrants if other measures had not been successful by then.

Regulating the language of education was the avenue half-heartedly embraced by the newly elected Liberal government, which in 1974 adopted the Official Language Act,[17] also known as Bill 22. Apart from declaratory provisions making French the official language of Quebec and the usual language of work and business, Bill 22 sought to restrict the access to English schools by limiting it to children who already spoke English. While in effect giving in to nationalist demands, the government tried to justify its position in pedagogical terms: it was useless to teach children in a language that they did not understand.[18] Knowledge of a language was believed to be a neutral, non-discriminatory criterion. The government was not ready to abandon explicitly the principle of personal choice that had prevailed until then. Section 41 thus expressed Bill 22's basic policy: "pupils must have a sufficient knowledge of the language of instruction to receive their instruction in that language." In order to implement that principle, section 43 allowed the minister of education to impose tests to verify the pupils' knowledge of their language of instruction.

However, section 41 also stated that "pupils who do not have a sufficient knowledge of any of the languages of instruction must receive their instruction in French." This was a clear departure from freedom of choice, a political decision that could not be explained in pedagogical terms. Moreover, section 40 prohibited school boards from increasing the number of pupils receiving instruction in English without the authorisation of the minister, which was to be given only if the number of pupils whose mother tongue was English within the territory of a school board warranted it. Regulations also provided, through an ambiguous formulation, that a pupil who had a sufficient knowledge of both English and French could attend English school only if English was his or her mother tongue; they also seemed to exempt pupils whose mother tongue was English from the testing regime.[19] Moreover, the minister of education was given the power to require the school boards to test the linguistic abilities of their pupils and to act accordingly.

The ambiguity and subjectivity of the criteria employed by Bill 22 for admission to the English schools caused severe difficulties in the administration of the scheme.[20] The number of parents declaring that English was the mother tongue of their children suddenly increased. Immigrant parents hastily taught English to their children, in the hope that they would pass the tests. Montreal's Italian community even organised clandestine schools for that purpose. The administration of the tests and the interpretation of their results was left to the discretion of each school board, and the regime was not applied in a consistent manner. It thus quickly became obvious that the testing of children's linguistic ability was a very impractical way of identifying the members of the English-speaking minority.

An election was held in Quebec in late 1976, and a new government was formed by the independentist Parti Québécois. One of the priorities of the new government was to adopt a law imposing the use of French in many sectors of public and private life. The Charter of the French Language,[21] as it was styled, or Bill 101, as it was commonly known in the media, went far beyond the provisions of Bill 22. While providing some exceptions in favour of English, it sought to make French the exclusive language of legislation, of the courts, and of public administration, as well as the normal language of work and of business. It also required commercial signs to be exclusively in French. More importantly, Bill 101 had a symbolic objective: Quebec was to become an essentially French society, where French would no longer be a subordinated language. The French language would become the main marker of Quebec identity, to the exclusion of religion or ancestry. That message is illustrated by the first paragraph of the Act's preamble, in which the National Assembly states that "the French language, the distinctive language of a people that is in the majority French-speaking, is the instrument by which that people has articulated its identity." Needless to say, Bill 101 spurred bitter reactions from the English-speaking community in Quebec, from the other provinces, and from the federal government.

In particular, Bill 101 sought to make French the normal language of education, although the government recognised that it was politically and practically impossible to abolish the English school system.[22] In particular, the government decided that all immigrants should send their children to French schools, at least until the end of high school. (Personal choice still prevails at the college and university levels.) Thus, contrary to Bill 22, which purported to uphold the principle of personal choice, while restricting it in some cases, Bill 101 stated clearly that education in French was the norm and education in English the exception. This led to the necessity of defining the ambit of the exception. In other words, who was a member of that long-standing English-speaking minority in Quebec for the benefit of which an exception was created? After the manifest failure of the testing regime of Bill 22, one possibility was to restrict admission to English schools to children whose mother tongue was English. However, determining the mother tongue of a child appeared to raise the same difficulties as the testing regime of Bill 22. There is no objective method of ascertaining what language a child learned first. Asking parents to provide that information would, in the words of the government, have been "open to deceit and to false declarations."[23] Thus, Bill 101 adopted a different criterion: section 73 stated that "the following children ... may receive their instruction in English: (*a*) a child whose father or mother received his or her elementary instruction in English, in Quebec."[24] This was thought to be an objective criterion that could be easily verified through school records and that reflected more accurately than alternative criteria a person's affiliation with the English-speaking community.[25]

Children of mixed marriages were dealt with in a flexible manner. It sufficed that one of a child's parents had been schooled in English at the primary level for that child to be allowed to attend English school. Moreover, as persons who are entitled to send their children to English school are not required to do so, this allowed mixed (English/French) couples to choose the language in which their children would be educated or, in effect, to choose, or influence in large part, their children's linguistic identity. This may be contrasted with the pre–1985 Indian Act, which operated on the (manifestly false) assumption that indigenous culture followed the male line and which left no discretion to mixed couples as to the culture with which their children would be legally associated. Hence, Bill 101 avoided the problems of discrimination that arise when the law employs gender distinctions to determine cultural identity. In resorting to a "one-parent rule," Bill 101 also eschewed the difficulties associated with requiring a fixed proportion of Anglophone ancestry, or even requiring that both parents of a child be Anglophones. As we have seen in chapter 4, requirements of that kind are likely to constitute discrimination.

Bill 101 excluded immigrants from the category of persons entitled to English schooling. This resulted from the requirement, in section 73, that a child's father or mother must have received his or her English elementary instruction *in Quebec*. Immigrants, who were presumably schooled in their country of origin and not in Quebec, could not meet that requirement. In terms of membership control, the law integrated them into the French-speaking majority in Quebec; it manifested the will of that community to include immigrants among its membership.

But the most controversial aspect of Bill 101 was that Anglophone Canadians from other provinces who had moved to Quebec were treated like immigrants from foreign countries and were not recognised to have any right to English-language schooling. (This rule has often been referred to as the "Quebec clause.") This reflected a conception of the identity of the English-speaking community in Quebec that was rejected by the members of that community. In effect, Bill 101 postulated that Anglophones in Quebec formed a community distinct from Anglophones elsewhere in Canada. However, most English-speaking Quebeckers would reject that distinction and would view themselves primarily as citizens of Canada.[26] There has always been a high degree of mobility among English-speaking Quebeckers between Quebec and the other provinces.

In a spirit of compromise, however, Bill 101 contained a provision (section 86) allowing the government to conclude reciprocity agreements with other provinces. Under those agreements, parents educated in English in a province that provided education in French to its minority would have the same rights as Anglophones educated in Quebec. Quebec's intent was to foster the development of French education in the other provinces. All the provinces refused to enter into such agreements, however, no doubt because at that time education in French was embryonic in many of them and because of the hostile reactions to Bill 101 in English-speaking Canada.[27] Bill 101 also contained acquired-rights provisions (section 73 (b) and (c)) in favour of immigrants who were already settled in Quebec when the law came into force and who had been educated in English outside Quebec or had already registered their children in English schools in Quebec. Moreover, persons staying tempo-rarily in Quebec (section 85) and the indigenous peoples (sections 87, 88, and 97) were exempted from the obligation to send their children to French schools.

Language Rights in the Canadian Constitution

The rise of nationalism in Quebec and the adoption of language laws did not go unchallenged. The federal government headed by Prime Minister Trudeau sought to respond with a policy of bilin-gualism designed to improve the poor state of French education in the English-speaking provinces and to raise the proportion of Francophones employed in the federal civil service. In Trudeau's mind, bilingualism also had the advantage of negating any exclu-sive link between French-speaking Canadians and the government of Quebec. Putting the emphasis on French-speaking minorities outside Quebec would make the federal government the legitimate representative of all French Canadians and therefore undercut Quebec nationalism. Accordingly, Parliament adopted the Official Languages Act in 1969,[28] making English and French the two offi-cial languages of Canada, while the federal government took measures to increase the services offered to the population in both languages.

Education, however, is a provincial matter. The federal govern-ment could not, acting alone, open French schools in the English-speaking provinces. This is why it proposed, rather, to include, in a constitutional charter of rights, a provision guaranteeing Canadian citizens the right to have their children educated in English or French, at their own choice. That position coincided with the rec-ommendations of the Laurendeau-Dunton Commission, which had been mandated to inquire into bilingualism.[29] The main deficiency at which that proposal was directed was the poor availability of French schools in the English-speaking provinces. But the right to choose education in English or French would have applied in Quebec as well, where it would have had the effect of allowing Quebeckers, irrespective of their native tongue, to send their chil-dren to English schools. Even if Bill 101 had not yet been enacted at that time, the Quebec government realised that such a constitu-tional right would restrict Quebec's autonomy and bar any future attempt to require immigrants to send their children to French schools. Hence, in 1971 Quebec rejected the proposed constitutional amendment.[30]

During the following decade, Quebec succeeded in persuading the other provinces that any constitutional guarantee concerning the language of education should be framed in terms of rights of minorities (that is, the linguistic minority in each province) rather than in terms of universal freedom of choice.[31] The agreement of the provinces on this principle forced the federal government to formulate its subsequent constitutional proposals in terms of minority rights. Quebec thus secured for itself the power to require its French-speaking majority to send their children to French schools. This being settled, the focus of the debate shifted from the principles of the linguistic regime to the criteria for membership in the provincial linguistic minorities, who would have special rights. The main objectives of the federal government were to reverse Bill 101's "Quebec clause," which denied English-speaking Canadians who had moved to Quebec the right to send their children to English schools, and, more generally, to ensure that children who began their instruction in one language could continue in that language if they moved to another province. To assess the degree to which Quebec's autonomy was restricted, it is important to understand the rationale behind the precise wording of the minority-language education guarantee finally enacted in 1982, section 23 of the Canadian Charter of Rights and Freedoms.

The Genesis of Section 23. The new constitution was finally enacted in 1982,[32] despite Quebec's opposition, and it includes the Charter, which, in addition to fundamental freedoms, due process rights, and the right to equality, contains a section devoted to language rights. Section 16 of the Charter declares English and French to be the official languages of Canada. Sections 17 and 18 provide for the equal use of both languages in Parliamentary proceedings. Section 19 confers on the individual the right to use English or French in proceedings before any federal court. Section 20 guarantees the right of the individual to communicate with, and to receive services from, certain federal institutions in English or French. Section 23 entrenches the right to minority-language instruction and, most importantly for our purposes, defines who is to be considered a member of the minority:

23. (1) Citizens of Canada

> *a*) whose first language learned and still understood is that of the English or French linguistic minority population of the province in which they reside, or

> *b*) who have received their primary school instruction in Canada in English or French and reside in a province where the language in which they received that instruction is the language of the English or French linguistic minority population of the province,
> have the right to have their children receive primary and secondary school instruction in that language in that province.

> (2) Citizens of Canada of whom any child has received or is receiving primary or secondary school instruction in English or French in Canada, have the right to have all their children receive primary and secondary school instruction in the same language.

Section 23 must be read in the light of section 59, which states that paragraph 23(1)(*a*) does not apply in Quebec until the Quebec government consents to its coming into force. So far, the Quebec government has not given its consent and is not likely to do so in the foreseeable future. The National Assembly has even adopted a law prohibiting the government from consenting to the coming into force of section 23(1)(*a*).[33]

Section 23 restricts provincial autonomy in matters of education by imposing on each province a duty to provide instruction to its official-language minority in its own language. But that duty relates not only to the general availability of minority-language schools but also to the identity of the members of the minority who may benefit from those schools. Thus, the first two paragraphs of section 23, coupled with section 59, delineate the categories of persons who have the right to send their children to minority-language schools. They require the provinces to consider those persons as members of their linguistic minority. In other words, the constitution sets out minimal membership criteria. This way of restricting provincial autonomy may be compared to the minimal membership criteria imposed on indigenous groups by most modern treaties or by section 10(4) of the Indian Act.

The multiple entitlements that section 23 provides reflect a complex compromise between several potential membership criteria, as well as a failed attempt to formulate them in terms that would apply uniformly throughout the country.

Mother language ("the first language learned and still understood") provides perhaps the most natural manner of identifying members of a linguistic minority. In the English-speaking provinces, it was often the only available indicator, as many French-speaking parents simply did not have the opportunity to attend French schools while they were young. Outside Quebec, any criterion based on the language of schooling of the parents would have been grossly under-inclusive. Applied in Quebec, mother tongue would displace the "Quebec clause" and allow (among others) English-speaking Canadians who move to Quebec to send their children to English schools. Hence, mother language could be seen as the obvious candidate for a criterion that would be applicable throughout the country and that would fulfil the political objectives of the federal government. This explains its presence in section 23(1)(a).

Yet the criterion of mother language was, in a sense, narrower than that of the language of the parents' instruction employed by Bill 101. Members of the Italian community who had attended primary school in English in Quebec pointed out that Italian, not English, was their mother language.[34] Thus, Bill 101 gave them more rights than the initial draft of section 23, which referred only to mother language. The solution was to include a reference to the language of primary instruction as an alternative way of establishing a connection with a linguistic minority, or, in other words, to add a replica of Bill 101's criterion to the proposed constitutional provision. As that criterion was to be applicable throughout the country, the reference to English instruction *in Quebec* was replaced with the mention of instruction in English or French anywhere *in Canada*. For that reason, this provision (now section 23(1)(b)) came to be known as the "Canada clause," in contrast to Bill 101's "Quebec clause."

However, resorting to mother language to identify members of the English-speaking minority would have caused two significant problems in Quebec, which explained in part the province's opposition to the proposed constitutional package. First, as I mentioned before, there is no objective method to determine the mother tongue of an individual. In a politically heated climate, because people may be tempted to make false declarations in order to secure a right for their children, the risk of false statements would prompt the government to establish procedures to assess their truth. It is not difficult to foresee that such procedures could consume much time and energy and could be very frustrating for the persons concerned, as the experience of Bill 22 has shown. Second, and most importantly, the criterion of mother language would have covered immigrants as soon as they obtained Canadian citizenship. Thus, immigrants from English-speaking countries would have had the right to send their children to English schools in Quebec upon being naturalized. This was in sharp contrast with Quebec's policy of requiring all immigrants, irrespective of their mother language, to have their children instructed in French. Mother language was thus, for political and practical reasons, unacceptable to Quebec.

Nevertheless, it was soon realised that most persons covered by paragraph (1)(*a*) of section 23 were also covered by paragraph (1)(*b*), the exception being naturalized immigrants having English as their mother tongue. Paragraph (1)(*b*) was sufficient to achieve the federal government's political objective of reversing the "Quebec clause." In a last-ditch effort to obtain Quebec's consent to its constitutional proposals, the federal government, through section 59, exempted Quebec from paragraph (1)(*a*). In the result, the language of primary education (received anywhere in Canada) remains the only criterion applicable in the province. Quebec retained the power to direct children of immigrants to the French school system, irrespective of the mother tongue of their parents. (This concession was not sufficient to overcome Quebec's opposition to the proposed new constitution.)

Section 23 and Quebec Autonomy. How can we assess the restrictions to Quebec's autonomy that flow from section 23 of the Charter? Of course, we may lament the fact that Quebec has lost the absolute power to regulate the language of education that it had under section 93 of the Constitution Act, 1867. However, some factors point towards a more nuanced assessment. First, sections 23 and 59 do not guarantee the freedom of choice with respect to language of schooling. Hence, the Charter does not impede the achievement of Bill 101's goals concerning education, namely, to require Francophones and immigrants to send their children to French school.[35] Second, the restrictions to autonomy resulting from section 23 may be offset if the criteria it imposes on Quebec reflect Quebec's interests and wishes. That situation could be compared to that of the indigenous peoples who signed land claims agreements containing a fixed definition of their membership that they can widen but not restrict. Indeed, the main substantive difference between the criteria initially found in Bill 101 and those imposed by section 23 is the replacement of the "Quebec clause" with the "Canada clause."[36] The balance of Bill 101's principles with respect to language of education was maintained.[37] The Canada clause did not have a significant impact and codified the intended result of the reciprocity agreements that were contemplated by Bill 101, except that the courts, rather than the Quebec government, would judge the other province's compliance with their obligation to provide schooling in French.[38] As historian Michael Behiels says: "It is evident in the Constitution Act, 1982 that the prime minister and the premiers did not want to unduly antagonize the government of Quebec on the matter of education rights for linguistic communities."[39] It also increased the correspondence between the law and the manner in which Quebec Anglophones viewed their identity, that is, as not forming a community separate from Anglophones in other provinces.

Yet the Supreme Court gave section 23 an interpretation that makes it more difficult for Quebec to ensure the respect of the "linguistic boundary" between Anglophones and Francophones. This difficulty flows from section 23(2) of the Charter, which, it will be remembered, grants to a child the right to go to English school in Quebec if that child "has received or is receiving primary or secondary school instruction in English ... in Canada." One possible interpretation of that phrase is that the right crystallises at the instant the child enters English school, so that the child immediately acquires the right to continue instruction in that language in the public system. Thus, certain parents argued that their children had acquired a right to English schooling by spending a very short period of time in a non-subsidized private English school (not regulated by Bill 101),[40] in an English school under the exemption for temporary workers (section 85 of Bill 101), or in an English school in another province. In an attempt to forestall these attempts at circumventing Bill 101's basic rules, the National Assembly amended the law in 1993 to provide that a child who has received or is receiving instruction in English anywhere in Canada is entitled to continue in English in Quebec only if "that instruction constitutes the *major part* of the elementary or secondary instruction received by the child in Canada."[41] In the *Solski* case,[42] certain parents contested the validity of those amendments to Bill 101 as being incompatible with their interpretation of section 23(2) of the Charter. It is interesting to contrast the decisions rendered by the Court of Appeal and by the Supreme Court. The Court of Appeal considered that the "major part" qualification was not in conflict with section 23(2). The Court noted that section 23 was a compromise exclusively directed at the protection of the linguistic minority in each province and that the constituent power consciously refrained from entrenching freedom of choice in the constitution. According to the Court, construing section 23(2) as requiring only a minimal time of English instruction would in practice constitute a return to the freedom of choice regime that both Quebec and Canada have rejected' and would thus depart from the 1982 compromise.[43] Thus, the Court of Appeal decided that flexibility in the definition of linguistic minorities must not jeopardize the very existence of a legal boundary between the two linguistic communities. In contrast, the Supreme Court decided that in order to comply with section 23(2), Bill 101's "major part" criterion had to be interpreted in "qualitative" rather than "quantitative" terms. The Court mandated a subjective test based on "the time spent in each program, at what stage of education the choice of language of instruction was made, what programs are or were available, and whether learning disabilities or other difficulties exist";[44] in the end, the decisive question was whether there was a "a genuine commitment to a minority language educational experience."[45]

The Supreme Court's decision has been criticised as being inconsistent, for it purports to give effect to the rejection of freedom of choice by the framers of the constitution, while adopting criteria that give significant weight to the parents' subjective intent.[46] Moreover, by "reading down" the concept of the "major part" of one's instruction, the Court deprived Quebec of the benefit of section 1 of the Charter, which allows legislatures to restrict rights (including section 23 rights) in a manner that is demonstrably justified in a free and democratic society. Thus, Quebec could not show that the general interest in policing the linguistic boundary and ensuring fairness in its application justified limits on section 23 rights. The case ended up being decided mostly on the basis of the interests of individual rights-holders.

Before the *Solski* case reached its ultimate conclusion, however, the National Assembly amended Bill 101 again, in 2002, to provide that education received in non-subsidized schools or pursuant to the exemption for temporary workers would not count when assessing whether a pupil has received the major part of his or her education in French.[47] Thus, Francophone or immigrant parents could not resort to the stratagem of paying for their children to attend a private non-subsidized school for a short period of time and then claiming a right to public education in English under section 23(2) of the Charter. The compatibility of the 2002 amendments with section 23 was not directly at issue in *Solski* but gave rise to another round of litigation. While the lower courts sustained the validity of the amendments, the Court of Appeal, in the *H.N.* and *T.B.* cases, has recently struck them down as being in breach of section 23 and not justifiable under section 1.[48]

The three judges who sat on the case each gave their own reasons. With respect to instruction received in private non-subsidized schools, Justice Hilton held that the 2002 amendments breached section 23 of the Charter because they precluded the case-by-case analysis mandated by the *Solski* decision.[49] Regarding section 1, he argued that the mere fact that a rigid criterion was employed by the law meant that the infringement of section 23 rights was not minimal and therefore not justified.[50] Justice Dalphond agreed that section 23 was breached but, with respect to the section 1 analysis, took pains to underline the importance of the purpose of the law: as about a thousand pupils each year gained the right to instruction in English through frequenting a private non-subsidized school for a period of one year or less and as some private schools were advertising their services as a way of sidestepping the requirements of Bill 101, he concluded that policing the language border was an objective that justified the curtailement of section 23 rights.[51] However, he was of the view that other, less intrusive means were open to the legislature, such as applying the provisions of Bill 101 to English-language private non-subsidized schools, so that children of Francophone or immigrant parents could not attend them. Thus, he concurred with Justice Hilton that the amendments were invalid. Justice Giroux dissented. He argued that legislatures had some margin of manoeuvre to flesh out the details of the right enshrined by section 23, in such a way that would promote the purpose of section 23, which he identified as the protection of linguistic groups.[52] Thus, in his view, the rule whereby instruction received in private non-subsidized schools does not count towards establishing a pupil's right to continue receiving instruction in English did not breach the Charter, as it was directed towards Quebec Francophones or immigrants, who were not among the groups protected by section 23. The Court of Appeal was unanimous, however, in deciding that the other rules adopted in 2002, namely the exclusion of instruction received pursuant to an exemption for temporary workers, for learning difficulties, or for humanitarian reasons, were invalid. In substance, the Court observed that these exemptions were much less frequently used than private non-subsidized schools, had been explicitly granted by the legislature, and had apparently not become a common strategy for wealthy parents to buy an exemption from Bill 101's requirements.[53] Leave to appeal has recently been granted by the Supreme Court.

The *Solski* and *H.N./T.B.* cases demonstrate the courts' difficulty in apprehending the interplay between the individual and collective interests that section 23 of the Charter seeks to reconcile, despite the Supreme Court's greater sensitiveness to that complexity in the *Gosselin* case,[54] which will be analyzed in detail below. The recent tendency of the Supreme Court to mandate a liberal interpretation of language rights and its rejection of the former view that the language rights enshrined in the Charter were a "political compromise"[55] obscures the incontrovertible fact that section 23, although couched in the language of individual rights, is indeed a complex political compromise between the interests of three linguistic groups, namely Quebec Francophones, Quebec Anglophones, and Francophones in other provinces, an essential term of which compromise is the curtailment of choice of language of instruction. Had this context been properly emphasized, judges would have seen that a test based in large part on the parents' subjective will is incompatible with section 23's compromise and that a legislative measure aimed at redressing class privilege by preventing wealthy parents from buying their children's passage through the linguistic boundary is justifiable under section 1. It is hoped that the Supreme Court will take better account of that context when it decides the *H.N./T.B.* appeals.

Section 23 and French-Speaking Minorities outside Quebec. While Quebec retains some autonomy to "police" the linguistic boundary separating Anglophones and Francophones, section 23 also limits the autonomy of the French-speaking minorities in the other provinces.[56] Two particular situations deserve our attention: the case of the French-speaking immigrants and the case of section 23 right-holders who do not speak French. From a membership control perspective, one raises a problem of inclusion and the other a problem of exclusion.

Under section 23, French-speaking immigrants do not have a constitutional right to send their children to French schools until they acquire Canadian citizenship. Even then, they will not gain that right if French is not their mother tongue. That can be problematic, for instance, for parents who come from countries where French is frequently spoken, although not the native language of the majority (for example, Algeria). Thus, persons who would "naturally" be attracted to the French language and culture cannot benefit from instruction in French in those provinces where the education legislation restricts admission to French schools to section 23 right-holders.[57] Yet in those provinces, English is not in a vulnerable position, so there is no need to restrict the choices of immigrants in order to promote English.

In Ontario that problem is partly resolved through a mechanism of discretionary admission: French school boards may admit children who do not satisfy the criteria of section 23.[58] This mechanism, although it is not constitutionally protected, gives the French-speaking minority of the province an increased measure of control over its membership. In New Brunswick, all children who actually have knowledge of French are admissible to French instruction, regardless of section 23.[59] There seems to be no constitutional impediment to such statutory enlargement of the categories of persons entitled to French education.[60]

The second problem derives from the fact that section 23 refers to the linguistic background of parents, not children. Children entitled to instruction in French may have English as their mother tongue and may even have a very limited knowledge of French. For instance, a person whose mother tongue is French may marry an Anglophone, and the couple may decide to teach only English to their children. If large numbers of Anglophone students attended the minority-language schools, those schools could lose their

French character and become immersion schools.[61] While French would remain the language of instruction, only English would be spoken in the schoolyard. This could jeopardise the right of French-speaking children to receive education "in minority language educational facilities," a right provided for in section 23(3)(b). Moreover, where the number of children warrants, the right guaranteed by section 23(3)(b) includes, according to the Supreme Court, the right of Francophone parents to manage their own school board.[62] However, if the minority-language school board received a majority of Anglophone students and if all parents had the right to vote in school commissioners' elections, Francophone parents could not then be said to control the school board.[63] This would result, in a sense, in a loss of autonomy. As the categories of section 23 cannot be modified downwards by a province, even with the support of its linguistic minority, it would be difficult to correct this problem. Courts have held that a province cannot, in its school legislation, reserve the French schools for pupils who are able to speak French, as this would amount to an addition to the conditions of section 23.[64] The inconveniences arising from that situation may, in practical terms, require French schools to provide special classes to teach French to those children so that they may later be integrated into the general French curriculum.[65]

COMPLIANCE WITH INDIVIDUAL RIGHTS

In contrast to the old Indian Act, the legal capture of linguistic identity took place in a context permeated by human rights. Thus, Bill 101 and section 23 avoid the most blatantly discriminatory rules that flowed from the sexist and racist conception of indigenous identity held by government officials in the late nineteenth century. Membership in a linguistic community does not depend on gender distinctions and conforms to a one-parent rule that, over time, has the effect of increasing the size of the part of population that may actually exercise a linguistic choice. These basic principles ensure that there is a large degree of correspondence between legal status (or legal rights) and actual linguistic identity. This is not to say, however, that the current regime is free from defects or that it is in total conformity with human rights. In particular, many groups who disagree with the current law's policies have framed their claims in terms of individual rights, in particular equality and the right to culture. Three such groups will be studied here: Francophones, non-English-speaking immigrants, and English-speaking immigrants. Some members of those three groups would like to have the choice, denied them under the current law, to send their children to English schools. However, the issues raised by these three groups are different, as identity interacts differently with the right to equality and the right to culture in each case. They will be reviewed in turn in this section.

Before I undertake that detailed assessment, however, it will be useful to identify some specific problems that bedevil the relationship between human rights and the regulation of language of schooling in Quebec and elsewhere in Canada. The first difficulty is that we are dealing with a situation of "nested minorities" within a federal system. In such a case, arguments based on human rights must be sensitive to the social, economic, and political context. That context informs not only the extent of the rights that should be attributed to a minority but also the ascription of minority status to a particular group. Thus, minority status should not be determined on a purely numerical basis. The pitfalls of such an approach are illustrated by the *Ballantyne* case of the United Nations Human Rights Committee.[66] In that case, Anglophone Quebeckers argued that certain provisions of Bill 101 that required them to put up commercial signs exclusively in French violated their rights under article 27 (among others) of the International Covenant. The committee, however, denied their claim on the basis that article 27 grants rights only to groups that form a minority within a sovereign state considered as a whole.[67] Thus, as Anglophones constitute a majority in Canada, they do not have rights under article 27, even though they are in a minority position in Quebec.

That holding, however, is problematic. As dissenting members of the committee noted, minorities cannot be defined only in numerical terms.[68] If the larger context is taken into account, it is apparent that Anglophone Quebeckers are vulnerable with respect to education, a jurisdiction controlled by the French-speaking majority of the province. There is no reason why they should not be recognised as a minority for the purposes of education, while they may properly be considered as a part of the Canadian majority for other purposes (say, employment in the private sector). Thus, minority rights for Quebec Anglophones should be defined according to their specific context, rather than granted or denied across the board for numerical reasons. An example of the flexible approach I am suggesting is found in the recent report concerning Finland of the Advisory Committee monitoring the application of the Council of Europe Framework Convention: that committee held that the Finnish-speakers within the predominantly Swedish-speaking region of the Åland Islands in Finland can properly benefit from the protection of the Framework Convention with respect to matters under the jurisdiction of the autonomous institutions of the region.[69] Therefore, the analysis that follows will assume that *Ballantyne* was wrongly decided and that Quebec Anglophones may invoke article 27, at least in matters of education. As a result, Anglophones and Francophones may both have (different) minority rights on the same territory.

The second difficulty is the fluid nature of minority rights in international law, especially with respect to education. Minority members' educational rights are often restricted in the name of state policies with respect to common or official languages. In this context, it is not surprising that international treaties protecting the right to education do not guarantee the right of parents to choose the language of instruction of their children.[70] Recent international instruments dealing specifically with minorities show a timid evolution towards the recognition of the right of minority members to receive instruction in their own language. For instance, article 4(3) of the United Nations Declaration on the Rights of Minorities, which purports to implement and develop the right to enjoy one's own culture guaranteed by article 27 of the Covenant, says that "States should take appropriate measures so that, wherever possible, persons belonging to minorities may have adequate opportunities to learn their mother tongue or to have instruction in their mother tongue."[71] However, this provision leaves a very wide margin of discretion to states, as obligations are only imposed "wherever possible," and teaching the minority language as a subject within an educational system where instruction is normally in the language of the majority seems to comply with the wording of the provision. Article 14(2) of the Council of Europe Framework Convention also uses this alternative formulation, suggesting that a state may always choose not to provide complete instruction in the language of the minority.[72]

For its part, the European Charter of Regional or Minority Languages,[73] in its article 8, imposes only alternative obligations on member states that they can fulfil by simply making a minority language a subject taught in primary, secondary, or technical schools; they are not required to provide complete instruction in that language. As de Varennes suggests, the general spirit of these instruments can be described as conforming to a "sliding-scale" approach, whereby the precise contents of the right are determined by an analysis of several factors, such as the size of the linguistic minority concerned, its political situation, and the availability of teaching materials.[74] For instance, those factors would tend to indicate that the Anglophone minority in Quebec (if it is to be considered a minority under article 27) does have such a right. Yet the issue is theoretical, as there has been a complete network of English educational institutions in Quebec for over two centuries.

The third difficulty, already encountered with respect to the indigenous peoples, is the conceptual tension between the right to equality, which is intuitively associated with identical treatment, and minority rights, which require some differentiation in legal entitlements.[75] This tension is exacerbated by the fact that Quebec's linguistic regime has repeatedly been challenged before the United Nations Human Rights Committee. The rule whereby the right to equality cannot be used to defeat a constitutional provision does not apply in international law. Thus, even though the Supreme Court has decided certain cases on that basis, we will have to analyse whether the manner in which the current law reflects linguistic identity is compatible with substantive equality.

Francophones and the "Right of Exit"

Francophone Quebeckers are not permitted to send their children to English schools. This restriction may be viewed, in formal terms, as differential treatment when compared to the treatment of Anglophones, who may choose between English and French. From a membership perspective, the restriction may also be considered as an attempt to constrain the identity choices of individuals. Quebec does not want Francophones to switch to the Anglophone community and sees the English schooling of Francophones as a significant step in that direction, which should be discouraged.

This central tenet of Bill 101's education policy may thus be assessed in terms of the right to equality (under the Canadian or

Quebec Charters) or of the right to culture (under section 27 of the International Covenant).

Francophones and Equality. The effects of the right to equality on choice of language are highlighted by a challenge brought by French-speaking Quebeckers against the provisions of Bill 101 that require them to have their children instructed in French (the *Gosselin* case).[76] They argued that these provisions are contrary to section 10 of the Quebec Charter,[77] which prohibits discrimination on the basis of language and civil status, among other grounds. In a judgment issued in 2005, the Supreme Court dismissed their claims.

The first issue raised by the *Gosselin* case, and which formed the main basis of the Supreme Court's decision, is the relationship between the constitutional right to minority-language education (found in section 23 of the Charter) and the right to equality. As discussed in chapter 2, the Supreme Court has said several times that a provision of the constitution cannot be construed so as to repeal another right and that minority rights contained in the constitution are an exception to the right to equality.[78] To avoid the application of that rule, the plaintiffs in *Gosselin* based their recourse on the Quebec Charter, which, contrary to the Canadian Charter, does not deal with language rights and is paramount over the provisions of other provincial statutes, such as Bill 101. Yet the Supreme Court held that the Quebec legislature could not be held to discriminate when it was simply reproducing the categories found in section 23 of the Canadian Charter. This is tantamount to saying that laws concerning the language of education enjoy an immunity from review under both the Quebec and the Canadian Charters, provided that they employ substantially the same categories as section 23 of the Canadian Charter. However, I have argued above that this "immunity" approach to the reconciliation of minority and equality rights is misguided and should be replaced with a review based on substantive equality, integrating the values embodied in constitutional guarantees of minority rights, such as section 23.[79] The Supreme Court adverted to that issue but did not offer a full analysis. Thus, it said that substantive equality may sometimes require the differential treatment of the members of a minority.[80] It also stressed the fact that the constitution clearly avoided granting all parents the choice of the language in which their children could be schooled but only afforded those rights to linguistic minorities, in particular to allow Quebec to protect the French language by requiring Francophones to send their children to French schools. According to the court, that scheme would be thwarted if the linguistic majority and minority were to be treated similarly.[81]

However, had the court undertaken a full analysis based on substantive equality, the result would have likely been the same. This issue may become particularly important if the *Gosselin* plaintiffs decide to bring their case before the United Nations Human Rights Committee, where the "immunity" approach taken by the Supreme Court is not recognized. The analysis of substantive equality may be divided, as usual, into the requirements of correspondence and of justification. With respect to correspondence, the criterion employed by Bill 101 and section 23 of the Charter with respect to Quebec, namely, the language of primary instruction of the parents, is an adequate, although admittedly not perfect, manner of distinguishing Anglophones from Francophones. The correspondence between that criterion and true linguistic identity depends on two assumptions: first, that minority-language instruction was available when the parents were of school age and, second, that most members of the minority indeed send their children to minority-language schools, which ensures that language of primary instruction is an accurate indicator of linguistic identity or mother tongue. These two assumptions hold true in Quebec, where a complete network of English schools has been in existence for more than two centuries and where, during the period 1971–98, about 98 percent of Francophones were schooled in French (at the primary and secondary levels) and from 82 percent to 92 percent of Anglophones were schooled in English.[82]

Moreover, the criterion is structured in a way that preserves the freedom of choice of mixed couples and that recognises that the law cannot determine, through a fixed rule, the linguistic identity of the children of those couples. Thus, by choosing to have their children instructed in English or French, parents indicate the linguistic community with which their children will be mainly associated. This amounts to a form of self-identification in marginal cases, which increases the correspondence between linguistic identity and the choices open to the parents. This avoids the discrimination resulting from rules based on a fixed degree of ancestry, such as those of the Indian Act, studied in the previous chapter.

One could argue that the law could resort to better criteria than the one found in Bill 101 and section 23 of the Charter. New Brunswick, for instance, recently adopted a law that allows all children who speak French or English to attend French or English school, respectively, regardless of the mother tongue or language of instruction of their parents, and that provides for the testing of children's linguistic abilities in doubtful cases.[83] However, if such a rule were transposed to Quebec, it would thwart Bill 101's purpose, because parents could teach some English to their children in order to qualify them for English instruction. (This is actually what happened when Bill 22 was in force, from 1975 to 1977.) One could also think of the criterion employed by section 23(1)(a) of the Charter: mother tongue of the parents. However, the legislature may legitimately want to avoid the evidentiary difficulties associated with the determination of the mother tongue of a person and to resort to a criterion based on facts that can be uncontrovertibly proved by documents. In Quebec, the failure of the testing regime of Bill 22 proved that criteria based on self-identification or a subjective assessment of one's linguistic abilities were unsuitable in a context where many people wished to circumvent the law.

In the result, the correspondence between the distinction employed by the law and the real linguistic identity of individuals must be assessed in light of all relevant factors, which include the feasibility of individual testing and the actual manner in which individuals manifest their linguistic identity. For instance, the language of the parents' primary schooling may be entirely irrelevant outside Quebec, where French schools were almost non-existent until the 1970s and where, still today, only about half the children eligible for minority-language instruction actually attend French school.[84]

The analysis then moves on to the question of justification. In this context of "nested" minorities, Bill 101 and section 23 of the Charter have a twin ameliorative purpose: they seek to reconcile the interests of the Anglophones, who constitute a minority in Quebec, and those of the Francophones, who constitute a minority in Canada (and in North America). Both groups have "minority interests" or needs that are related to the minority situation of the group. On the one hand, Quebec Anglophones do not control the provincial government, which has jurisdiction over education. They need guarantees that the English school system will remain in existence and that they will have the right to send their children to it. On the other hand, Francophones control the provincial government, but they face socio-economic pressures that flow from their minority situation in the larger North American context (a fact that was recognised by the Supreme Court in *Gosselin*).[85] As a group, they need measures to ensure that those pressures do not lead to the marginalisation of French. Reconciling the needs of those two minorities is made possible by the adoption of a system of membership control: distinguishing between Anglophones and Francophones allows the law to grant rights to or to impose burdens on the right persons according to their ethnolinguistic identity, thus furthering the objectives of both groups.

It should be pointed out that the courts have recognized that the promotion and the protection of the French language in Quebec is a valid ameliorative purpose.[86] In particular, Chief Justice Deschênes, the trial judge in the *Quebec Association of Protestant School Boards* case, specifically recognized that the Quebec legislature could require French-speaking Quebeckers to send their children to French school.[87] The validity of that objective is also recognized by the constituent power itself, which drafted section 23 of the Charter in a way that allowed Quebec to curtail the linguistic choices of Francophones and immigrants. Similar objectives have been upheld in the international context. By way of comparison, in the *Belgian Linguistics* case, the European Court of Human Rights stated that the preservation of the "linguistic unity" of Belgium's two main regions was a legitimate objective that could justify restrictions on individual rights.[88] In Switzerland, the courts have concluded that the protection of a language that is in danger of disappearing is a legitimate public purpose justifying restrictions on freedom of expression in matters of commercial advertising.[89] In *Lovelace* v. *Canada*, the United Nations Human Rights Committee also suggested, without deciding the issue, that preserving the identity of an indigenous people could be a goal that would justify restrictions on the right to enjoy one's own culture.[90]

In this context, it is likely that the impacts of Quebec's linguistic regime on Francophones will be considered proportional to the importance of the legislative purpose. The Francophones' right to education is not affected as such. What is really denied to them is the right to choose a language of instruction different from their mother tongue. As we have seen above, this is generally not understood as a basic human right. At most, the recent evolution of international law suggests that members of a minority, when they are in sufficient numbers, would have a right to be educated in *their own* language. Moreover, the complainants are members of a group, the French-speaking majority in Quebec, that cannot be said to have suffered from historical stereotyping or prejudice in the realm of education. Education is a provincial jurisdiction and has always been controlled by the French-speaking majority. Francophones who wish to have their children instructed in English do not constitute an oppressed group or an ethnic group on their own who would have different linguistic claims than Francophones at large. Thus, the analysis of those factors shows that the duty imposed on Francophones (but not on Anglophones) to send their children to French school does not breach human dignity and is not substantively discriminatory.

Francophones and the Right to Culture. Is there a violation of article 27 of the International Covenant where the law forbids Francophones to send their children to English schools? Surely, Francophones are not thereby deprived of the right to use their own language (French) in common with other members of their linguistic group. To find a violation of article 27, one must rely on the additional proposition that this article entails a "right of exit," that is, that members of a linguistic minority must be given the right not to associate with other members of their group and to assimilate into the linguistic majority.

An argument to that effect could be based on the Declaration on the Rights of Persons Belonging to Religious, Ethnic or Linguistic Minorities,[91] a non-binding resolution of the United Nations General Assembly that purports to detail the rights guaranteed by article 27 of the International Covenant. Section 3(2) of that Declaration states: "No disadvantage shall result for any person belonging to a minority as the consequence of the exercise or non-exercise of the rights set forth in the present Declaration." According to that rule, an individual would have, so to speak, a right to assimilate to the majority or, at least, not to be treated as a member of the minority. In the present case, that would arguably mean that French-speaking Quebeckers would have the right to assimilate to the Canadian English-speaking majority. However, it is not clear that Francophone Quebeckers suffer a "disadvantage" from not having the choice of the language of instruction of their children.

Anglophone Canadians from other provinces, after all, do not have that choice either. Being instructed in one's own language is not, as such, a disadvantage.

In reality, this concept of disadvantage suggests that the recognition of a right of exit would make more sense where being associated with a minority subjects the individual to important constraints. That may be the case with minorities that attempt to regulate many aspects of the lives of their members (for example, religious groups), minorities whose language does not provide sufficient opportunities for education or work, or minorities whose members are constantly subjected to stereotypes, prejudice, or mistreatment. In contrast, Quebec does not purport to interfere with the cultural choices of its residents (except for the use of French in public settings), the French language provides enough educational or occupational opportunities in Quebec (and in the world generally), and in today's context, Francophone Quebeckers are not subjected to prejudice or oppression. Hence, considering the relevant context shows that Quebec's situation does not call for a "right of exit" for its French-speaking population.[92]

Moreover, recognising a right of exit would subvert the federal arrangement that aims at placing French-speaking Quebeckers in a majority position with respect to some areas of jurisdiction important to their culture. As I have shown above, the linguistic majority in any country may pursue policies that aim at the preservation of its language if it is in a disadvantaged situation compared to the language of a neighbouring country (think of the example of Polish and German in Poland after World War I).[93] In that case, individual members of the majority do not have a "right of exit" or a right to have their children instructed in the language of the neighbouring country. A "right of exit" does not come into existence because the group that adopts cultural protection measures is a minority within a sovereign state, rather than a majority. In fact, the federal arrangement aims precisely at providing the minority with some of the benefits or powers that state majorities enjoy as a matter of course. Recognising a "right of exit" in that case would simply negate the minority's power to impose duties on its members in order to promote its culture, subject to conditions that are easily met in Quebec's case. Thus, when the situation is analysed in the entire socio-political context, we come to the conclusion that the "right of exit" (if it flows from article 27 at all) does not apply to the situation of Quebec.

Most of the arguments made above with respect to the linguistic choices of Quebec Francophones may be transposed to the situation of Anglophones in the other provinces, with the qualification that English is not a language in need of protection. However, the fact that Anglophones have no constitutional right to send their children to French minority-language schools may be justified by the need to preserve the French character of those schools and the autonomy of the French-speaking minorities with respect to education.

Non-English-Speaking Immigrants

The Canadian linguistic regime does not offer immigrants any freedom to choose the language of education of their children. Section 23 of the Charter grants rights to Canadian citizens only. Moreover, in Quebec, where only section 23(1)(b) is in force, immigrants cannot base an entitlement on schooling received in Canada, as they were presumably living abroad when they were young.

In this section, I will analyse the situation of immigrants whose mother tongue is not one of the official languages of Canada. Their situation raises the complex issue of claims to use a language that is not a person's mother tongue. In the Canadian constitution, language rights are usually structured in terms of individual choice and not by reference to the individual's linguistic affiliation. For instance, a Francophone may request a trial in English if he so chooses.[94] However, section 23 rights are not granted to every individual, and its drafters were careful not to entrench freedom of choice. Section 23 entitlements are based on affiliation with an official-language community, which immigrants usually cannot establish. In this section, I will assess the compatibility of this regime with equality and the right to culture. The situation of English-speaking immigrants in Quebec will be dealt with in a later section.

Immigrants and Equality. As usual, the analysis of substantive equality will be broken down into the requirements of correspondence and of justification. The requirement of correspondence is difficult to apply in the case of immigrants. In the membership context, correspondence usually means that the distinctions employed by the law must reflect actual ethnic (or, in this case, linguistic) identity. Yet immigrants whose mother tongue is neither English nor French can hardly argue that they are misclassified as between French and English. In fact, the law makes no attempt at assessing their linguistic identity. Rather, it enforces policies aimed at maintaining a balance between French and English in Canada. Thus, justification is more relevant than correspondence in this regard.

The justification for restricting the immigrants' linguistic choices lies in the preservation of the equilibrium between French and English, and more specifically in maintaining territorial solutions aimed at making Quebec an essentially French-speaking territory. In particular, Quebec sought (with success) to reverse the trend whereby a large proportion of immigrants sent their children to English schools, which, in the long term, jeopardised Quebec's French character. As mentioned above, legislative objectives related to the preservation of a vulnerable language are usually considered valid. Moreover, the restriction on individual rights or interests appears proportional to this goal. Immigrants do not have any particular claim to integrate into one of the country's two official-language communities. Immigrants may also choose to settle in a province where English-language instruction is the norm.

In fact, a country's right to adopt one or several official languages is usually considered an acceptable explanation of language-based distinctions. One apparent exception is the recent *Diergaardt* decision of the United Nations Human Rights Committee, which dealt with the adoption of English as the sole official language in post-apartheid Namibia.[95] The Namibian state sought to prohibit its public servants from communicating, even verbally, with its citizens in any language other than English. In effect, this prohibition meant that Afrikaans-speaking civil servants could not have a telephone conversation with Afrikaans-speaking citizens, even if both parties to the conversation consented. A majority of the committee held this to be discrimination based on language, contrary to article 26 of the International Covenant. However, several members dissented and emphasised the state's liberty to determine its own official languages and to treat differently official and non-official languages. It seems that the majority opinion is explained by the fact that Afrikaans was Namibia's former official language and that the post-apartheid government took other measures destined to curtail the autonomy of Afrikaans-speaking communities. In any event, it seems difficult to extend *Diergaardt*'s holding to the linguistic claims of immigrants.

Immigrants and the Right to Culture. The situation of immigrants can also be viewed from the perspective of the right to culture. If we assume that in the factual circumstances of Quebec, article 27 includes a right to education in the minority's language only for the English-speaking minority, can immigrants avail themselves of the rights recognised for the Anglophones? More often than not, the immigrants' claims relate to English-language schooling, not to instruction in their own language. However, article 27 does not guarantee a right to choose one's language of instruction or to choose the language of a different minority. Thus, non-English speaking immigrants can make such a claim only if they can argue that they have become part of the Anglophone minority in Quebec.

Who, then, can claim to be a member of the English linguistic minority in Quebec that is protected by article 27? The most useful guidance on that subject is found in the *Lovelace* decision of the Human Rights Committee. To determine that Sandra Lovelace was a member of an ethnic minority (the Maliseet people), the committee referred to a blend of objective and subjective factors:

> Persons who are born and brought up on a reserve, who have kept ties with their community and wish to maintain those ties must normally be considered as belonging to that minority within the meaning of the Covenant. Since Sandra Lovelace is ethnically a Maliseet Indian and has only been absent from her home reserve for a few years during the existence of her marriage, she is, in the opinion of the Committee, entitled to be regarded as "belonging" to this minority and to claim the benefits of article 27 of the Covenant.[96]

Of course, those criteria cannot be integrally applied to a linguistic minority. Nevertheless, by referring to persons born and brought up on the community's land, the committee indicates that a person's ethnic identity is determined mainly during childhood. If we transpose this reasoning to the case of linguistic minorities, we would come to the conclusion that linguistic identity is defined by a person's mother tongue, or perhaps by any language learned during childhood.

Applying this principle to the case of Quebec, we would be driven to conclude that immigrants whose mother tongue is English are members of the province's English-speaking minority. Their children would thus have the right to be schooled in English, according to article 27. The fact that those persons are not born in Canada does not disentitle them to the protection of article 27. However, under that approach, non-English-speaking immigrants would have no particular right to be treated as if they were Anglophones. Under the test set out in *Lovelace*, the law does not afford the individual a right to adopt a new ethnicity or a new language.

More general philosophical perspectives about immigration and minority rights are also relevant to the issue. One view is that a state (or a region of a state) is entitled to decide what its official language(s) will be, according to factors such as the historical presence and size of a linguistic group. Immigrants, then, are presumed to consent to this state of things and to accept to adopt the state's official language, at least in public settings.[97] If a state chooses to promote its official language through policies such as those of Quebec, immigrants are bound to follow. On the other hand, one could argue that individuals do not waive their rights, especially their cultural rights, when they migrate to a new country and that this is especially true of children of immigrants, who did not choose their situation at all. Thus, immigrants would constitute minorities that are no less deserving of rights than minorities that have a long-standing presence; both kinds of minorities are equally entitled to cultural autonomy and linguistic choice. It would follow that Bill 101 could not treat Anglophones and immigrants differently without discriminating between linguistic minorities, much like the distinction between Indians and Métis studied in the previous chapter.

The first of those two perspectives is preferable. Despite the problems associated with the idea that immigrants "consent" to the language policies of their new country, there is a kernel of truth in the proposition that immigrants do not have a fundamental right to change the public institutions of their new country, except through participation in the democratic process. *A fortiori* there seem to be no grounds for an immigrant's claim to change the equilibrium or compromises between his or her new country's existing linguistic or ethnic groups. For instance, if I were to move to Barcelona, it would be difficult to see on what basis I should be able to insist that my children be taught Spanish but not Catalan, contrary to Catalonia's linguistic policies. (The situation would be different if Spanish were my mother tongue.) Thus, non-English-speaking immigrants in Quebec cannot claim to choose the linguistic group to which they will assimilate.

English-Speaking Immigrants

The situation is more problematic where an immigrant's mother tongue is English. For instance, citizens of the United States who settle in Quebec can certainly be considered as members of Quebec's Anglophone minority. Yet according to Bill 101 and section 23 of the Charter, they must send their children to French school. The question, then, is whether those persons' existing linguistic and cultural affiliation prevails over Quebec's language policy.

In this regard, the *Bickel*[98] case of the European Court of Justice is instructive. This case dealt with the German-speaking minority in the Italian region of Trentino–Alto Adige. Italian law grants several rights to that minority, including the right to have judicial proceedings conducted entirely in the citizen's mother tongue (Italian or German). Bickel, an Austrian citizen who did not speak Italian, was arrested in that region and requested a trial in German. As he was neither an Italian citizen nor a member of the German-speaking minority in Trentino–Alto Adige, doubts arose as to whether he was entitled to request a trial in German. The European Court of Justice decided that the state's refusal to grant his request would constitute discrimination on the basis of citizenship, which was prohibited by the European Union Treaty. In the same fashion, the fact that Bill 101 (as well as section 23 of the Charter) takes into account only primary instruction received in Canada in order to determine who is entitled to send his or her children to English school (thus excluding immigrants from English-speaking countries) constitutes a distinction based on national origin.

What the *Bickel* case shows is that it is difficult to transpose the analysis developed above, concerning non-English-speaking immigrants, to the case of English-speaking immigrants. The main difference is that the lack or correspondence between legal distinctions and actual linguistic identity is much more apparent where children of English-speaking immigrants are not allowed into English schools. It would be hard to explain to an immigrant coming from, say, Australia that while there exists a complete network of English primary and secondary schools in Montreal, his or her children cannot attend them. That person would reply that he or she is no less an Anglophone than someone who was born in Montreal. While immigrants who speak a language other than English have no special claim to a right to choose English over French, Anglophones certainly have a strong interest in having their children educated in their own language. Thus, with respect to Anglophone immigrants, the criterion employed in Bill 101 and section 23 of the Charter would be substantively discriminatory.

What arguments can the Quebec government invoke in order to justify its treatment of Anglophone immigrants? First, it can point to the difficulty of reaching an adequate definition of the Anglophone immigrant. Criteria such as mother tongue (of the parent) or language of education may be difficult to verify. It is true that immigrants from certain specified countries could be presumed to be Anglophones.[99] However, the potential basis of inclusion in that list of countries is unclear: would it include only countries where English is the language of the majority of the population (for example, the United States, the United Kingdom, Australia, and so on), or also countries where English is an official language (for example, South Africa) or an important vehicular language (for example, India)? In any event, an approach based on a closed list of countries could be said to discriminate on the basis of national origin. The second argument would be that any enlargement of the categories of persons entitled to English instruction would threaten the fragile equilibrium between French and English in Quebec. But this is doubtful: if a proper criterion was selected, the number of persons gaining access to the English schools would likely be small. For instance, in the last decade, only 3.5 percent of recent immigrants to Quebec had English as their mother tongue.[100] Yet this assumes that individual assertions of mother tongue can be effectively verified, as about 35 percent of recent immigrants have some knowledge of English and could conceivably make such a claim.

Those two obstacles, however, do not appear insuperable, and it seems possible to devise a criterion, or a combination of criteria, that would identify the genuinely Anglophone immigrants while avoiding an important impact on Quebec's linguistic equilibrium. For instance, the definition could include all immigrants from countries where English is spoken by a large majority of the population, as well as immigrants from other countries who can demonstrate that they received their primary education in English.

This would mean that the current regime (Bill 101 and section 23 of the Charter) discriminates in an unjustifiable manner when it denies access to English school to the children of Anglophone immigrants. Of course, Canadian courts would probably not reach that conclusion, as it would be tantamount to saying that a part of the constitution is unconstitutional. Nevertheless, the exclusion of English-speaking immigrants could be held to violate article 26 of the International Covenant on Civil and Political Rights, as national constitutions do not constitute a defence against allegations of discrimination heard by the Human Rights Committee.

One might think that the solution to this problem would be for Quebec to consent to the coming into force of section 23(1)(*a*) of the Charter, which would mean that immigrants whose mother tongue is English would have, upon gaining Canadian citizenship, the right to send their children to English schools. Yet one might fear that, given the judgment of the Supreme Court in *Solski*, Quebec would thereupon lose its autonomy to "fine-tune" its definition of the Anglophone immigrant, with the courts substituting a test emphasising individual choice. Thus, from Quebec's perspective, a statutory solution would probably be preferable.

My study of the system of membership control that regulates access to minority-language schools in Canada shows that it is possible to reconcile the autonomy of a linguistic group and its need to define its own membership with individual human rights. In this case, the need for membership control arose because the French-speaking community in Quebec desired to enlarge its membership through the inclusion of immigrants. Quebec's autonomy in this regard initially flowed from its jurisdiction over education. While the 1982 Canadian constitution does allow Quebec to pursue policies of protection of the French language, it restricts Quebec's autonomy to define the identity of its main linguistic groups and the eligibility to English-language schooling. This impingement on autonomy is not dramatic, as it codified the intended result of reciprocity agreements with other provinces. Yet recent decisions of the Supreme Court throw some doubt on Quebec's ability to ensure compliance with its language laws, by emphasising individual choice as a major factor in assessing the entitlement to minority-language schooling.

The criteria employed by Bill 101 and section 23 of the Charter raise no major human rights problems of the kind encountered in the discussion of the old Indian Act. Language rights do not depend on "blood quantum" or gender distinctions, and a measure of choice is preserved in the case of mixed marriages. A single problem remains: that of the Anglophone immigrants to Quebec, whose linguistic identity is not accurately reflected by the current framework. Those persons would likely be successful in arguing that the current régime is contrary to the prohibition on discrimination in article 26 of the International Covenant. This shows that it is difficult to find a single defining marker of identity and that human rights requirements may force legal definitions to employ several alternative criteria.

Conclusion: Judging Identity

The aim of this book has been to analyse the interplay between human rights and the legal rules that control membership in minorities. Two cases have been studied: those of the indigenous peoples and of the official-language minorities of Canada. In the introduction, I identified two main consequences of human rights for membership control systems: the autonomy or self-determination of the minority with respect to its membership rules and the compliance of those criteria with equality and individual rights.

The first issue is the allocation of the power to decide membership issues. There are convincing reasons for recognising the autonomy of the representative institutions of the minority itself. Those institutions are in a better position than the state to define what constitutes the ethnicity of the group. Moreover, while a state may adopt membership criteria that result in the oppression of the minority (for example, the criteria of the old Indian Act), a minority is less likely to do so. The right to self-determination in international law, as well as its domestic manifestations (such as the aboriginal right to self-government), also militate for the recognition of a power of self-definition for minorities. Yet the cases studied in this book show that the right of a minority to define its membership has often been denied and has never been totally free of intervention by the state.

My analysis of the right to equality (and of the right to culture, which raises similar issues) shows that it is possible to define membership in an ethnic group without discriminating. The difficulty is to draw a line between those criteria that accurately define an ethnic group and those that simply perpetuate stereotypes and prejudice and result in discrimination. The right to equality requires a certain degree of correspondence between the criteria employed by the law to ascribe identity and the actual, sociological criteria used by members of the group to define themselves. In other words, there is discrimination if the gap between legal status and actual ethnic identity is too wide.

The social science concept of ethnic identity helps us to understand the application of the right to equality to membership control systems. I have distinguished between racial, cultural, and relational conceptions of ethnic identity. A racial conception is based on the belief that cultural traits are transmitted biologically, an assumption contradicted by modern science. Membership rules that rely exclusively on a specified degree of ancestry reflect such a conception of identity and are very difficult to justify. For instance, the rules of the present Indian Act deny Indian status to children of two successive mixed marriages without reference to other factors that might indicate a person's identification with an indigenous community. A cultural conception of identity relies on cultural traits or markers that prove an individual's attachment to an ethnic group. Ancestry is not decisive but may be a relevant factor, as culture is usually, but not exclusively, transmitted through the family; it is then used as a "proxy for culture." Rules based on a cultural conception of identity are more likely to be compatible with equality, as they increase the correspondence between legal status and actual identity. An example would be the rules found in the membership codes of certain First Nations that allow someone to be admitted into the group upon consideration of several factors, including knowledge of the group's language, history and customs, family ties, residence on the group's territory, and so forth. A relational conception of identity is based not on fixed cultural traits but on group members' perceptions about what makes someone else a group member. This conception underlies membership rules based on group recognition, such as the rules adopted by certain Métis organisations or those set out in the *Powley* decision. They usually minimise human rights problems, unless the group adopts a racial conception of its own identity.

The cases studied in this book show the difficulties encountered by courts when assessing the conformity of membership rules with human rights standards. Initially, the focus on formal equality made the very concept of membership control appear discriminatory.

However, the shift to a substantive conception of equality required judges to focus on the twin requirements of correspondence and justification. Judges are showing an increasing grasp of the concept of ethnic identity (which helps to assess correspondence) and the various justifications of minority rights. Courts are now able to reach a more informed assessment of membership rules, recognising the necessity of a legal definition of membership in appropriate circumstances, while identifying rules that are based on objectionable conceptions of identity. The right to equality can be used to differentiate membership rules that contribute to the improvement of the situation of a disadvantaged minority from those that simply oppress or stereotype the members of such a group.

Thus, self-determination of minority groups is not at odds with the individual rights of their members. Judicial review based on human rights does not bring about the dismantling of membership control systems. Conversely, recognising the autonomy of minority groups to define their own membership rules does not necessarily lead to breaches of human rights. Autonomy and individual rights can be seen as being mutually reinforcing, rather than necessarily antagonistic.

Notes

INTRODUCTION

1 R.S.Q., C. C–12.

2 *Parasiuk* v. *Québec (Ministre de l'Éducation)*, REJB 2004–70101 (C.A.).

3 I. Lordon, "NDP's Brault in Hotseat after Smith Metis Comments," and M. Caesar, "Metis Grand Chief Condemns Status Question," *The Low Down to Hull and Back News*, 14 December 2005.

4 "Indian" was the legal term used to describe the indigenous population. The derogatory character of the term is illustrated by the fact that in the nineteenth century, it was translated in French as *sauvage*, meaning savage or uncivilised. The term "Indian" (now translated as *indien*) is still in use today in federal legislation and will be employed in this book to refer to the category of persons whose status is recognised by the Indian Act. The term "indigenous" (*autochtone*), more in line with current international usage, will be employed in other contexts, but the reader should be aware that "aboriginal" (also translated as *autochtone*) is often employed in the Canadian context.

5 *Buhs* v. *Leroy (Rural Municipality No. 339)* (2002), 211 D.L.R. (4th) 55 (Sask. C.A.), esp. at para. 32; *Yellowknife Public Denominational District Education Authority* v. *Northwest Territories (Local Authorities Election Act, Returning Officer)* (2007), 283 D.L.R. 400 (N.W.T.S.C.); *Syndicat Northcrest* v. *Amselem*, [2004] 2 S.C.R. 551 at 580–83.

6 McHugh, *Aboriginal Societies*, 305; Kingsbury, "Reconciling Five Competing Conceptual Structures"; Daes, *Working Paper*, para. 59; Koubi and Schulte-Tenckhoff, "'Peuple autochtone' et 'minorité.'"

7 Kymlicka, *Multicultural Odysseys*; Roy, *Vers un droit de participation*, 25–33; *Tsilhqot'in Nation c. British Columbia*, [2008] 1 C.N.L.R. 112 (B.C.S.C.) at 203.

8 With respect to indigenous peoples, see Peterson and Brown, *New Peoples*; Nagel, *American Indian Ethnic Renewal*; Garroutte, *Real Indians*; Sturm, *Blood Politics*; Schouls, *Shifting Boundaries*. With respect to linguistic communities, see Juteau, *L'ethnicité*.

9 For a first step in that direction, see Grammond, "Equality."

10 *A.G. Canada* v. *Lavell; Isaac* v. *Bédard*, [1974] S.C.R. 1349.

11 *Lovelace* v. *Canada*, U.N. DOC. CCPR/C/13/D/24/1977 (1981).

12 *R.* v. *Powley*, [2003] 2 S.C.R. 207.

CHAPTER ONE

1 See, e.g., Dworkin, *Law's Empire*; Côté, *Interpretation*.

2 International Astronomical Union, 2006 General Assembly Resolution Votes, online at http://www.iau.org/iau0603.414.0.html (accessed 29 May 2007).

3 For instance, in *Canada (A.G.)* v. *Canard*, [1976] 1 S.C.R. 170 at 207, Justice Beetz wrote that the mention of "Indians" in the *Constitution Act, 1867* "creates a racial classification and refers to a racial group." In *Lovelace* v. *Ontario*, [1998] 2 C.N.L.R. 36 (Ont. C.A.), the Ontario Court of Appeal said of the indigenous peoples that "They are a race distinct from all other racial and cultural groups in our society" (at para. 75).

4 Banton, *Racial Theories*.

5 Smedley, *Race in North America*, 28; see also Appiah, "Race, Culture, Identity."

6 Jenkins, *Rethinking Ethnicity*, 83.

7 *Re Eskimos*, [1939] S.C.R. 104; the evidence put before the Court is discussed in Backhouse, *Color-Coded*, 39–52.

8 Jacquard, *Au péril de la science?* 56–72.

9 Appiah, "Race, Culture, Identity," 71ff.

10 Rosenberg et al., "Genetic Structure"; Bamshad et al., "Deconstructing the Relationship."

11 Jorde and Wooding, "Genetic Variation."

12 Tylor, *Origins of Culture*, 1.

13 Parekh, *Rethinking Multiculturalism*, 143; see also Cuche, *La notion de culture*; as well as the UNESCO Universal Declaration on Cultural Diversity (2001), online <http://unesdoc.unesco.org/images/0012/001271/127160m.pdf> (accessed 26 October 2004).

14 *Convention (No. 169) Concerning Indigenous and Tribal Peoples in Independent Countries* (International Labour Organisation, 27 June 1989, 28 I.L.M. 1382).

15 Capotorti, *Study of the Rights*, 7; the Capotorti definition closely paral-
lels that given by the Permanent Court of International Justice in *The
Greco-Bulgarian "Communities,"* (1930) P.C.I.J. Rep. Ser. A, No. 17 at
21; see also Deschênes, "Qu'est-ce qu'une minorité?"; Rouland,
Pierré-Caps and Poumarède, *Droit des minorités et des peuples
autochtones*, 218, 232–8, 428–43; Fenet, Koubi, and Schulte-Tenckhoff,
Le droit et les minorités, 20–32; Roy, *Vers un droit de participation*,
17–76.

16 Quoted in Tremblay, *La réforme*, 463.

17 *R. v. Van der Peet*, [1996] 2 S.C.R. 507; the test was reformulated somewhat in terms of "way of life" in *R. v. Sappier*; *R. v. Gray*, [2006] 2
S.C.R. 686 at 711–14.

18 Barsh and Henderson, "The Supreme Court's *Van der Peet* Trilogy";
Asch, "The Judicial Conceptualization of Culture"; Schulte-Tenckhoff,
La question des peuples autochtones, 155–7; Niezen, "Culture and the
Judiciary"; Macklem, *Indigenous Difference*, 167–9.

19 See, e.g., *R. v. Pamajewon*, [1996] 2 S.C.R. 821.

20 Barsh and Henderson, "The Supreme Court's *Van der Peet* Trilogy."

21 Barth, "Introduction"; Cashmore, *Dictionary of Race and Ethnic Rela-
tions*, 85–90; Eriksen, *Ethnicity and Nationalism*, 10–12, 36–58; Jenkins,
Rethinking Ethnicity; Eller, *From Culture to Ethnicity to Conflict*, 8–41;
Juteau, *L'ethnicité et ses frontières*; Cuche, *Le concept de culture*; Glenn,
Legal Traditions of the World, 12–25, 31–7.

22 Eriksen, *Ethnicity and Nationalism*, 12.

23 Barth, "Introduction," 11.

24 Chartrand, "Re-Conceptualizing Equality"; Kingsbury, "Reconciling Five
Competing Conceptual Structures."

25 Schouls, *Shifting Boundaries*, 8–16, 51–9.

26 Nagel, *American Indian Ethnic Renewal*; see also Garroutte, *Real Indians*; Sturm, *Blood Politics*.

27 *Reference re Secession of Quebec*, [1998] 2 S.C.R. 217 at 261–3; *R. v.
Advance Cutting & Coring Ltd.*, [2001] 3 S.C.R. 209 at 307–8 (LeBel J.).

28 *R. v. Van der Peet*, [1996] 2 S.C.R. 507 at 538–9.

29 Kymlicka, *Multicultural Citizenship*, 95–9.

30 J. Hitt, "Ça vous dirait d'être indien?" *Courrier international*, no. 815,
15 June 2006, 50–2; M. Perreault, "Le boom de la généalogie
génétique," *La Presse* (Montreal), 2 October 2006, Actuel 2.

31 Juteau, *L'ethnicité et ses frontières*, 86–102.

32 See the review in Griffiths, "Equality and Egalitarianism."

33 See, e.g., Perelman, "Égalité et justice"; Rosenfeld, "Equality."

34 Fredman, "Discrimination," 204.
35 *Bliss* v. *A.G. Canada*, [1979] 1 S.C.R. 183.
36 *Brooks* v. *Canada Safeway Ltd.*, [1989] 1 S.C.R. 1219.
37 MacKinnon, *Feminism Unmodified*, 32–45; Rhode, "Definitions of Difference."
38 Turpel, "Patriarchy and Paternalism."
39 Crenshaw, "Race, Reform and Retrenchment," 1376–81; Rosenfeld, "Equality."
40 See, e.g., Rawls, *Theory of Justice*; Dworkin, *Sovereign Virtue*.
41 Collins, "Discrimination, Equality and Social Inclusion," 20; Arnardóttir, *Equality and Non-Discrimination*, 31.
42 See, e.g., Dworkin, *Sovereign Virtue*.
43 See, *e.g.*, *Canadian National Railway Co.* v. *Canada (Canadian Human Rights Commission)*, [1987] 1 S.C.R. 1114 at 1143–45; see also Fredman, *Discrimination Law*, 150–8.
44 *Lau* v. *Nichols*, 414 U.S. 563, 94 S.Ct. 786 (1974).
45 A discussion of minority-language education in the United States is found in several of the essays in Kymlicka and Patten, *Language Rights and Political Theory*.
46 Jaggar, "Sexual Difference and Sexual Equality," 243–5; Rosenfeld, "Equality," 162–3.
47 See, e.g., Young, *Justice and the Politics of Difference*, 157ff; Arnardóttir, *Equality and Non-Discrimination*, 27–8.
48 Fredman, *Discrimination Law*, 106–15.
49 *Scherbert* v. *Verner*, 374 U.S. 398, 83 S.Ct. 1790 (1963); *Commission scolaire régionale de Chambly* v. *Bergevin*, [1994] 2 S.C.R. 525.
50 *Griggs* v. *Duke Power Co.*, 401 U.S. 424, 91 S.Ct. 849 (1971).
51 *British Columbia (Public Service Employee Relations Commission)* v. BCGSEU, [1999] 3 S.C.R. 3.
52 MacKinnon, *Feminism Unmodified*, 40–5.
53 Jaggar, "Sexual Difference and Sexual Equality," 249–52.
54 Ibid., 248; see also Fredman, "A Difference with Distinction."
55 *Eldridge* v. *British Columbia (A.G.)*, [1997] 3 S.C.R. 624.
56 See below, chapter 5; the link between substantive equality and minority-language education was recognised by the Supreme Court in *Arsenault-Cameron* v. *Prince Edward Island*, [2000] 1 S.C.R. 3 at 27–8.
57 Harris, "Race and Essentialism"; Iyer, "Categorical Denials."
58 Crenshaw, "Mapping the Margins"; Sheppard, "Grounds of Discrimination"; Hannett, "Equality at the Intersections."
59 Rhode, "Definitions of Difference," 204–7.

60 *Plessy* v. *Ferguson*, 163 U.S. 537 (1896) (Harlan J., dissenting).

61 U.N. G.A. Res. 217/A (III).

62 (1965), 660 U.N.T.S. 195.

63 *International Convention on the Elimination of All Forms of Racial Discrimination* (21 December 1965, 660 U.N.T.S. 195), art. 2(2); *Canadian Charter of Rights and Freedoms*, part I of the *Constitution Act, 1982*, R.S.C. 1985, app. II, No. 44, s. 15(2).

64 Gutmann, "Responding to Racial Injustice"; Dworkin, *Sovereign Virtue*, 409 ff.

65 For instance, the U.S. Supreme Court requires that affirmative action programs be tightly linked to evidence of past racial prejudice in a particular firm or branch of the industry: *City of Richmond* v. *J.A. Croson Co.*, 488 U.S. 469 (1989).

66 *International Convention on the Elimination of All Forms of Racial Discrimination* (21 December 1965, 660 U.N.T.S. 195), art. 2(2): "These measures shall in no case entail as a consequence the maintenance of unequal or separate rights for different racial groups after the objectives for which they were taken have been achieved."

67 *R.* v. *Williams*, [1998] 1 S.C.R. 1128 at 1158.

68 *R.* v. *Drybones*, [1970] S.C.R. 282.

69 Flanagan, *First Nations*, 194.

70 *Rice* v. *Cayetano* 528 U.S. 495, 120 S.Ct. 1044 (2000).

71 Kymlicka, *Multicultural Citizenship*, 82–4; see also Raz, *Ethics in the Public Domain*, 161–2.

72 Kymlicka, *Multicultural Citizenship*, 84–9.

73 Tamir, *Liberal Nationalism*, 145–50; Taylor, "The Politics of Recognition," 43–4.

74 Noël, *L'intolérance*; Young, *Justice and the Politics of Difference*, 96–121.

75 Kymlicka, *Multicultural Citizenship*, 111; Réaume and Green, "Education and Linguistic Security," 782; Woehrling, "Minority Cultural and Linguistic Rights," 63.

76 See the section on substantive equality, above.

77 Kymlicka, *Multicultural Citizenship*, 35–44.

78 See the review in Newman, "Exit, Voice and 'Exile.'"

79 Patten, "Rights of Internal Linguistic Minorities"; Newman, "Exit, Voice and 'Exile.'"

80 Taylor, "The Politics of Recognition," 41–4, 63–4; Réaume, "Official-Language Rights"; Réaume, "The Demise of the Policital Compromise Doctrine," 612–23; Gutmann, *Identity in Democracy*, 73–80.

81 Tamir, *Liberal Nationalism*, 73, 96.
82 Raz, *Ethics in the Public Domain*, 116–19, 162–3.
83 Parekh, *Rethinking Multiculturalism*, 156.
84 Schouls, *Shifting Boundaries*, 120.
85 Ibid., 69.
86 Moore, *The Ethics of Nationalism*, 70.
87 For a summary, see Macklem, *Indigenous Difference*, 153–5.
88 See, e.g., *R. v. Van der Peet*, [1996] 1 S.C.R. 507 at 538–9.
89 A survey of the critics of original acquisition can be found in Simmons, "Original-Acquisition Justifications of Private Property"; see also Flanagan, *First Nations?* 11–26.
90 Kymlicka, *Politics in the Vernacular*, 148; see also Macklem, *Indigenous Difference*, 83–5.
91 Waldron, "Superseding Historic Injustice"; Waldron, "Redressing Historic Injustice"; Føllesdal, "Indigenous Minorities and the Shadow of Injustice Past"; Kymlicka, *Multicultural Citizenship*, 220; Newman, "Prior Occupation," 791–5.
92 Simmons, "Historical Rights"; Meisels, "Corrective Justice," 73–8; Hill, "Compensatory Justice."
93 Spinner-Halev, "Land, Culture and Justice."
94 Newman, "Prior Occupation," 795–801.
95 See, e.g., Grammond, *Aménager la coexistence*, 32–52, 74–7; Brisson, "L'appropriation du Canada"; Morin, *L'usurpation*; Martínez, *Study on Treaties*.
96 Macklem, *Indigenous Difference*, 119–28.
97 Tully, *Strange Multiplicity*; Parekh, *Rethinking Multiculturalism*, 194; Maaka and Fleras, "Engaging with Indigeneity," 89; Macklem, *Indigenous Difference*, 153–5.
98 Alfred, *Peace, Power and Righteousness*, 85–8.
99 Lawrence, *"Real" Indians*, 58.

CHAPTER TWO

1 See, e.g., Cassese, *Self-Determination*; Crawford, "The Right to Self-Determination."
2 Roy, *Vers un droit de participation*.
3 Kymlicka, "Minority Rights."
4 See, e.g., *Final Observations of the Human Rights Committee: Canada*, U.N. Doc. CCPR/C/79/Add.105 (7 April 1999) at para. 8.

5 United Nations, *Declaration on the Rights of Indigenous Peoples*, U.N. G.A. Resol. 61/295, online at <http://www2.ohchr.org/english/issues/indigenous/declaration.htm> (accessed 12 May 2008).

6 *Reference re Secession of Quebec*, [1998] 2 S.C.R. 217 at 282–7; see also Crawford, "The Right of Self-Determination."

7 *Convention concerning Indigenous and Tribal Peoples in Independent Countries* (1989), 28 I.L.M. 1382.

8 Martínez Cobo, *Study of the Problem of Discrimination against Indigenous Populations*, paras. 380–1.

9 Government of Canada, *Aboriginal Self-Government*.

10 See, e.g., House of Commons, Minutes of Proceedings and Evidence of the Sub-committee on Indian Women and the *Indian Act* (8 September 1982), 1:64ff, testimony of David Ahenakew, National Chief of the AFN.

11 *Roff v. Burney*, 168 U.S. 218, 18 S.Ct. 60 (1897).

12 *Sawridge Band v. Canada*, [1996] 1 F.C. 3 (T.D.); an appeal was allowed on the grounds of the partiality of the trial judge: *Sawridge Band v. Canada*, [1997] 3 F.C. 580 (C.A.); ten years later, the new trial has not yet come to its conclusion.

13 *R. v. Pamajewon*, [1996] 2 S.C.R. 821.

14 See, e.g., Barsh and Henderson, "The Supreme Court's *Van der Peet* Trilogy"; Asch, "The Judicial Conceptualization of Culture."

15 *Campbell v. British Columbia (A.G.)* (2000), 189 D.L.R. (4th) 333 (B.C. s.c.); *Mitchell v. M.N.R.*, [2001] 1 S.C.R. 911 at 976–81 (Binnie J.); see also Slattery "Making Sense of Aboriginal and Treaty Rights," 211–15; but see *Mississaugas of Scugog Island First Nation v. National Automobile, Aerospace, Transportation and General Workers Union of Canada (CAW-Canada), Local 444* (2007), 287 D.L.R. (4th) 452 (Ont. C.A.).

16 Kymlicka, "Minority Rights."

17 Roy, *Vers un droit de participation*, 158–65.

18 *Declaration on the Rights of Persons Belonging to National or Ethnic, Religious or Linguistic Minorities*, U.N. G.A. Res. 47/135 (18 December 1992, 32 I.L.M. 911).

19 See, e.g., Thornberry, *International Law and the Rights of Minorities*, 175–6; Fenet, Koubi, and Schulte-Tenckhoff, *Le droit et les minorités*, 439–40; see also Benhabib, *The Claims of Culture*, 131; Otis, "Territoriality."

20 *Lovelace v. Canada*, U.N. Doc. CCPR/C/13/D/24/1977 (1981); *Kitok v. Sweden*, U.N. Doc. CCPR/C/33/D/197/1985 (1988).

21 *Declaration on the Rights of Persons Belonging to National or Ethnic, Religious or Linguistic Minorities*, U.N. G.A. Res. 47/135 (18 December 1992, 32 I.L.M. 911), art. 3(2).

22 *Framework Convention for the Protection of National Minorities* (Strasbourg, 1 February 1995, 34 I.L.M. 351), art. 3(1).

23 *Explanatory Memorandum to the Framework Convention for the Protection of National Minorities*, (1995) 16 H.R.L.J. 92.

24 Committee on the Elimination of Racial Discrimination, *General Recommendation No. 8*, U.N. Doc. A/45/18 (1990).

25 *Indian Act*, R.S.C. 1985, c. I-5, s. 20.

26 *Indian Act*, R.S.C. 1985, c. I-5, ss. 18–28, 58; see also *Devereux v. R.*, [1965] S.C.R. 567.

27 See, e.g., *R. v. Gladstone*, [1996] 2 S.C.R. 723; *R. v. Marshall*, [1999] 3 S.C.R. 456.

28 See, e.g., *Blueberry River Indian Band v. Canada (Department of Indian and Northern Affairs)* (2001), 201 D.L.R. (4th) 35 (F.C.A.).

29 *Indian Act*, R.S.C. 1985, c. I-5, s. 87.

30 Clifton, "Alternate Identities and Cultural Frontiers," 17; see also Constant, *La citoyenneté*, 100, 135–7.

31 *Kitok v. Sweden*, U.N. Doc. CCPR/C/33/D/197/1985 (1988).

32 *Indian Act*, R.S.C. 1985, c. I-5, ss. 74 ff.

33 See, e.g., *Cree-Naskapi (of Quebec) Act*, S.C. 1984, c. 18.

34 *Yukon First Nations Self-Government Act*, S.C. 1994, c. 35, s. 11 and sch. III.

35 Otis, "Territoriality," 148–51.

36 Ibid., 144–5.

37 Newman, "Exit, Voice, and 'Exile.'"

38 Kaeckenbeeck, *The International Experiment of Upper Silesia*, 298–344.

39 *German Schools in Upper Silesia*, (1928) P.C.I.J. Rep., Ser. A, no. 12.

40 *Indian Act*, R.S.C. 1985, c. I-5, s. 24.

41 *Indian Act*, R.S.C. 1985, c. I-5, s. 87.

42 *Canada (Minister of Employment and Immigration) v. Chiarelli*, [1992] 1 S.C.R. 711 at 736; *Charkaoui v. Canada (Citizenship and Immigration)*, [2007] 1 S.C.R. 350 at 416.

43 See, in this regard, *Reference re Bill 30, An Act to Amend the Education Act (Ont.)*, [1987] 1 S.C.R. 1148; *Adler v. Ontario*, [1996] 3 S.C.R. 609.

44 *Joslin v. New Zealand*, U.N. Doc. CCPR/C/75/D/902/1999 (2002).

45 *Van Oord v. Netherlands*, U.N. Doc. CCPR/C/60/D/658/1995 (1997).

46 *A.G. Canada v. Lavell; Isaac v. Bédard*, [1974] S.C.R. 1349 at 1359 (Ritchie J.), 1390 (Pigeon J.); that case is studied in detail in chapter 3;

see also the subsequent cases of *R.* v. *Rocher* (1984), 14 D.L.R. (4th) 210 (N.W.T. C.A.) at 215; *R.* v. *Campbell* (1996), 142 D.L.R. (4th) 496 (Manitoba C.A.).

47 *Canadian Bill of Rights*, R.S.C. 1985, app. III.

48 *Morton* v. *Mancari*, 417 U.S. 535, 94 S.Ct. 2474 (1974); *U.S.* v. *Antelope*, 430 U.S. 641, 97 S.Ct. 1395 (1977); but see *Rice* v. *Cayetano*, 528 U.S. 495, 120 S.Ct. 1044 (2000).

49 *Canadian Human Rights Act*, R.S.C. 1985, c. H-5, s. 67.

50 Newman, "Understanding Language Rights," 366, 385–7, 395–8.

51 *Mahe* v. *Alberta*, [1990] 1 S.C.R. 342 at 369.

52 *Lalonde* v. *Ontario (Commission de restructuration des services de santé)* (2001), 208 D.L.R. (4th) 577 (Ontario C.A.) at paras. 280–4.

53 *Westmount (Ville de)* v. *Québec (Procureur général)*, [2001] R.J.Q. 2520 (C.A.) at 2545.

54 Newman, "Understanding Language Rights," 366.

55 See, e.g., *Drybones* v. *The Queen*, [1970] S.C.R. 282.

56 *Arsenault-Cameron* v. *Prince Edward Island*, [2000] 1 S.C.R. 3 at 28; Newman, "Understanding Language Rights," 388–94.

57 Kirk, "Discrimination and Difference."

58 *Lovelace* v. *Ontario*, [2000] 1 S.C.R. 950 at 1003–11.

59 See *R.* v. *Kapp*, 2008 SCC 41; Otis, "Aboriginal Governance."

60 *Conseil de la nation huronne wendat* v. *Gagnon*, [1992] R.D.J. 71 (C.A.) at 84 (Rousseau-Houle J., dissenting on other grounds); *R.* v. *Campbell* (1996), 142 D.L.R. (4th) 496 (Manitoba C.A.); *Scrimbitt* v. *Sakimay Indian Band Council*, [2000] 1 F.C. 513 (T.D.); *Hall* v. *Dakota Tipi Indian Band*, [2000] 4 C.N.L.R. 108 (F.C.T.D.); *Francis* v. *Mohawk Council of Kanesatake*, [2003] 4 F.C. 1133 (T.D.) at para. 15; *Horse Lake First Nation* v. *Horseman* (2003), 223 D.L.R. (4th) 184 (Alberta Q.B.); *Clifton* v. *Hartley Bay Indian Band*, [2006] 2 F.C.R. 24 (F.C.); *Thompson* v. *Leq?á:mel First Nation* (2007), 284 D.L.R. (4th) 80 (F.C.).

61 Royal Commission on Aboriginal Peoples, *Report*, vol. 2, ch. 3, section 2.3, recommendation 17; see also Hogg and Turpel, "Implementing Aboriginal Self-Government," 213–215; *Corbiere* v. *Canada (Minister of Indian and Northern Affairs)*, [1999] 2 S.C.R. 203 at 249 (L'Heureux-Dubé J.).

62 *Waldman* v. *Canada*, U.N. Doc. CCPR/C/67/D/694/1996 (1999).

63 *Adler* v. *Ontario*, [1996] 3 S.C.R. 609.

64 Turpel, "Patriarchy"; McNeil, "Aboriginal Governments"; Wilkins, "... But We Need the Eggs."

65 Deveaux, "A Deliberative Approach."

66 Borrows, "Contemporary Traditional Equality."

67 See above, note 60.

68 Otis, "Aboriginal Governance."

69 Arnardóttir, *Equality and Non-Discrimination*; Gerards, *Judicial Review*; Vandenhole, *Non-Discrimination and Equality*.

70 Arnardóttir, *Equality and Non-Discrimination*, 13–16, 183; Gerards, *Judicial Review*, 60–72.

71 Arnardóttir, *Equality and Non-Discrimination*, even argues that it is the main concept that explains equality decisions; Gerards, *Judicial Review*, 696–711; Fredman, "From Deference to Democracy," 73–6; *R. (ex rel. Carson) v. Secretary of State for Work and Pensions*, [2005] 4 All E.R. 545 (H.L.), at paras. 15–16. In the United States, contrast *Fitzgerald v. Racing Association of Central Iowa*, 123 S.Ct. 2156 (2003) at 2159 (rational basis review); *Nguyen v. Immigration and Naturalization Service*, 533 U.S. 53, 121 S.Ct. 2053 (2001) (intermediate scrutiny); *Grutter v. Bollinger*, 123 S.Ct. 2325 (2003) at 2337–8 (strict scrutiny).

72 See especially Arnardóttir, *Equality and Non-Discrimination*, 184–6.

73 R.S.C. 1985, C. H-5.

74 R.S.C. 1985, app. III.

75 R.S.Q., C. C-12.

76 *Law v. Canada (Minister of Employment and Immigration)*, [1999] 1 S.C.R. 497.

77 *Eldridge v. British Columbia (A.G.)*, [1997] 3 S.C.R. 624; see also *Vriend v. Alberta*, [1998] 1 S.C.R. 493; *British Columbia (Public Service Employee Relations Commission) v. BCGSEU*, [1999] 3 S.C.R. 3.

78 Sheppard, "Grounds of Discrimination."

79 *Egan v. Canada*, [1995] 2 S.C.R. 513 at 548–52.

80 *Andrews v. Law Society of British Columbia*, [1989] 1 S.C.R. 143 at 152 (Wilson J.), 183 (McIntyre J., dissenting on other grounds); *Miron v. Trudel*, [1995] 2 S.C.R. 418 at 494–6 (McLachlin J.); *Egan v. Canada*, [1995] 2 S.C.R. 513 at 599–603 (Cory and Iacobucci JJ.).

81 *Hodge v. Canada (Minister of Human Resources Development)*, [2004] 3 S.C.R. 357.

82 Gilbert and Majury, "Critical Comparisons"; Moreau, "Equality Rights"; Réaume, "Relevance"; Fredman, "From Deference to Democracy," 64; Baker, "Comparison Tainted by Justification."

83 *Canada (A.G.) v. Hislop*, [2007] 1 S.C.R. 429.

84 *Benner v. Canada (Secretary of State)*, [1997] 1 S.C.R. 358 at 397–400; see also *Brossard (Town) v. Quebec (Commission des droits de la personne)*, [1988] 2 S.C.R. 279.

85 *Brooks* v. *Canada Safeway Ltd.*, [1989] 1 S.C.R. 1219 at 1247; *Janzen* v. *Platy Enterprises Ltd.*, [1989] 1 S.C.R. 1252 at 1289.

86 *Andrews* v. *Law Society of British Columbia*, [1989] 1 S.C.R. 143 at 181–2 (McIntyre J.).

87 *Miron* v. *Trudel*, [1995] 2 S.C.R. 418 at 440–4 (Gonthier J.); *Egan* v. *Canada*, [1995] 2 S.C.R. 513 at 530–9 (La Forest J.).

88 See, e.g., Beatty, "The Canadian Conception of Equality," 354–9.

89 *Law* v. *Canada (Minister of Employment and Immigration)*, [1999] 1 S.C.R. 497 at 529.

90 See, e.g., Hogg, *Constitutional Law*, 52–6; Robitaille, "Vous êtes victime de discrimination"; Ryder, Cidalia, and Lawrence, "What's Law Good For?" 122.

91 *Gosselin* v. *Quebec (A.G.)*, [2002] 4 S.C.R. 429; for criticism, see Kim and Piper, "Back to the Poorhouse"; McIntyre, "The Supreme Court."

92 *Gosselin*, 563–5.

93 *Gosselin*, 471–81.

94 See also *Canadian Foundation for Children, Youth and the Law* v. *Canada (A.G.)*, [2004] 1 S.C.R. 76 at paras. 59–69 (McLachlin C.J.), 74ff. (Binnie J., dissenting).

95 *Granovsky* v. *Canada (Minister of Employment and Immigration)*, [2000] 1 S.C.R. 703; *Lovelace* v. *Ontario*, [2000] 1 S.C.R. 950; see also Grabham, "*Law* v. *Canada*: New Directions for Equality," 658–60.

96 Proulx, "Les droits à l'égalité revus et corrigés"; Greschner, "Does *Law* Advance the Cause of Equality?"

97 *R.* v. *Oakes*, [1986] 1 S.C.R. 103; see also *Canada (A.G.)* v. *JTI-Macdonald Corp.*, [2007] 2 S.C.R. 610 at 629.

98 *Thomson Newspapers Co.* v. *Canada (A.G.)*, [1998] 1 S.C.R. 877 at 939–46 (Bastarache J.); *Harper* v. *Canada (A.G.)*, [2004] 1 S.C.R. 827 at paras. 77–88 (Bastarache J.); *R.* v. *Bryan*, [2007] 1 S.C.R. 527 at 540–7; Martin, "Balancing Individual Rights," 366; Wiseman, "Competence Concerns."

99 *Irwin Toy Ltd.* v. *Quebec (A.G.)*, [1989] 1 S.C.R. 927 at 993–4, 999.

100 *Libman* v. *Quebec (A.G.)*, [1997] 3 S.C.R. 569 at 605–6; *Harper* v. *Canada (A.G.)*, [2004] 1 S.C.R. 827.

101 *R.* v. *Kapp*, 2008 SCC 41, paras. 43–9.

102 *Irwin Toy Ltd.* v. *Quebec (A.G.)*, [1989] 1 S.C.R. 927 at 993–4; *Thomson Newspapers Co.* v. *Canada (A.G.)*, [1998] 1 S.C.R. 877 at 942–3 (Bastarache J.); *R.* v. *Sharpe*, [2001] 1 S.C.R. 45 at 96 (McLachlin C.J.); *R.* v. *Bryan*, [2007] 1 S.C.R. 527 (Bastarache J.); *Canada (A.G.)* v. *JTI-Macdonald Corp.*, [2007] 2 S.C.R. 610 at 631–2.

103 See, e.g., *Granovsky* v. *Canada (Minister of Employment and Immigration)*, [2000] 1 S.C.R. 703; *Gosselin* v. *Quebec (A.G.)*, [2002] 4 S.C.R. 429; *Hodge* v. *Canada (Minister of Human Resources Development)*, [2004] 3 S.C.R. 357; *Auton (Guardian ad litem of)* v. *British Columbia (A.G.)*, [2004] 3 S.C.R. 657.

104 *Universal Declaration of Human Rights*, U.N. G.A. Res. 217/A (III) art. 1, 2, 7.

105 Schabas, "Canada and the Adoption of the Universal Declaration."

106 *International Covenant on Civil and Political Rights* (19 December 1966, 999 U.N.T.S. 107).

107 *International Convention on the Elimination of all Forms of Racial Discrimination* (21 December 1965, 660 U.N.T.S. 195).

108 *Convention on the Elimination of All Forms of Discrimination Against Women* (18 December 1979, 1249 U.N.T.S. 13).

109 *Broeks* v. *Netherlands*, U.N. Doc. CCPR/C/29/D/172/1984 (1987) at para. 12.4; *Wackenheim* v. *France*, U.N. Doc. CCPR/C/75/D/854/1999 (2002).

110 Choudhury, "Interpreting the Right to Equality," 30–1; see, e.g., *Kavanagh* v. *Ireland*, U.N. Doc. CCPR/C/71/D/819/1998 (2001), at para. 10.2.

111 *South West Africa, Second Phase*, [1966] I.C.J. Reports 6 at 305–9 (Judge Tanaka); see also *Minority Schools in Albania*, P.C.I.J. Rep. Ser. A/B, no. 64 (1935) at 19.

112 *International Convention on the Elimination of all Forms of Racial Discrimination* (21 December 1965, 660 U.N.T.S. 195), art. 1(4); *Convention on the Elimination of All Forms of Discrimination Against Women* (18 December 1979, 1249 U.N.T.S. 13), art. 4.

113 Vandenhole, *Non-Discrimination and Equality*, 58–60; Choudhury, "Interpreting the Right to Equality," 37–9; see, e.g., *Ballantyne* v. *Canada*, U.N. Doc. CCPR/C/47/D/359/1989 (1993), at para. 11.5; see, however, *Althammer* v. *Austria*, U.N. Doc. CCPR/C/78/D/998/2001 (2003), at para. 10.2.

114 See, e.g., *Broeks* v. *Netherlands*, U.N. Doc. CCPR/C/29/D/172/1984 (1987), at para. 13; *Müller* v. *Namibia*, U.N. Doc. CCPR/C/74/D/919/2000 (2002), at para. 6.7.

115 *Love* v. *Australia*, U.N. Doc. CCPR/C/77/D/983/2001 (2003).

116 Vandenhole, *Non-Discrimination and Equality*, 45–6.

117 Ibid., 47.

118 *Drybones* v. *The Queen*, [1970] S.C.R. 282; *Bear* v. *Canada (A.G.)*, [2003] 3 F.C. 456 (C.A.) at 477; *R.* v. *Bob* (1991), 3 C.R. (4th) 348 (Sask. C.A.) at 360; *T. (R.) (Re)* (2004), 248 D.L.R. (4th) 303 (Sask. Q.B.); *R.* v. *Kapp*, [2006] 3 C.N.L.R. 282 (B.C.C.A.), aff'd 2008 SCC 41.

119 *Québec (Commission des droits de la personne et de la jeunesse)* v. *Montréal (City)*, [2000] 1 s.c.r. 665 at 685–97; *Granovsky* v. *Canada (Minister of Employment and Immigration)*, [2000] 1 s.c.r. 703 at 720.

120 *Charter of Human Rights and Freedoms*, r.s.q., c. c-12, s. 10.

121 *Fletcher Challenge Canada Ltd.* v. *British Columbia (Council of Human Rights)* (1992), 97 d.l.r. (4th) 550 (b.c.s.c.).

122 Weaver, "Indigenous Identity"; Garroute, *Real Indians*; Strum, *Blood Politics*; Lawrence, *"Real" Indians.*

123 Dorais, "Language, Culture and Identity."

124 Royal Commission on Aboriginal Peoples, *Report*, vol. 2, 251; Sharp, "Blood, Custom and Consent."

125 *Ford* v. *Quebec (A.G.)*, [1988] 2 s.c.r. 712 at 777–9.

126 *Nova Scotia (Workers' Compensation Board)* v. *Martin*, [2003] 2 s.c.r. 504 at 574.

127 See *R.* v. *Beaulac*, [1999] 1 s.c.r. 768, which holds that any accused may request a criminal trial in French, even though he speaks English.

128 Domenichelli, *Constitution et régime linguistique*; Delpérée, *Le droit constitutionnel de la Belgique.*

129 Bauböck, "Pourquoi rester unis?" ; Bauböck, "Autonomie territoriale."

130 Eisenberg, "Diversity and Equality," 59.

131 *Thomson Newspapers Co.* v. *Canada (A.G.)*, [1998] 1 s.c.r. 877 at 942 (Bastarache J.).

132 See above, n61.

133 *Gosselin* v. *Quebec (A.G.)*, [2002] 4 s.c.r. 429 at 508–12 (L'Heureux-Dubé J., dissenting).

134 *Trociuk* v. *British Columbia (A.G.)*, [2003] 1 s.c.r. 835.

135 In assuming that the right to communicate with government officials in one's own language is protected by article 27, I go beyond the present state of the Human Rights Committee case law.

136 *Lovelace* v. *Canada*, u.n. Doc. ccpr/c/13/d/24/1977 (1981).

137 Ibid., para. 14.

138 Ibid., para. 17.

139 *Kitok* v. *Sweden*, u.n. Doc. ccpr/c/33/d/197/1985 (1988).

140 *R.* v. *Trotchie*, [2003] 1 c.n.l.r. 288 (Saskatchewan Prov. Ct.); see also *R.* v. *Fowler*, [1993] 3 c.n.l.r. 178 (n.b. Prov. Ct.); *Tsilhqot'in Nation* v. *British Columbia*, [2008] 1 c.n.l.r. 112 (b.c.s.c.), at para. 444; *R.* v. *Kapp*, 2008 scc 41 at para. 4; this principle would apparently not apply to treaty rights; admissibility to treaty benefits would be governed by Indian status: *Chief Chipeewayan Band* v. *The Queen*, [2003] 1 c.n.l.r. 54 (f.c.a.).

141 Ibid., para. 21.

CHAPTER THREE

1 See, e.g., the *Royal Proclamation of 7 October 1763*, R.S.C. 1985, app. II, no. 1; the *Ordinance to prevent the selling of strong liquors to Indians in the province of Quebec*, 1777, c. 7 (Quebec); the *Act to prevent the Sale of Spirituous Liquors to Indians*, 1835, c. 9 (Upper Canada).

2 *Act to prevent certain Wild Fowl and Snipes from being destroyed at improper seasons of the year, and to prevent the trapping of Grouse and Quail in this Province*, S. Prov. C. 1845, c. 44, s. 5.

3 See, e.g., *R. v. Verdi* (1914), 23 C.C.C. 47, 4 C.N.L.C. 444 (N.S. Co. Ct.); *Brossard v. D'Aillebout* (1914), 15 R.P. 412, 4 C.N.L.C. 39 (Quebec S.C.).

4 *Bay v. Registrar of Indians* (1976), 9 C.N.L.C. 36 (F.C.T.D.) at 42; *Re O'Bomsawin*, [1981] 4 C.N.L.R. 76 (Quebec S.C.).

5 Leslie, *Assimilation, Integration or Termination*, 80, 117.

6 On the process of reserve creation, see *Ross River Dena Council Band v. Canada*, [2002] 2 S.C.R. 816.

7 *Report on the Affairs of the Indians in Canada*, Journals of the Legislative Assembly of the Province of Canada, 1844–45, app. EEE (20 March 1845); 1847, app. T (24 June 1847).

8 *Act for the better protection of the Lands and Property of the Indians in Lower Canada*, S. Prov. C. 1850, c. 42; *Act for the protection of the Indians in Upper Canada from imposition, and the property occupied or enjoyed by them from trespass and injury*, S. Prov. C. 1850, c. 74.

9 For the present provisions, see the *Indian Act*, R.S.C. 1985, c. I-5, ss. 18–41, 53–60.

10 *Constitution Act, 1867*, R.S.C. 1985, app. II, no. 5, s. 91(24).

11 *Indian Act 1876*, S.C. 1876, c. 18.

12 McHugh, *Aboriginal Societies*, 255–62.

13 *St Ann's Island Shooting and Fishing Club Ltd v. The King*, [1950] S.C.R. 211 at 219.

14 *Indian Act 1876*, S.C. 1876, c. 18, ss. 61–3.

15 *Act further to amend "The Indian Act, 1880,"* S.C. 1884, c. 27, s. 5.

16 *Indian Act 1876*, S.C. 1876, c. 18, ss. 79–85.

17 Harring, *White Man's Law*, 265–8.

18 *Indian Act 1876*, S.C. 1876, c. 18, ss. 64–6.

19 *Mitchell v. Peguis Indian Band*, [1990] 2 S.C.R. 85 at 130–1.

20 Bartlett, "Citizens Minus"; McHugh, *Aboriginal Societies*, 262–4.

21 Royal Commission on Aboriginal Peoples, *Report*, vol. 1, 137ff; McHugh, *Aboriginal Societies*, 216.

22 Titley, *A Narrow Vision*, 50.
23 Royal Commission on Aboriginal Peoples, *Report*, vol. 1, 333–409.
24 *Act further to amend "The Indian Act, 1880,"* S.C. 1884, c. 27, s. 3.
25 Enfranchisement is discussed in detail below, in the final subsection of this chapter.
26 *R. v. Howson* (1894), 1 Terr. L.R. 492, 3 C.N.L.C. 553 (N.W.T. S.C., en banc); *R. v. Mellon* (1900), 7 C.C.C. 179, 3 C.N.L.C. 580 (N.W.T. S.C.); *R. v. Hughes* (1906), 12 B.C.R. 290, 3 C.N.L.C. 559 (B.C. Co. Ct.); *R. v. Pickard* (1908), 14 C.C.C. 33, 3 C.N.L.C. 603 (Alberta Dist. Ct.); *R. v. Verdi* (1914), 23 C.C.C. 47, 4 C.N.L.C. 444 (N.S. Co. Ct.). See also Backhouse, *Color-Coded*, 21–7; Mawani, "In Between."
27 With respect to the prohibition of alcohol, see Mawani, "In Between."
28 *Drybones v. The Queen*, [1970] S.C.R. 282.
29 *Canadian Bill of Rights*, R.S.C. 1985, app. III.
30 *Act to encourage the gradual Civilization of the Indian Tribes in this Province, and to amend the Laws respecting Indians*, S. Prov. C. 1857, c. 26.
31 *Indian Act*, S.C. 1951, c. 29; see Leslie, *Assimilation, Integration or Termination*.
32 Minutes of the Joint Special Committee of the Senate and House of Commons regarding the *Indian Act* (21 April 1947), Appendix EL.
33 The report is printed in the Journals of the House of Commons (22 June 1948) 647.
34 Delâge and Sawaya, *Les traités des Sept-Feux*, 191–4; Rozon, *Un dialogue identitaire*, 131–56.
35 Rozon, *Un dialogue identitaire*, 152–5; see also Gélinas, *Les autochtones*, 132, 145–8.
36 See, e.g., Alfred, *Heeding the Voices*, 163–4, 173; Weaver, "First Nations Women," 96, 98; Lawrence, *"Real" Indians*, 51, 58, 69.
37 See, e.g., the submission of the Indian Association of Alberta, reprinted in the Minutes of the Joint Special Committee of the Senate and House of Commons regarding the *Indian Act* (21 April 1947), appendix EM, at para. 50; the similar submission of the Union of Saskatchewan Indians, same minutes (8 May 1947) appendix ES. See also Leslie, *Assimilation, Integration or Termination*, 147–8; Jamieson, *Indian Women*, 57–8.
38 *Act to amend "the Indian Act,"* S.C. 1887, c. 33, s. 1.
39 *Indian Act*, S.C. 1951, c. 29, s. 9.

40 Smith, "Western Woods Cree," 259.
41 Clifton, "Alternate Identities and Cultural Frontiers," 11.
42 Sioui, *Les Wendats*, 222.
43 Colleyn, *Éléments d'anthropologie*, 89–96.
44 Fenton, "Northern Iroquoian Culture Patterns"; Viau, *Femmes de personne*, 33, 145ff; Napoleon, "Extinction by Numbers," 142–3.
45 See, e.g., Viau, *Femmes de personne*, 79ff.
46 Van Kirk, *Many Tender Ties*, 28 ff.
47 Alfred, *Heeding the Voices*, 163.
48 MacLeod, "Plains Cree Identity."
49 Émond, "Quels sont les partenaires," 138–42; Napoleon, "Extinction by Numbers," 126.
50 *Indian Act*, R.S.C. 1985, c. 1-5, s. 2(1).
51 *Ross River Dena Council Band* v. *Canada*, [2002] 2 S.C.R. 816.
52 Von Gernet, "Iroquoians," 155–60; Richter, *The Ordeal of the Longhouse*, 118–32.
53 Tobias, "Canada's Subjugation of the Plains Cree," 216–17.
54 Rogers and Leacock, "Montagnais-Naskapi," 172, 180–1; Preston, "East Main Cree," 197; Smith, "Western Woods Cree," 258–9.
55 Groves, "The Curious Instance."
56 Bell, "Who Are the Métis"; Chartrand and Giokas, "Defining 'The Métis People'"; Isaac, *Métis Rights*.
57 Eriksen, *Ethnicity and Nationalism*, 78ff; Rousseau, "Les études sur l'ethnogénèse"; Peterson and Brown, *The New Peoples*; the concept of the ethnogenesis of the Métis nation was recognised by the Court of Appeal in *R.* v. *Powley* (2001), 196 D.L.R. (4th) 221 (Ontario C.A.) at 231–2; see also the decision of the Supreme Court: *R.* v. *Powley*, [2003] 2 S.C.R. 207 at 215–16.
58 Royal Commission on Aboriginal Peoples, *Report*, vol. 4, 220–32; Dickason, *Canada's First Nations*, 236–9; Purich, *The Métis*.
59 *Manitoba Act 1870*, R.S.C. 1985, app. II, no. 8, s. 31.
60 Chartrand, "Aboriginal Rights: The Dispossession of the Métis."
61 Rayner, *The Creation of a "Non-Status" Indian Population*, 37–45; Morris, *The Treaties of Canada*, 20, 41, 222, 269.
62 *Act to amend "The Indian Act 1876*," S.C. 1879, c. 34, s. 1.
63 Devine, *The People Who Own Themselves*, 169–84.
64 McHugh, *Aboriginal Societies*, 250–5; see also *R.* v. *Powley* (2001), 196 D.L.R. (4th) 221 (Ontario C.A.) at 233, where it is said that large numbers of the Sault Ste Marie Métis joined neighbouring Indian bands during the nineteenth century.

65 *Métis Population Betterment Act*, S.A. 1938 (2d session), c. 6; *Métis Population Betterment Act*, S.A. 1940, c. 6; *Metis Settlements Act*, R.S.A. 1990, c. M–14.3; Isaac, *Métis Rights*, 52.

66 *R.* v. *Blais*, [2003] 2 S.C.R. 236; see also *Manitoba Métis Federation Inc.* v. *Canada (A.G.)*, 2007 MBQB 293; Isaac, *Métis Rights*, 13–15.

67 See, e.g., *R.* v. *Powley*, [2003] 2 S.C.R. 207.

68 Dickason, *Canada's First Nations*, 7, 11; Dorais, "Inuit," 130.

69 Memorandum from W.H.B. Hoare of the Department of the Interior, N.A.C., RG85, vol. 1127, file 250–1–1 (10 May 1927).

70 *Re Eskimos*, [1939] S.C.R. 104.

71 Backhouse, *Color-Coded*, 39–52.

72 *Hamlet of Baker Lake* v. *Minister of Indian Affairs and Northern Development*, [1980] 1 F.C. 518 (T.D.).

73 Inuk is the singular form of Inuit.

74 Dickason, *Canada's First Nations*, 73–4; Marshall, *History and Ethnography of the Beothuk*.

75 Tanner, "Aboriginal Peoples of Newfoundland"; Wetzel, "Liberal Theory."

76 *Order Declaring a Body of Indians at Conne River, Newfoundland, to be a Band of Indians for Purposes of the Act*, SOR/84–501 (1984) 118 Canada Gazette 1 2935; *Miawpukek Band Order*, SOR/89–533 (1989) 123 Canada Gazette 4692.

77 *Mushuau Innu First Nation Band Order*, SOR/2002–415; *Sheshatshiu Innu First Nation Band Order*, SOR/2002–414.

78 *Labrador Inuit Land Claims Agreement* (Ottawa: Department of Indian Affairs and Northern Development 2005), c. 3.

79 *Agreement for the Recognition of the Qailpu Mi'kmaq Band* (30 November 2007), online at http://www.mamka.ca/Downloads/Agreement%20for%20the%20Recognition%20of%20the%20Qalipu%20Mikmaq%20Band.pdf (accessed 12 May 2008).

80 *Canadian Bill of Rights*, R.S.C. 1985, app. III.

81 *Act for the better protection of the Lands and Property of the Indians in Lower Canada*, S. Prov. C. 1850, c. 42.

82 *Indian Act 1876*, S.C. 1876, c. 18, s. 3(3).

83 *Indian Act*, S.C. 1951, c. 29.

84 It should be noted in this connection that "marriage" meant not only Christian marriage (which would be prevalent only in indigenous communities in frequent contact with missionaries) but also indigenous customary marriage: *Re Wah-Shee* (1975), 57 D.L.R. (3d) 743 (N.W.T. S.C.).

The leading case in this regard is *Connolly* v. *Woolrich* (1867), 17 R.J.R.Q. 75, 1 C.N.L.C. 70 (Quebec S.C.), confirmed by *Johnstone* v. *Connolly* (1869), 17 R.J.R.Q. 266, 1 C.N.L.C. 151 (Quebec C.A.), which recognised the validity of a marriage between an Irish fur trader and a Cree woman that had been celebrated according to Cree custom. The judge noted that Cree marriage, which was monogamous and based on the consent of both spouses, was sufficiently similar to Christian marriage to deserve recognition. See also Zlotkin, "Judicial Recognition of Aboriginal Customary Law"; Sanders, "Indian Women."

85 *Act for the better protection of the Lands and Property of the Indians in Lower Canada*, S. Prov. C. 1850, c. 42, s. 5; *Act for the protection of the Indians in Upper Canada from imposition, and the property occupied or enjoyed by them from trespass and injury*, S. Prov. C. 1850, c. 74, s. 4, 5, 10; see also the *Act to encourage the gradual Civilization of the Indian Tribes in this Province, and to amend the Laws respecting Indians*, S. Prov. C. 1857, c. 26, s. 1, and the *Act providing for the organisation of the Department of the Secretary of State of Canada, and for the management of Indian and Ordnance Lands*, S.C. 1868, c. 42, s. 17.

86 Delâge and Sawaya, *Les traités des Sept-Feux*, 191–4; see also Royal Commission on Aboriginal Peoples, *Report*, vol. 1, 269–70.

87 See above, n44.

88 *Act to repeal in part and to amend an Act, intituled, An Act for the better protection of the Lands and property of the Indians in Lower Canada*, S. Prov. C. 1851, c. 59, s. 2; see also the *Act providing for the organisation of the Department of the Secretary of State of Canada, and for the management of Indian and Ordnance Lands*, S.C. 1868, c. 42, s. 15.

89 *Civil Code of Lower Canada* (1866), art. 175–7.

90 *Civil Code of Lower Canada* (1866), art. 243.

91 Parent, *Le nom patronymique*.

92 *Indian Act 1876*, S.C. 1876, c. 18, s. 3(3); *Indian Act*, S.C. 1951, c. 29, s. 11(f).

93 *Benner* v. *Canada (Secretary of State)*, [1997] 1 S.C.R. 358 at 402–3.

94 See, e.g., *Müller* v. *Namibia*, U.N. Doc. CCPR/C/74/D/919/2000 (2002).

95 Taylor, "The Politics of Recognition," 66–73; Kymlicka, *Multicultural Citizenship*, 152ff.

96 *Martin* v. *Chapman*, [1983] 1 S.C.R. 365; see also *Re Merasty* (1956), 5 C.N.L.C. 286 (Saskatchewan Dist. Ct.).

97 *Kemp* v. *Rath* (1996), 141 D.L.R. (4th) 25 (Alberta C.A.) at 32.

98 *Act for the better protection of the Lands and Property of the Indians in Lower Canada*, S. Prov. C. 1850, c. 42, s. 5.

99 *Sahanatien* v. *Smith*, [1982] 2 F.C. 807 (T.D.); *Tuplin* v. *Canada (Indian and Northern Affairs)*, [2002] 1 C.N.L.R. 350 (Prince Edward Island S.C.) at 368.

100 Those adoptions have been recognised by the courts for purposes other than the transmission of Indian status, such as inheritance or survivor benefits; see, e.g., *Casimel* v. *Insurance Corp of British Columbia* (1993), 106 D.L.R. (4th) 720 (B.C. C.A.).

101 *Canadian Human Rights Act*, R.S.C. 1985, c. H-5.

102 *Jacobs* v. *Mohawk Council of Kahnawake*, [1998] 3 C.N.L.R. 68 (Can. Hum. Rts. Trib.).

103 Leslie, *Assimilation, Integration or Termination*, 36.

104 *Act for the gradual enfranchisement of Indians, the better management of Indian affairs, and to extend the provisions of the Act 31st Victoria, Chapter 42*, S.C. 1869, c. 6.

105 *Indian Act 1876*, S.C. 1876, c. 18, s. 3(3)(c).

106 *Indian Act*, S.C. 1951, c. 29, s. 12(1)(b).

107 *Martin* v. *Chapman*, [1983] 1 S.C.R. 365 at 379 (Lamer J., dissenting); *Corbiere* v. *Canada (Minister of Indian and Northern Affairs)*, [1999] 2 S.C.R. 203 at 268 (L'Heureux-Dubé J.); see also the argument put forward by Canada in *Lovelace* v. *Canada*, U.N. Doc. CCPR/C/13/D/24/1977 (1981) at para. 5; Weaver, "First Nations Women," 95; Jamieson, *Indian Women*.

108 Gélinas, *Les autochtones*, 145–8.

109 Krosenbrink, *Sexual Equality*, 52; Freeman, "Attitudes towards 'Miscegenation.'"

110 Debates of the House of Commons (27 April 1869), 83–5 (Langevin); see also Jamieson, *Indian Women*, 31–3.

111 Quoted in Jamieson, *Indian Women*, 30–1.

112 Minutes of the Joint Council of the Garden River and Batchewana Bands (6 August 1875), N.A.C., RG 10, vol. 1967, file 5184; see also Jamieson, *Indian Women*, 34–7.

113 For a more detailed analysis of the policy reasons favouring a narrow definition of "Indian" in late nineteenth-century British Columbia, see Mawani, "In Between," 31.

114 See, e.g., the explicit agreement on that question in a memorandum to W.E. Harris, Minister of Citizenship and Immigration, from the Indian Association of Alberta (7 September 1950), N.A.C., RG2, series B–2, vol. 164, file I-14.

115 Weaver, "First Nations Women," 96, 98.

116 *Indian Act 1876*, S.C. 1876, c. 18, s. 61.

117 See, e.g., the testimony of Chief William Scow of the Native Brotherhood
of British Columbia, Minutes of the Joint Special Committee of the Senate and House of Commons regarding the *Indian Act* (1 May 1947); the
same concerns were expressed a few years later: Summary of the Proceedings of a Conference held by the Hon. Walter Harris, Minister of Citizenship and Immigration, with Representative Indians, in Ottawa, 26–28
October 1953, N.A.C., RG26, vol. 70, file 10.

118 *Divorce Act*, S.C. 1967–68, c. 24.

119 See, e.g., *Report of the Royal Commission on the Status of Women in
Canada* (Ottawa 1970) at 237–8.

120 *Canadian Bill of Rights*, R.S.C. 1985, app. III.

121 Lavell-Harvard and Corbiere Lavell, "Aboriginal Women."

122 *A.G. Canada v. Lavell; Isaac v. Bédard*, [1974] S.C.R. 1349.

123 *Drybones v. The Queen*, [1970] S.C.R. 282.

124 Jamieson, *Indian Women*, 2.

125 Weaver, "First Nations Women," 99–100.

126 Cardinal, *The Rebirth of Canada's Indians*, 109.

127 *A.G. Canada v. Lavell; Isaac v. Bédard*, [1974] S.C.R. 1349 at 1359.

128 Ibid., at 1361.

129 Ibid., at 1365–7.

130 Ibid., at 1390–1.

131 Ibid., at 1389.

132 Ibid., at 1382, 1388.

133 Ibid., at 1385.

134 Ibid., at 1386; see also Eisenberg, "Diversity and Equality," 59.

135 Ibid., at 1388.

136 Although, as we have seen above, this is more likely to be the goal of the
rule of descent through the male line rather than that of the exclusion of
women who have "married out."

137 Ibid., at para. 14.

138 *Lovelace v. Canada*, U.N. Doc. CCPR/C/13/D/24/1977 (1981) at para. 15.

139 Ibid., at para. 17.

140 In a different case, the committee held a similar distinction in Mauritius's
citizenship rules to be discriminatory on the basis of sex, in violation of
article 26 of the Covenant: *Aumeeruddy-Cziffra v. Mauritius*, U.N. Doc.
CCPR/C/12/D/35/1978 (1981).

141 *Act to encourage the gradual Civilization of the Indian Tribes in this
Province, and to amend the Laws respecting Indians*, S. Prov. C. 1857, c.
26, s. 3; *Act for the gradual enfranchisement of Indians, the better management of Indian affairs, and to extend the provisions of the Act 31st*

Victoria, Chapter 42, s.c. 1869, c. 6, s. 13, 16; *Indian Act 1876*, s.c. 1876, c. 18, s. 86; *Indian Act,* s.c. 1951, c. 29, s. 108.

142 Royal Commission on Aboriginal Peoples, *Report,* vol. 1, 145–8.

143 Leslie, *Assimilation, Integration or Termination,* 39, 64, 150–1.

144 Gélinas, *Les autochtones,* 125–8.

145 *Act further to amend "The Indian Act, 1880,"* s.c. 1884, c. 27, s. 16.

146 *Act to Amend the Indian Act,* s.c. 1919–20, c. 50; *Act to Amend the Indian Act,* s.c. 1922, c. 26.

147 *Act to Amend the Indian Act,* s.c. 1932–33, c. 42.

148 Titley, *A Narrow Vision,* 49.

149 *Indian Act 1880,* s.c. 1880, c. 28, s. 99(1).

150 Brownlie, "A Better Citizen."

151 Memorandum to the Cabinet by W.E. Harris, Minister of Citizenship and Immigration, Cabinet Document 133–50 (1 May 1950), N.A.C., RG2, series B–2, vol. 137; see also *Martin* v. *Chapman,* [1983] 1 s.c.r. 365 at 371 (Wilson J.), 379 (Lamer J., dissenting); Leslie, *Assimilation, Integration or Termination,* 225.

152 *Martin* v. *Chapman,* [1983] 1 s.c.r. 365 at 372.

153 *Indian Act 1876,* s.c. 1876, c. 18, s. 26(1); *Indian Advancement Act 1884,* s.c. 1884, c. 28, s. 5; *Indian Act,* s.c. 1951, c. 29, ss. 2 (definition of "elector"), 39 and 76.

154 *Corbiere* v. *Canada (Minister of Indian and Northern Affairs),* [1999] 2 s.c.r. 203.

155 Ibid. at 220 (McLachlin and Bastarache JJ.).

156 Ibid. at 222 (McLachlin and Bastarache JJ.).

157 Ibid. at 224–5 (McLachlin and Bastarache JJ.).

158 Ibid. at 254 (L'Heureux-Dubé J.).

159 Ibid. at 266–9 (L'Heureux-Dubé J.).

CHAPTER FOUR

1 Weaver, *Making Canadian Indian Policy,* 171–89.

2 *Constitution Act, 1982,* R.S.C. 1985, app. II, no. 44, s. 35.

3 See, e.g., *R.* v. *Sparrow,* [1990] 1 s.c.r. 1075; *Delgamuukw* v. *British Columbia,* [1997] 3 s.c.r. 1010; *R.* v. *Marshall,* [1999] 3 s.c.r. 456.

4 See, e.g., *R.* v. *Sparrow,* [1990] 1 s.c.r. 1075; *R.* v. *Adams,* [1996] 3 s.c.r. 101.

5 *R.* v. *Sappier; R.* v. *Gray,* [2006] 2 s.c.r. 686.

6 *R.* v. *Gladstone,* [1996] 2 s.c.r. 723; *R.* v. *Marshall,* [1999] 3 s.c.r. 456.

7 R. v. *Pamajewon*, [1996] 2 S.C.R. 821; *Delgamuukw* v. *British Columbia*, [1997] 3 S.C.R. 1010.

8 Government of Canada, *Aboriginal Self-Government*. See, for an example of a self-government agreement, the *Nisga'a Final Agreement* (Ottawa 1999), c. 11, 12, 16.

9 Concluding Observations of the Committee on Economic, Social and Cultural Rights: Canada, U.N. Doc. E/C.12/1/Add.31 (10 December 1998) at para. 17; Concluding Observations of the Committee on the Elimination of Racial Discrimination: Canada, U.N. Doc. A/57/18 (1 November 2002) at paras. 329–34.

10 Beavon and Cook, "An Application"; this figure is calculated for on-reserve First Nations.

11 McHugh, *Aboriginal Societies*, 360.

12 See, in general, Jamieson, "Sex Discrimination and the *Indian Act*," 126–31; Weaver, "First Nations Women"; NWAC, *Aboriginal Women's Rights*; Hartley, "Search for Consensus."

13 House of Commons, Minutes of Proceedings and Evidence of the Sub-committee on Indian Women and the *Indian Act* (9 September 1982) 2:52–5, testimony of Jane Gottfriedson, president of NWAC.

14 Senate and House of Commons, Minutes of Proceedings and Evidence of the Special Joint Committee of the Senate and House of Commons on the Constitution of Canada (16 December 1980) 27:114ff, testimony of Bill Badcock of the AFN; House of Commons, Minutes of Proceedings and Evidence of the Sub-committee on Indian Women and the *Indian Act* (8 September 1982) 1:64ff, testimony of David Ahenakew, National Chief of the AFN.

15 See, e.g., Borrows, "Contemporary Traditional Equality," 36–7.

16 Members of the Treaty Eight Group of Indian Bands, *Presentation to the House of Commons Standing Committee on Indian Affairs and Northern Development* (25 March 1985) [on file with author]; note that this group includes the Sawridge Band, which contests the validity of Bill C-31.

17 Weaver, "First Nations Women," 121–2; NWAC, Aboriginal Women's Rights, 9; *McIvor* v. *Registrar, Indian and Northern Affairs Canada*, [2007] 3 C.N.L.R. 72 (B.C.S.C.) at 97.

18 *Act to Amend the Indian Act*, R.S.C. 1985, c. 32 (1st supp).

19 House of Commons, Minutes of Proceedings and Evidence of the Standing Committee on Indian Affairs and Northern Development, 14 March 1985 (Wally McKay of the AFN), 28 March 1985 (Marlyn Kane of NWAC); Krosenbrink, *Sexual Equality*, 160–1; Weaver, "First Nations Women," 113, 118; Hartley, "Search for Consensus."

20 Weaver, "First Nations Women," 118.
21 Clatworthy, "Impact of the 1985 Amendments," 67–8.
22 *James Bay and Northern Quebec Agreement and Complementary Agree-ments* (Sainte-Foy: Publications du Québec 1998). See also the compan-ion legislation: *Cree-Naskapi (of Quebec) Act*, s.c. 1984, c. 18; *Act Respecting Cree, Inuit and Naskapi Native Persons*, R.S.Q., c. A–33.1.
23 *The Western Arctic Claim: The Inuvialuit Final Agreement* (Ottawa: Department of Indian Affairs and Northern Development 1984).
24 *Gwich'in Comprehensive Land Claim Agreement* (Ottawa: Department of Indian Affairs and Northern Development 1992).
25 *Sahtu Dene and Métis Comprehensive Land Claim Agreement* (Ottawa: Department of Indian Affairs and Northern Development 1993).
26 *Tlicho Agreement* (Ottawa 2003).
27 *Council of Yukon Indians – Umbrella Final Agreement* (Ottawa: Depart-ment of Indian Affairs and Northern Development 1993); see also the companion legislation implementing self-government: *Yukon First Nations Self-Government Act*, s.c. 1994, c. 35.
28 *Agreement Between the Inuit of the Nunavut Settlement Area and Her Majesty the Queen in right of Canada* (Ottawa: Tungavik and Depart-ment of Indian Affairs and Northern Development 1993).
29 *Nisga'a Final Agreement* (Ottawa: Department of Indian Affairs and Northern Development 1999).
30 *Labrador Inuit Land Claims Agreement* (Ottawa: Department of Indian Affairs and Northern Development 2005).
31 *Cree-Naskapi (of Quebec) Act*, s.c. 1984, c. 18, s. 5; *Yukon First Nations Self-Government Act*, s.c. 1994, c. 35, s. 17(2).
32 *Cree-Naskapi (of Quebec) Act*, s.c. 1984, c. 18, s. 188ff.
33 *Yukon First Nations Self-Government Act*, s.c. 1994, c. 35, s. 8(2); *Nisga'a Final Agreement*, c. 11, s. 9p).
34 *Nunavut Agreement*, s. 35.3.1.
35 Ibid., ss. 35.4.1–35.4.5.
36 Ibid., ss. 35.5.1–35.5.10.
37 *Complementary Agreement No. 18 to the James Bay and Northern Que-bec Agreement* (2005) [on file with author]; *Act Respecting Cree, Inuit and Naskapi Native Persons*, R.S.Q., c. A–33.1, ss. 25.1ff; *Labrador Inuit Land Claims Agreement* (Ottawa: Department of Indian Affairs and Northern Development 2005), c. 3.
38 See, in this regard: *Première nation des Abénakis d'Odanak v. Canada (Minister of Indian Affairs and Northern Development)*, 2007 FC 30; 2008 FCA 126.

39 Krosenbrink, *Sexual Equality*, 195–200.

40 That exclusion was later declared unconstitutional in the *Corbiere* case; see above, chap. 3.

41 Department of Indian and Northern Affairs, *Répercussions des modifications de 1985 à la Loi sur les Indiens (Projet de loi c–31)*, vol. 3, *Études des bandes et collectivités indiennes* (Ottawa 1990), 80–1; *Raphaël v. Conseil des Montagnais du Lac Saint-Jean* (Can. Hum. Rts. Trib., 9 June 1995).

42 *Statutory Instruments Regulations Amendment*, SOR/87–398, (1987) 121 Canada Gazette II 2728.

43 The Department of Indian Affairs refused my request for copies of membership codes of Ontario bands, invoking exemptions in the *Access to Information Act*, despite the fact that the Federal Court, in *Twinn v. Canada (Minister of Indian Affairs and Northern Development)*, [1987] 3 F.C. 368 (T.D.), appears to have held that there was no reason not to communicate membership codes to the public. Only after the intervention of the information commissioner did the department agree to provide me with copies of those codes. Of the fifteen Indian bands that I contacted directly in writing, only one answered my request.

44 See, e.g., *Omeasoo v. Canada (Minister of Indian Affairs and Northern Development)*, [1989] 1 C.N.L.R. 110 (F.C.T.D.); apparently, fifty-three bands had their requests rejected: Weaver, "First Nations Women," 141.

45 Membership codes of the Sawridge Band and the Ermineskin Band, reprinted in Gilbert, *Entitlement to Indian Status*, 153-6; membership code of the Wapekeka Band [on file with author].

46 *Sawridge Band v. Canada*, [2003] 4 F.C. 748 (T.D.), affirmed [2004] 3 F.C.R. 274 (C.A.).

47 Krosenbrink, *Sexual Equality*, 200–8; Weaver, "First Nations Women," 128.

48 Department of Indian and Northern Affairs, *Répercussions des modifications de 1985 à la Loi sur les Indiens (Projet de loi C-31)*, vol. 3, *Études des bandes et collectivités indiennes* (Ottawa 1990), 25–8; NWAC, *Aboriginal Women's Rights*, 13–15.

49 *Raphaël v. Conseil des Montagnais du Lac Saint-Jean* (Can. Hum. Rts. Trib., 9 June 1995); *Courtois v. Canada (Department of Indian and Northern Affairs)*, [1991] 1 C.N.L.R. 40 (Can. Hum. Rts. Trib.).

50 *Scrimbitt v. Sakimay Indian Band Council*, [2000] 1 F.C. 513 (T.D.).

51 *Sawridge Band v. Canada*, [1996] 1 F.C. 3 (T.D.); as to that case, see Dick, "The Politics of Intragroup Difference."

52 *Sawridge Band v. Canada*, [1997] 3 F.C. 580 (C.A.).

53 *R. v. Powley* (2001), 196 D.L.R. (4th) 221 (Ontario C.A.) at 230; confirmed by *R. v. Powley*, [2003] 2 S.C.R. 207.

54 The question of group recognition is analyzed more fully in Grammond, "Equality."

55 Royal Commission on Aboriginal Peoples, *Report*, vol. 4, 229; Morse and Groves, "Canada's Forgotten Peoples," 147–8.

56 For instance, a group called the Confederation of Aboriginal Peoples recently split from the Native Alliance of Quebec (CAP's provincial organisation in Quebec), leading to protracted litigation between the two sides: *Communauté autochtone Muskwa de Mistassini (Communauté de l'Ours)* v. *Bérubé*, 2006 QCCS 4212; 2007 QCCA 1804; *Carle v. Nault*, 2006 QCCS 2902.

57 For a province-by-province summary, see Isaac, *Métis Rights*, 50–67.

58 Available at <http://www.metisnation.ca/MNA/defining1.html> (accessed 10 May 2004); or Isaac, *Métis Rights*, 6.

59 See, e.g., the Métis Nation of Saskatchewan Constitution, <http://www.metisnation-sask.com/ governance/constitution.html> (accessed 10 May 2004), s. 10, or the Métis Nation of Ontario's membership rules, <http://www.metisnation.org/insideMNO/PDF/MNO%Code_By-laws%20 Mar_ 2002.pdf> (accessed 10 May 2004), ss. 2.2, 2.3.

60 Sawchuk, "Negotiating an Identity."

61 Chartrand and Giokas, "Defining 'The Métis People.'"

62 Information about CAP's affiliates' membership criteria may be found on CAP's website: <http://www.abo-peoples.org/affiliates/index.html>.

63 *R. v. Powley*, [2003] 2 S.C.R. 207; Isaac, *Métis Rights*, 8–13.

64 *R. v. Powley*, [2003] 2 S.C.R. 207 at 223.

65 Ibid. at 224.

66 Ibid. at 215–16.

67 *R. v. Daigle*, [2003] 3 C.N.L.R. 232 (N.B. Prov. Ct.), affirmed (2004), 271 N.B.R. (2d) 384 (Q.B.).

68 *R. v. Powley*, [2003] 2 S.C.R. 207 at 224.

69 The *Powley* test has been applied in *R. v. Laviolette*, [2005] 3 C.N.L.R. 202 (Sask. Prov. Ct.); *R. v. Willison*, [2006] 4 C.N.L.R. 253 (B.C.S.C.); *Labrador Métis Nation v. Newfoundland and Labrador (Minister of Transportation and Works)*, [2006] 4 C.N.L.R. 94 (N.L.S.C.T.D.) aff'd [2008] 1 C.N.L.R. 48 (N.L.C.A.); *R. v. Kelley*, [2006] 3 C.N.L.R. 324 (Alberta Prov. Ct.), rev'd on other grounds [2007] 2 C.N.L.R. 332 (Alberta Q.B.); *R. v. Norton*, [2005] 3 C.N.L.R. 268 (Sask. Prov. Ct.); *Ontario (Minister of Natural Resources) v. Beaudry*, 2006 ONCJ 59; *R. v. Hopper*, 2004 NBPC 7; 2005 NBQB 399; 2008 NBCA 42; *R. v. Lavigne*,

[2007] 4 C.N.L.R. 268 (N.B.Q.B.); *R. c. Belhumeur*, 2007 SKPC 114; *R. v. Brideau*, 2008 NBQB 74; for an overview of those cases, see Isaac, *Métis Rights*, 21–5, 50–67. In *Tsilhqot'in Nation* c. *British Columbia*, [2008] 1 C.N.L.R. 112 (B.C.S.C.) at para. 444, the court suggested that the *Powley* test would also apply to identify persons entitled to exercise aboriginal rights, as opposed to rights flowing from the *Indian Act*.

70 *R. v. Chiasson*, [2002] 2 C.N.L.R. 220 (N.B. Prov. Ct.), affirmed, (2004) 270 N.B.R. (2d) 357 (Q.B.), leave to appeal refused, 2005 NBCA 82; *R. v. Castonguay*, [2003] 1 C.N.L.R. 177 (N.B. Prov. Ct.), aff'd by 2006 NBCA 43.

71 *R. v. Willison*, [2006] 4 C.N.L.R. 253 (B.C.S.C.) at para. 57.

72 *R. v. Powley*, [2003] 2 S.C.R. 207 at 221.

73 See, e.g., *Ontario (Minister of Natural Resources)* v. *Beaudry*, 2006 ONCJ 59.

74 Horton and Mohr, "*R. v. Powley*," 808–16; Chartrand, "Hard Case."

75 Ibid. at 225.

76 *R. v. Lavigne*, [2007] 4 C.N.L.R. 268 (N.B.Q.B.).

77 *R. v. Laviolette*, [2005] 3 C.N.L.R. 202 (Sask. Prov. Ct.).

78 Holmes, *Equality or Disparity?*; Weaver, "First Nations Women," 117–18, 121, 125; McIvor, "Aboriginal Women Unmasked"; RCAP, *Report*, vol. 4, 43–8; NWAC, *Aboriginal Women's Rights*.

79 See the section entitled "The Double-Mother Rule," above, chap. 3.

80 Clatworthy, "Impacts of the 1985 Amendments," 73–8.

81 *Gehl* v. *Canada (A.G.)*, [2002] 4 C.N.L.R. 108 (Ont. S.C.J.); [2002] 4 C.N.L.R. 115 (Ont. C.A.).

82 Mann, "Indian Registration."

83 *McIvor* v. *Registrar, Indian and Northern Affairs Canada*, [2007] 3 C.N.L.R. 72 (B.C.S.C.).

84 Ibid. at para. 268.

85 Ibid. at paras. 123–43.

86 Ibid. at paras. 231, 314.

87 Ibid. at paras. 306–7.

88 Ibid. at paras. 309, 314; for another expression of that view by government officials, see Hartley, "Search for Consensus," 19.

89 See, in this regard, *Ardoch Algonquin First Nation* v. *Canada (A.G.)*, [2004] 2 F.C.R. 108 (C.A.); Grammond, "Equality."

90 See the Health Canada website concerning eligibility for this program: http://www.hc-sc.gc.ca/fnih-spni/nihb-ssna/bene-fit-prestation/index_e.html (accessed 29 May 2007).

91 Grammond, *Aménager la coexistence*, 378–80, 389–90.

92 Clatworthy, "Impacts of the 1985 Amendments."

93 See, e.g., Fiske and George, "Bill C–31"; Cannon, "Revisiting Histories."

94 *McIvor v. Registrar, Indian and Northern Affairs Canada*, [2007] 3 C.N.L.R. 72 (B.C.S.C.) at 158, 166–8.

95 *Moses v. Canada*, [2003] 1 C.N.L.R. 100 (F.C.); [2004] 2 C.N.L.R. 135 (F.C.); see also *McIvor v. Registrar, Indian and Northern Affairs Canada*, 2007 BCSC 26; see McIvor, "Aboriginal Women Unmasked."

96 *Perron v. Canada (A.G.)*, [2003] 3 C.N.L.R. 198 (Ont. S.C.J.).

97 *James Bay Agreement*, ss. 3.2.2 and 3.2.5; *Gwich'in Agreement*, s. 4.1.1; *Yukon Umbrella Final Agreement*, s. 3.2.2; *Nisga'a Final Agreement*, c. 20; *Tlicho Agreement*, c. 1, definition of "Tlicho person."

98 *Nisga'a Final Agreement*, c. 20.

99 *James Bay Agreement*, s. 3.2.1.

100 *Gwich'in Agreement*, s. 4.3.2; *Nunavut Agreement*, ss. 35.3.5, 35.3.6; *Nisga'a Final Agreement*, c. 20, s. 17; *Tlicho Agreement*, s. 3.4.2.

101 *James Bay Agreement*, s. 3.4; *Gwich'in Agreement*, s. 4.6; *Nunavut Agreement*, ss. 35.4, 35.5; *Yukon Umbrella Final Agreement*, ss. 3.7, 3.11; *Nisga'a Final Agreement*, c. 20, s. 26; *Tlicho Agreement*, ss. 3.4.6, 3.5.

102 Personal communications with Pierre Kolit (13 November 2002), Leetia Itidloie (20 November 2002), and Wendy Abalak (2 December 2002), members of the local enrolment committees of the communities of Rankin Inlet, Cape Dorset, and Cambridge Bay, respectively.

103 However, in one community two non-Inuit women who married Inuit men and who have adopted the Inuit way of life have been enrolled: personal communication with Leetia Itidloie (20 November 2002).

104 PriceWaterhouseCoopers, *Second Independent Five Year Review of the Implementation of the Nunavut Land Claims Agreement, Final Report*, 11 May 2006. Online: <http://www.tunngavik.com/english/pdfs-english/Second%20Five%20Year%20Review%20of%20the%20Nunavut%20Land%20Claims%20Agreement.pdf> (accessed 29 May 2007).

105 *Act Respecting Cree, Inuit and Naskapi Native Persons*, R.S.Q., c. A–33.1, s. 25.5; *Labrador Inuit Land Claims Agreement* (Ottawa: Department of Indian Affairs and Northern Development 2005), ss. 3.3.2(c), 3.3.4(c).

106 See, e.g., *Scrimbitt v. Sakimay Indian Band Council*, [2000] 1 F.C. 513 (T.D.).

107 The categories that follow are borrowed from Clatworthy, "Impacts of the 1985 Amendments," 78–86.

108 Membership code of the Adams Lake Band, reprinted in Gilbert, *Entitlement to Indian Status*, 160–1.

109 See, e.g., the membership code of the Lac La Croix Band [on file with author].

110 See, e.g., the membership code of the Big Island Band, reprinted in Gilbert, *Entitlement to Indian Status*, 157–9.

111 See, e.g., the membership code of the Chippewas of Georgina Island First Nation [on file with author].

112 See, e.g., the membership code of the Moose Cree Band, reprinted in Gilbert, *Entitlement to Indian Status*, 164–5.

113 See, e.g., the membership code of the Chapleau Cree Band, reprinted in Gilbert, *Entitlement to Indian Status*, 169–71.

114 *Jacobs* v. *Mohawk Council of Kahnawake*, [1998] 3 C.N.L.R. 68 (Can. Hum. Rts. Trib.); see also *Six Nations of the Grand River Band Council* v. *Henderson*, [1997] 1 C.N.L.R. 202 (Ont. Ct., Gen. Div.).

115 *Grismer* v. *Squamish First Nation*, [2007] 1 C.N.L.R. 146 (F.C.).

116 The decision is unclear about the precise technical reasons for Jacobs's exclusion. When he was born and adopted, the old *Indian Act*, then in force, denied Indian status to non-Indian children adopted by Indians. He appears to have gained Indian status only upon the coming into force of Bill C–31, in 1985. However, the Kahnawake rules recognise band membership only for persons who had Indian status when they came into force, in 1981. Thus, Jacobs was not included at that time and the Kahnawake refused to grant membership to persons who were reinstated in 1985. In addition, the Kahnawake rules explicitly deny membership to non-Indians adopted by Kahnawake Mohawks. One should note that the Kahnawake membership rules predate Bill C–31 and have never been submitted for the approval of the Minister of Indian Affairs pursuant to section 10 of the *Indian Act*. Their legal status thus remains unclear.

117 *Jacobs* v. *Mohawk Council of Kahnawake*, [1998] 3 C.N.L.R. 68 (Can. Hum. Rts. Trib.) at 95–7.

118 *Grismer* v. *Squamish First Nation*, [2007] 1 C.N.L.R. 146 (F.C.) at 163.

119 *Grismer* v. *Squamish First Nation*, [2007] 1 C.N.L.R. 146 (F.C.) at 164.

120 See, e.g., the membership code of the Garden River Ojibway Band [on file with author], part IX.

121 *Sawridge Band* v. *Canada*, [2003] 4 F.C. 748 (T.D.), affirmed [2004] 3 F.C.R. 274 (C.A.).

122 *Scrimbitt* v. *Sakimay Indian Band Council*, [2000] 1 F.C. 513 (T.D.).

123 *Grismer* v. *Squamish First Nation*, [2007] 1 C.N.L.R. 146 (F.C.).

124 *Eaton* v. *Brant County Board of Education*, [1997] 1 S.C.R. 241 at 272; see also *Winko* v. *British Columbia (Forensic Psychiatric Institute)*, [1999] 2 S.C.R. 625 at 678–82.

125 *Lovelace* v. *Canada*, U.N. Doc. CCPR/C/13/D/24/1977 (1981) at paras. 14, 17.

126 Membership code of the Chapleau Cree Band, reprinted in Gilbert, *Entitlement to Indian Status*, 169–71.

127 *Sawridge Band* v. *Canada*, [2003] 4 F.C. 748 (T.D.), affirmed [2004] 3 F.C.R. 274 (C.A.).

128 Dick, "The Politics of Intragroup Difference."

129 Membership code of the Chapleau Cree Band, reprinted in Gilbert, *Entitlement to Indian Status*, 169–71, s. 37.

130 *Sauvé* v. *Canada (Chief Electoral Officer)*, [2002] 3 S.C.R. 519.

131 *Indian Act*, R.S.C. 1985, c. I-5, s. 81(1)(p.1).

132 *Gamblin* v. *Norway House Cree Nation*, [2003] 1 C.N.L.R. 49 (F.C.A.); see also, in the context of a criminal conviction, *R. c. Taylor* (1997), 122 C.C.C. (3d) 376, [1998] 2 C.N.L.R. 140 (Sask. C.A.).

133 Membership Code of the Wapekeka Band, reprinted in Gilbert, *Entitlement to Indian Status*, 189.

134 The relevant documents are reprinted in *Jacobs* v. *Mohawk Council of Kahnawake*, [1998] 3 C.N.L.R. 68 (Can. Hum. Rts. Trib.).

135 *Universal Declaration of Human Rights*, U.N. G.A. Res. 217/A (III), art. 16; *International Covenant on Civil and Political Rights* (19 December 1966, 999 U.N.T.S. 107), art. 23; *Convention on the Elimination of All Forms of Discrimination Against Women* (18 December 1979, 1249 U.N.T.S. 13), art. 16.

136 See, by analogy, *R.* v. *Morgentaler*, [1988] 1 S.C.R. 30 at 166–72 (Wilson J.).

137 *Convention on the Elimination of All Forms of Discrimination Against Women* (18 December 1979, 1249 U.N.T.S. 13).

138 *Lovelace* v. *Canada*, U.N. Doc. CCPR/C/13/D/24/1977 (1981).

139 P. Chartrand, speech delivered at the *Canadian Rights and Freedoms: 25 Years under the Charter* conference, University of Ottawa, 16 April 2007.

140 See, e.g., the Métis Nation of Saskatchewan's constitution: "a descendant of those Métis who received or were entitled to receive land grants and/or Scrip under the provision of the *Manitoba Act, 1870* or the *Dominion Lands Act*, as enacted from time to time"; Online: http://metna.sasktelwebhosting.com/governance/acts/const.html#link10 (accessed 1 June 2007).

141 Information provided by Karole Dumont-Beckett, registrar of the Métis Nation of Ontario, 7 September 2006.

142 Sawchuk, "Negotiating an Identity."

143 Lawrence, *"Real" Indians*, 85.

144 Ibid.

145 See, e.g., http://www.winnipegmetis.ca/docs/membership_application_package.pdf (accessed 1 June 2007).

146 *R. v. Powley*, [2003] 2 S.C.R. 207 at 225.

147 *R. v. Laviolette*, [2005] 3 C.N.L.R. 202 (Sask. Prov. Ct.); *R. v. Lavigne*, [2007] 4 C.N.L.R. 268 (N.B.Q.B.).

148 R.S.A. 2000, C. M–14.

149 *Vicklund and Peavine Métis Settlement and Willier*, M.S.A.T. Order No. 160 (3 October 2004).

150 *Peavine Métis Settlement* v. *Alberta (Minister of Aboriginal Affairs and Northern Development)*, [2007] 4 C.N.L.R. 179 (Alta. Q.B.).

151 Ibid. at para. 168.

152 Ibid. at paras. 204, 206.

153 See above, chap. 3.

154 *R. v. Powley*, [2003] 2 S.C.R. 207 at 225–6.

155 See, e.g., *Nunavut Agreement*, s. 35.3.3; *Council of Yukon Indians Umbrella Final Agreement*, s. 3.4.1; *Nisga'a Final Agreement*, c. 20, s. 3; *Tlicho Agreement*, s. 3.1.2.

156 *Indian Act*, R.S.C. 1985, C. I–5, s. 13.

157 *R. v. Powley*, [2003] 2 S.C.R. 207 at 225–6.

CHAPTER FIVE

1 For an overview of the debate concerning Quebec identity, see Mathieu, *Qui est Québécois?*; see also Williams, "Recognition."

2 *Reference re Secession of Quebec*, [1998] 2 S.C.R. 217 at 252.

3 Carignan, "Les résolutions de Québec," 14–15.

4 Morin and Woehrling, *Les constitutions du Canada et du Québec*, 153–62; McRoberts, *Misconceiving Canada*; Tierney, *Constitutional Law*, 139–40; Romney, "Compact Theory."

5 These religious guarantees are now a thing of the past with respect to Quebec, as the guarantees of section 93 of the *Constitution Act, 1867*, concerning denominational school boards were repealed with respect to that province in 1997: *Constitution Amendment 1997 (Quebec)*, SI/97–141; school boards are now organised on a linguistic rather than a religious basis.

6 For a historical overview of the use of French in education, see the
   Report of the Royal Commission on Bilingualism and Biculturalism
   (Ottawa 1967), vol. 2, 39ff; Hayday, *Bilingual Today*, 16–28; as for the
   situation in Ontario, see *Reference re Education Act of Ontario and
   Minority Language Education Rights* (1984), 10 D.L.R. (4th) 491
   (Ontario C.A.) at 506–17.

7 *City of Winnipeg v. Barrett*, [1892] A.C. 445 (P.C.); *Brophy v. A.G. of
   Manitoba*, [1895] A.C. 202 (P.C.).

8 A poignant account of the difficulties encountered by the
   Franco-Manitobans of that period may be found in novelist Gabrielle
   Roy's autobiography: Roy, *La Détresse et l'Enchantement*, 67–88.

9 *Ottawa Separate School Trustees v. Mackell*, [1917] A.C. 62 (P.C.); for
   other narrow interpretations of section 93, see *Reference re Education
   Act (Que.)*, [1993] 2 S.C.R. 511; *Ontario English Catholic Teachers' Assn
   v. Ontario (A.G.)*, [2001] 1 S.C.R. 470.

10 Behiels, *Francophone Communities*, 7–8

11 *Report of the Royal Commission on Bilingualism and Biculturalism*
   (Ottawa 1967), vol. 2, 52.

12 In *Ballantyne v. Canada*, U.N. Doc. CCPR/C/47/D/359/1989 (1993), the
   United Nations Human Rights Committee denied that Quebec
   Anglophones constituted a "minority" whose members were entitled to
   rights under article 27 of the *International Covenant on Civil and Political Rights*; the appropriateness of that ruling is discussed later in this
   chapter, in the section "Compliance with Individual Rights."

13 The account that follows is largely based upon Proulx, "Le choc des
   Chartes," and Garant, *Droit scolaire*, 101–46.

14 See above, note 9.

15 *Act to promote the French language in Québec*, S.Q. 1969, c. 9, s. 2.

16 Gendron Commission, *La situation de la langue française au Québec*,
   vol. 2, 72.

17 S.Q. 1974, c. 6; the constitutional validity of the Act was upheld in
   *Bureau métropolitain des écoles protestantes de Montréal v. Ministre de
   l'Éducation du Québec*, [1976] C.S. 430, 83 D.L.R. (3d) 645 (Quebec
   S.C.).

18 See the remarks of Minister François Cloutier, cited in Proulx, "Le choc
   des Chartes," 107–8.

19 *Regulation respecting knowledge of the language of instruction*, O.C.
   1347–75 (1975) 107 Quebec Official Gazette 1589.

20 Taddeo and Taras, *Le débat linguistique au Québec*, 155–89.

21 R.S.Q., c. C–11 (initially adopted as S.Q. 1977, c. 5).

22 Government of Quebec, *Québec's Policy*, 71 ff.
23 Ibid., 74.
24 *Charter of the French Language*, R.S.Q., c. C–11, S. 73.
25 Government of Quebec, *Québec's Policy*, 74–5.
26 MacMillan, *The Practice of Language Rights*, 123ff.
27 Behiels, *Francophone Communities*, 39–40.
28 *Official Languages Act*, S.C. 1968–69, c. 54.
29 *Report of the Royal Commission on Bilingualism and Biculturalism*, vol. 2, 157 ff.
30 Proulx, "Le choc des Chartes," 132–3; Behiels, *Francophone Communities*, 23–4.
31 Behiels, *Francophone Communities*, 41–3.
32 *Constitution Act, 1982*, R.S.C. 1985, app. II, no. 44.
33 *Act respecting the Constitution Act, 1982*, R.S.Q., c. L–4.2, S. 4.
34 Proulx, "Le choc des Chartes," 152–7.
35 This was recently confirmed in *Gosselin (Tutor of)* v. *Quebec (A.G.)*, [2005] 1 S.C.R. 238, a case studied in more detail below.
36 The effectiveness of that change was confirmed by the Supreme Court in *A.G. Quebec* v. *Quebec Association of Protestant School Boards*, [1984] 2 S.C.R. 66.
37 Brouillet, *La négation de la nation*, 352.
38 *Quebec Association of Protestant School Boards* v. *A.G. Quebec*, [1982] C.S. 673, 140 D.L.R. (3d) 33 (Quebec S.C.) at 708.
39 Behiels, *Francophone Communities*, 80.
40 See Woehrling, "L'évolution du cadre juridique," 268–72.
41 *Act to amend the Charter of the French Language*, S.Q. 1993, c. 40, s. 24.
42 *Québec (Procureure générale)* v. *Solski*, [2002] R.J.Q. 1285 (C.A.); *Solski (Tutor of)* v. *Quebec (A.G.)*, [2005] 1 S.C.R. 201.
43 See also *G.P.* v. *Comité de révision sur la langue d'enseignement*, [2001] T.A.Q. 50 at 65–6.
44 *Solski (Tutor of)* v. *Quebec (A.G.)*, [2005] 1 S.C.R. 201 at para. 33.
45 Ibid. at para. 47.
46 Brouillet, *La négation de la nation*, 357; Woehrling "L'évolution du cadre juridique," 276–85; Braën, "La Cour suprême"; see also *Ministre de l'Éducation, du Loisir et du Sport du Québec* v. *Tribunal administratif du Québec*, 2007 QCCS 1870.
47 *Act to amend the Charter of the French Language*, S.Q. 2002, c. 28, s. 3.
48 *H.N.* v. *Québec (Ministre de l'Éducation)*, [2007] R.J.Q. 2097 (C.A.); *T.B.* v. *Québec (Ministre de l'Éducation)*, [2007] R.J.Q. 2150 (C.A.).

49 *H.N.* v. *Québec (Ministre de l'Éducation)*, [2007] R.J.Q. 2097 (C.A.) at 2122–3.

50 Ibid. at 2128–9.

51 Ibid. at 2131–2, 2140.

52 Ibid. at 2146–9.

53 *T.B.* v. *Québec (Ministre de l'Éducation)*, [2007] R.J.Q. 2150 (C.A.) at 2162–4.

54 *Gosselin (Tutor of)* v. *Quebec (A.G.)*, [2005] 1 S.C.R. 238.

55 *R.* v. *Beaulac*, [1999] 1 S.C.R. 768.

56 Aquilino, "Qui suis-je?"

57 See, e.g., the *School Act*, R.S.A. 2000, c. S–3, s. 10; the *School Act*, R.S.B.C. 1996, c. 412, s. 5.

58 *Education Act*, R.S.O. 1990, c. E.2, s. 293; see also the *Education Act*, R.S.S. 1995, c. E–0.2, s. 144.

59 R.S.N.B., c. E–1.12, s. 5.

60 Le Bouthiller, "Le droit à l'instruction en français;" *Lavoie* v. *Nova Scotia (A.G.)* (1989), 58 D.L.R. (4th) 293 (Nova Scotia C.A.) at 311–12.

61 Foucher, "Les droits linguistiques," 294–6.

62 *Mahe* v. *Alberta*, [1990] 1 S.C.R. 342.

63 In this regard, Major and Bastarache JJ. in *Arsenault-Cameron* v. *Prince Edward Island*, [2000] 1 S.C.R. 3, speak of the minority parents' *exclusive* power of management; see also *Gosselin (Tutor of)* v. *Quebec (A.G.)*, [2005] 1 S.C.R. 238, at paras. 31–2; *Solski (Tutor of)* v. *Quebec (A.G.)*, [2005] 1 S.C.R. 201, at paras. 49–50.

64 *Reference re Education Act of Ontario and Minority Language Education Rights* (1984), 10 D.L.R. (4th) 491 (Ontario C.A.) at 519; *Reference re Minority Language Educational Rights (P.E.I.)* (1988), 49 D.L.R. (4th) 499 (P.E.I. C.A.) at 514–15.

65 This situation is expressly contemplated by the *Education Act*, R.S.N.B., c. E–1.12, s. 5; see also *Lau* v. *Nichols*, 414 U.S. 563, 94 S.Ct. 786 (1974).

66 *Ballantyne* v. *Canada*, U.N. Doc. CCPR/C/47/D/359/1989 (1993).

67 Ibid. at para. 11.2.

68 Ibid., separate opinion of Ms. Evatt.

69 Advisory Committee on the Framework Convention for the Protection of National Minorities, *Opinion on Finland* (20 April 2006), online: <http://www.coe.int/t/e/human_rights/minorities/2._framework_convention_%28monitoring%29/2._monitoring_mechanism/4._opinions_of_the_advisory_committee/1._country_specific_opinions/2._second_cycle/PDF_2nd_OP_Finland_eng.pdf>, at paras. 20–6; *Opinion on Switzerland* (20 February 2003), online: <http://www.coe.int/t/e/human_

rights/minorities/2._framework_convention_%28monitoring%29/2._
monitoring_mechanism/4._opinions_of_the_advisory_committee/1._
country_specific_opinions/1._first_cycle/PDF_1st_OP_Switzerland.pdf>, at
para. 21 (accessed 10 August 2006).

70 *International Covenant on Economic, Social and Cultural Rights* (19
December 1966, 943 U.N.T.S. 13), art. 13; *Convention against Discrimi-
nation in Education* (Paris, 14 December 1960, 429 U.N.T.S. 93); *Case
Relating to Certain Aspects of the Laws on the Use of Languages in Edu-
cation in Belgium* (1968) 1 E.H.R.R. 252 at 282; see also de Varennes,
Language, Minorities and Human Rights, 198–9; Woehrling,
"L'évolution du cadre juridique."

71 *Declaration on the Rights of Persons Belonging to National or Ethnic,
Religious or Linguistic Minorities*, U.N. G.A. Res. 47/135 (18 December
1992, 32 I.L.M. 911), art. 4(3).

72 *Framework Convention for the Protection of National Minorities*
(Strasbourg, 1 February 1995, 34 I.L.M. 351), art. 14(2).

73 *European Charter of Regional or Minority Languages* (Strasbourg, 5
November 1992, European Treaty Series 148), art. 8.

74 de Varennes, *Language, Minorities and Human Rights*, 204–6; Beiter,
Right to Education, 420–7.

75 See the section "Minority Rights and Equality," chapter 2, above.

76 *Gosselin (Tutor of)* v. *Quebec (A.G.)*, [2005] 1 S.C.R. 238.

77 *Charter of Human Rights and Freedoms*, R.S.Q., c. C–12.

78 See above, chap. 2, "Minority Rights and Equality."

79 See above, chap. 2, "Minority Rights and Equality."

80 *Gosselin (Tutor of)* v. *Quebec (A.G.)*, [2005] 1 S.C.R. 238 at para. 15; on
the application of substantive equality to language issues, see Newman,
"Understanding Language Rights."

81 Ibid. at para. 31.

82 St-Germain, *La situation linguistique.*

83 *Education Act*, R.S.N.B., c. E–1.12, s. 5(1) (adopted in 2000).

84 Martel, *Rights, Schools and Communities*, 58.

85 *Gosselin (Tutor of)* v. *Quebec (A.G.)*, [2005] 1 S.C.R. 238 at para. 31.

86 *Ford* v. *Quebec (A.G.)*, [1988] 2 S.C.R. 712 at 777–9; *Reference re Secession of Quebec*, [1998] 2 S.C.R. 217 at 252; see also, for a philosophical
discussion of those issues, Patten and Kymlicka, "Language Rights,"
42–8.

87 *Quebec Association of Protestant School Boards* v. *A.G. Quebec*, [1982]
C.S. 673, 140 D.L.R. (3d) 33 (Quebec S.C.) at 695–7.

88 *Case Relating to Certain Aspects of the Laws on the Use of Languages in Education in Belgium* (1968), 1 E.H.R.R 252 at 293.

89 *Société anonyme Bar Amici* v. *Disentis/Mustér, commune* (1992), 140 Journal des tribunaux 1–616.

90 *Lovelace* v. *Canada*, U.N. Doc. CCPR/C/13/D/24/1977 (1981) at para. 17; see also United Nations Human Rights Committee, *ICCPR General Comment No. 23*, at para. 6.2.

91 U.N. G.A. Res. 47/135 (18 December 1992, 32 I.L.M. 911), art. 3(2); see also the *Framework Convention for the Protection of National Minorities* (Strasbourg, 1 February 1995, 34 I.L.M. 351), art. 3(1).

92 For a fuller discussion of the right to exit, see Newman, "Exit, Voice and 'Exile.'"

93 See chap. 2, above, section entitled "Individual Burdens and Collective Interests."

94 See, e.g., *R.* v. *Beaulac*, [1999] 1 S.C.R. 768.

95 *Diergaardt* v. *Namibia*, U.N. Doc. CCPR/C/69/D/760/1997 (2000); for comments on this case, see Woehrling, "L'évolution du cadre juridique," 312–14.

96 *Lovelace* v. *Canada*, U.N. Doc. CCPR/C/13/D/24/1977 (1981); for more details concerning this case see above, chap. 3, section entitled "Women 'Marrying Out.'"

97 This is the basis of Kymlicka's distinction between national minorities and "ethnic groups" resulting from immigration: Kymlicka, *Multicultural Citizenship*, 10–11, 95–9.

98 Case C–274/96, *Bickel* v. *Italy*, [1998] E.C.R. 1–7650.

99 MacMillan, *The Practice of Language Rights*, 121–4.

100 Ministère des relations avec les citoyens et de l'immigration, *Caractéristiques de l'immigration au Québec* (Quebec City 2003), online : <http://www.mrci.gouv.qc.ca/publications/pdf/0507_caracteristiques_immigration.pdf> (accessed 10 August 2006).

Bibliography

Alfred, Gerald R. *Heeding the Voices of Our Ancestors*. Toronto: Oxford University Press 1995.

Alfred, Taiaiake. *Peace, Power, Righteousness: An Indigenous Manifesto*. Toronto: Oxford University Press 1999.

Appiah, K. Anthony. "Race, Culture, Identity: Misunderstood Connections." In *Color Conscious: The Political Morality of Race*, ed. K. Anthony Appiah and Amy Gutmann. Princeton: Princeton University Press 1996.

Aquilino, Michel. "Qui suis-je? Identité linguistique et exclusion des non-ayants droit par l'article 23 de la *Charte*." *Ottawa Law Review* 38 (2007): 65.

Arnardóttir, Oddný Mjöll. *Equality and Non-Discrimination under the European Convention on Human Rights*. The Hague: Martinus Nijhoff 2003.

Asch, Michael. "The Judicial Conceptualization of Culture After *Delgamuukw* and *Van der Peet*." *Review of Constitutional Studies* 5 (2000): 119.

Backhouse, Constance. *Color-Coded: A Legal History of Racism in Canada 1900–1950*. Toronto: University of Toronto Press 1999.

Baker, Aaron. "Comparison Tainted by Justification: Against a "Compendious Question" in Art. 14 Discrimination." *Public Law* (2006): 476.

Bamshad, Michael, et al. "Deconstructing the Relationship between Genetics and Race." *Nature Reviews Genetics* 5 (2004): 598.

Banton, Michael. *Racial Theories*, 2d ed. Cambridge: Cambridge University Press 1998.

Barman, Jean. "At the Edge of Law's Empire: Aboriginal Interraciality, Citizenship, and the Law in British Columbia." *Windsor Yearbook of Access to Justice* 24 (2006): 3.

Barsh, Russel L., and James Youngblood Henderson. "The Supreme Court's *Van der Peet* Trilogy: Naïve Imperialism and Ropes of Sand." *McGill Law Journal* 42 (1997): 993.

Bartels, Dennis, and Alice Bartels. "Mi'gmaq Lives: Aboriginal Identity in Newfoundland." In *Walking a Tightrope: Aboriginal Peoples and Their Representations*, ed. Ute Lischke and David T. McNab. Waterloo: Wilfrid Laurier University Press 2005.

Barth, Fredrik. "Introduction." In *Ethnic Groups and Boundaries*. Prospect Heights, IL: Waveland Press 1998.

Bartlett, Richard. "Citizens Minus: Indians and the Right to Vote." *Saskatchewan Law Review* 44 (1980): 163.

Bauböck, Rainer. "Pourquoi rester unis?" In *Altérité et droit : Contributions à l'étude du rapport entre droit et culture*, ed. Isabelle Schulte-Tenckhoff. Brussels: Bruylant 2002.

– "Autonomie territoriale ou culturelle pour les minorités nationales." In *La Constellation des Appartenances : Nationalisme, libéralisme et pluralisme*, ed. Alain Dieckhoff. Paris: Presses de Sciences Po 2004.

Beatty, David M. "The Canadian Conception of Equality." *University of Toronto Law Journal* 46 (1996): 349.

Beavon, Dan, and Martin Cooke. "An Application of the United Nations Human Development Index to Registered Indians in Canada, 1996." In *Aboriginal Conditions: Research as a Foundation for Public Policy*, ed. Jerry P. White, Paul S. Maxim, and Dan Beavon. Vancouver: UBC Press 2003.

Behiels, Michael D. *Canada's Francophone Minority Communities: Constitutional Renewal and the Winning of School Governance*. Montreal and Kingston: McGill-Queen's University Press 2004.

Beiter, Klaus Dieter. *The Protection of the Right to Education by International Law*. Leiden: Martinus Nijhoff 2006.

Bell, Catherine. "Who Are the Métis in Section 35(2)." *Alberta Law Review* 29 (1991) 351.

Benhabib, Seyla. *The Claims of Culture: Equality and Diversity in the Global Era*. Princeton: Princeton University Press 2002.

Borrows, John. "Contemporary Traditional Equality: The Effect of the *Charter* on First Nation Politics." *University of New Brunswick Law Journal* 43 (1994): 19.

Braën, André. "Les droits linguistiques." In *Les droits linguistiques au Canada*, ed. Michel Bastarache. Montreal: Éditions Yvon Blais 1986.

– "La Cour suprême et l'accès à l'école anglaise au Québec." *Revue générale de droit* 35 (2005): 363.

Brisson, Jean-Maurice. "L'appropriation du Canada par la France de 1534 à 1760 ou les rivages inconnus du droit." In *Le statut juridique des peuples autochtones au Québec et le pluralisme*, ed. Andrée Lajoie et al. Cowansville: Yvon Blais 1996.

Brouillet, Eugénie. *La négation de la nation : L'identité culturelle québécoise et le fédéralisme canadien.* Sillery: Septentrion 2005.

Brown, Desmond H. "They Do Not Submit Themselves to the King's Law: Amerindians and Criminal Justice during the French Regime." *Manitoba Law Journal* 28 (2002): 377.

Brownlie, Robert Jarvis. "'A better citizen than lots of white men': First Nations Enfranchisement – an Ontario Case Study, 1918–1940." *Canadian Historical Review* 87 (2006): 29.

Cannon, Martin. "Revisiting Histories of Legal Assimilation, Racialized Injustice, and the Future of Indian Status in Canada." In *Aboriginal Policy Research: Moving Forward, Making a Difference*, ed. Jerry P. White, Erick Anderson, Wendy Cornet, and Dan Beavon. Toronto: Thompson Educational Publishing 2006.

Capotorti, Francesco. *Study of the Rights of Persons Belonging to Ethnic, Religious and Linguistic Minorities.* U.N. Doc. E/CN.4/Sub.2/384.

Carasco, Emily F. "Canadian Native Children: Have Child Welfare Laws Broken the Circle?" *Canadian Journal of Family Law* 5 (1986): 111.

Cardinal, Harold. *The Rebirth of Canada's Indians.* Edmonton: Hurtig Publishers 1979.

Cardinal, Linda. "Langue, droit et politique: La théorie libérale et le débat sur les langues minoritaires." In *Languages, Constitutionalism and Minorities*, ed. André Braën, Pierre Foucher, and Yves Le Bouthiller. Toronto: LexisNexis Butterworths 2006.

Carignan, Pierre. "Les résolutions de Québec et la compétence législative en matière d'éducation." *Revue juridique Thémis* 23 (1989): 1.

Cashmore, E. Ellis. *Dictionary of Race and Ethnic Relations.* London: Routledge & Kegan Paul 1984.

Cassese, Antonio. *Self-Determination of Peoples: A Legal Reappraisal.* Cambridge: Cambridge University Press 1996.

Chartrand, Larry. "Métis Identity and Citizenship." *Windsor Review of Legal and Social Issues* 12 (2001): 5.

– "Re-Conceptualizing Equality: A Place for Indigenous Political Identity." *Windsor Yearbook of Access to Justice* 19 (2001): 243.

Chartrand, Paul L.A.H. "Aboriginal Rights: The Dispossession of the Métis." *Osgoode Hall Law Journal* 29 (1991): 457.

– "The Hard Case of Defining 'The Métis People' and Their Rights: A Commentary on *R. v. Powley*." *Constitutional Forum* 12:3 (2003): 84.

– ed. *Who Are Canada's Aboriginal Peoples? Recognition, Definition and Jurisdiction*. Saskatoon: Purich Publishing 2002.

Chartrand, Paul L.A.H., and John Giokas. "Defining 'The Métis People': The Hard Case of Canadian Aboriginal Law." In *Who Are Canada's Aboriginal Peoples? Recognition, Definition and Jurisdiction*, ed. Paul L.A.H. Chartrand. Saskatoon: Purich Publishing 2002.

Choudhury, T. "Interpreting the Right to Equality under Article 26 of the International Covenant on Civil and Political Rights." *European Human Rights Law Review* (2003): 24.

Clatworthy, Stewart. "Impacts of the 1985 Amendments to the Indian Act on First Nations Populations." In *Aboriginal Conditions: Research as a Foundation for Public Policy*, ed. Jerry P. White, Paul S. Maxim, and Dan Beavon. eds., Vancouver: UBC Press 2003.

Clifton, James A. "Alternate Identities and Cultural Frontiers." In *Being and Becoming Indian*. Chicago: Dorsey Press 1989.

Colleyn, Jean-Pierre. *Éléments d'anthropologie sociale et culturelle*. 5th ed. Brussels: Éditions de l'Université de Bruxelles 1990.

Collins, Hugh. "Discrimination, Equality and Social Inclusion." *Modern Law Review* 66 (2003): 16.

Constant, Fred. *La citoyenneté*, 2d ed. Paris: Montchrestien 2000.

Cornell, Stephen. "The Transformation of Tribe: Organization and Self-Concept in Native American Ethnicities." *Ethnic & Racial Studies* 11 (1988): 27.

Cornet, Wendy. "First Nations Governance, the *Indian Act* and Women's Equality Rights." In *First Nations Women, Governance and the Indian Act*. Ottawa: Status of Women Canada 2001.

Côté, Pierre-André. *The Interpretation of Legislation in Canada*, 3d ed. Scarborough: Carswell 2000.

Crawford, James. "The Right of Self-Determination in International Law: Its Development and Future." In *Peoples' Rights*, ed. Philip Alston. Oxford: Oxford University Press 2001.

Crenshaw, Kimberlé W. "Race, Reform and Retrenchment: Transformation and Legitimation in Antidiscrimination Law." *Harvard Law Review* 101 (1988): 1331.

– "Mapping the Margins: Intersectionality, Identity Politics and Violence against Women of Color." *Stanford Law Review* 43 (1991): 1241.

Cuche, Denys. *La notion de culture dans les sciences sociales*, 3d ed. Paris: La Découverte 2004.

Cummings, Peter A., and Neil H. Mickenberg. *Native Rights in Canada*, 2d ed. Toronto: Indian-Eskimo Association of Canada 1972.

Daes, Erica-Irene. *Indigenous Peoples and Their Relationship to Land.* U.N. Doc. E/CN.4/Sub.2/2000/25.

– *Working Paper by the Chairperson-Rapporteur, Erica-Irene A. Daes, on the Concept of "Indigenous People."* U.N. Doc. E/CN.4/Sub.2/AC.4/1996/2.

Dauvergne, Catherine. *Humanitarianism, Identity and Nation: Migration Laws in Canada and Australia.* Vancouver: UBC Press 2005.

Delâge, Denys, and Jean-Pierre Sawaya. *Les traités des Sept-Feux avec les Britanniques.* Sillery: Septentrion 2001.

Delpérée, Francis. *Le droit constitutionnel de la Belgique.* Brussels/Paris: Bruylant/LGDJ 2000.

Department of Indian and Northern Affairs Canada. *The Elimination of Sex Discrimination from the Indian Act.* Ottawa 1982.

– *Répercussions des modifications de 1985 à la loi sur les Indiens (Projet de loi C–31), vol. 3 : Études des bandes et collectivités indiennes.* Ottawa 1990.

– *Federal Policy for the Settlement of Native Claims.* Ottawa 1993.

Deschênes, Jules. "Qu'est-ce qu'une minorité? " *Cahiers de Droit* 27 (1986): 255.

de Varennes, Fernand. *Language, Minorities and Human Rights.* The Hague: Martinus Nijhoff 1996.

Deveaux, Monique. "A Deliberative Approach to Conflicts of Culture." In *Minorities within Minorities: Equality, Rights and Diversity*, ed. Avigail Eisenberg and Jeff Spinner-Halev. Cambridge: Cambridge University Press 2005.

Devine, Heather. *The People Who Own Themselves: Aboriginal Ethnogenesis in a Canadian Family, 1660–1900.* Calgary: University of Calgary Press 2004.

Dick, Caroline. "The Politics of Intragroup Difference: First Nations' Women and the Sawridge Dispute." *Canadian Journal of Political Science* 39 (2006): 97.

Dickason, Olive P. *Canada's First Nations*, 2d ed. Toronto: Oxford
University Press 1997.
Domenichelli, Luisa. *Constitution et régime linguistique en Belgique et au
Canada*. Brussels: Bruylant 1999.
Dorais, Louis-Jacques. "Language, Culture and Identity: Some Inuit
Examples." *Canadian Journal of Native Studies* 15 (1995): 293.
Dworkin, Ronald M. *Law's Empire*. Oxford: Hart Publishing 1986.
– *Sovereign Virtue: The Theory and Practice of Equality*. Cambridge:
Harvard University Press 2000.
Eisenberg, Avigail. "Diversity and Equality: Three Approaches to
Cultural and Sexual Difference." *Journal of Political Philosophy* 11
(2003): 41.
Eller, Jack D. *From Culture to Ethnicity to Conflict*. Ann Arbor:
University of Michigan Press 1999.
– "La culture au cœur du conflit : L'anthropologie, la différence
culturelle et l'argument 'ethnique.'" In *Altérité et droit : Contributions
à l'étude du rapport entre droit et culture*, ed. Isabelle
Schulte-Tenckhoff. Brussels: Bruylant 2002.
Émond, André. "Quels sont les partenaires autochtones avec lesquels la
Couronne entretient une relation historique? " *Canadian Bar Review*
76 (1997): 130.
Eriksen, Thomas H. *Ethnicity and Nationalism*. London: Pluto Press
1993.
Fenet, Alain, Geneviève Koubi, and Isabelle Schulte-Tenckhoff. *Le droit
et les minorités*, 2d ed. Brussels: Bruylant 2000.
Fenton, William N. "Northern Iroquoian Culture Patterns." In
Handbook of North American Indians: Northeast. Vol. 15, ed. Bruce
G. Trigger. Washington, DC: Smithsonian Institution 1978.
Fiske, Jo-Anne, and Evelyn George. "Bill C–31: A Study of Cultural
Trauma." In *Aboriginal Policy Research: Moving Forward, Making a
Difference*, ed. Jerry P. White, Erick Anderson, Wendy Cornet, and
Dan Beavon. Toronto: Thompson Educational Publishing 2006.
Flanagan, Tom. *First Nations? Second Thoughts*. Montreal and
Kingston: McGill-Queen's University Press 2000.
Føllesdal, Andreas. "Indigenous Minorities and the Shadow of Injustice
Past." *International Journal of Minority & Group Rights* 7
(2000): 19.
Foucher, Pierre. "Les droits linguistiques en matière scolaire." In *Les
droits linguistiques au Canada*, ed. Michel Bastarache. Cowansville:
Yvon Blais 1986.

Fredman, Sandra. "A Difference with Distinction: Pregnancy and Parenthood Reassessed." *Law Quarterly Review* 110 (1994): 106.

– "Discrimination." In *Oxford Handbook of Legal Studies*, ed. Peter Cane and Mark Tushnet. Oxford: Oxford University Press 2002.

– *Discrimination Law*. Oxford: Oxford University Press 2002.

– "From Deference to Democracy: The Role of Equality under the Human Rights Act 1998." *Law Quarterly Review* 122 (2006): 53.

Freeman, Victoria. "Attitudes toward 'Miscegenation' in Canada, the United States, New Zealand, and Australia, 1860–1914." *Native Studies Review* 16 (2005): 41.

Garant, Patrice. *Droit scolaire*. Cowansville: Éditions Yvon Blais 1992.

Garroutte, Eva Marie. *Real Indians: Identity and the Survival of Native America*. Berkeley: University of California Press 2003.

Gélinas, Claude. *Les autochtones dans le Québec post-confédéral, 1867–1960*. Quebec City: Septentrion 2007.

Gendron Commission. *La situation de la langue française au Québec: Rapport de la Commission d'enquête sur la situation de la langue française et sur les droits linguistiques au Québec*. Québec 1972.

Gerards, Janneke H. *Judicial Review in Equal Treatment Cases*. The Hague: Martinus Nijhoff 2005.

Gilbert, Daphne, and Diana Majury. "Critical Comparisons: The Supreme Court of Canada Dooms Section 15." *Windsor Yearbook of Access to Justice* 24 (2006): 111.

Gilbert, Larry. *Entitlement to Indian Status and Membership Codes in Canada*. Toronto: Carswell 1996.

Glenn, H. Patrick. *Legal Traditions of the World*. Oxford: Oxford University Press 2000.

Government of Canada. *Aboriginal Self-Government: The Government of Canada's Approach to Implementation of the Inherent Right and the Negotiation of Aboriginal Self-Government*. Ottawa: Department of Indian Affairs and Northern Development 1995.

Government of Quebec. *Québec's Policy on the French Language*. Quebec 1977.

Grabham, Emily. "*Law v. Canada*: New Directions for Equality under the *Canadian Charter?*" *Oxford Journal of Legal Studies* 22 (2002): 641.

Grammond, Sébastien. *Aménager la coexistence: Les peuples autochtones et le droit Canadien*. Brussels/Montréal: Bruylant/Yvon Blais 2003.

– 2008. "Equality between Indigenous Groups." *Supreme Court Law Review* (forthcoming).

Green, Leslie. "Are Language Rights Fundamental?" *Osgoode Hall Law Journal* 25 (1987): 639.
– "Internal Minorities and Their Rights." In *The Rights of Minority Cultures*, ed. Will Kymlicka. Oxford: Oxford University Press 1995.
Greschner, Donna. "Does *Law* Advance the Cause of Equality?" *Queen's Law Journal* 27 (2001): 299.
Griffiths, William B. "Equality and Egalitarianism: Framing the Contemporary Debate." *Canadian Journal of Law and Jurisprudence* 7 (1994): 5.
Groves, Robert K. "The Curious Instance of the Irregular Band: A Case Study of Canada's Missing Recognition Policy." *Saskatchewan Law Review* 70 (2007): 153.
Gutmann, Amy. "Responding to Racial Injustice." In *Color Conscious: The Political Morality of Race*, ed. K. Anthony Appiah and A. Gutmann. Princeton: Princeton University Press 1996.
– *Identity in Democracy*. Princeton: Princeton University Press 2003.
Hannett, Sarah. "Equality at the Intersections: The Legislative and Judicial Failure to Tackle Multiple Discrimination." *Oxford Journal of Legal Studies* 23 (2003): 65.
Harring, Sidney L. *White Man's Law: Native People in Nineteenth-Century Canadian Jurisprudence*. Toronto: University of Toronto Press 1998.
Harris, Angela P. "Race and Essentialism in Feminist Legal Theory." *Stanford Law Review* 42 (1990): 581.
Hartley, Gerard. "The Search for Consensus: A Legislative History of Bill C-31, 1969–1985." In *Aboriginal Policy Research: Moving Forward, Making a Difference*, ed. Jerry P. White, Erick Anderson, Wendy Cornet, and Dan Beavon. Toronto: Thompson Educational Publishing 2006.
Havard, Gilles. *La Grande Paix de Montréal de 1701*. Montréal: Recherches amérindiennes au Québec 1992.
Hayday. Matthew *Bilingual Today, United Tomorrow: Official Languages in Education and Canadian Federalism*. Montreal and Kingston: McGill-Queen's University Press 2005.
Hill, Renée A. "Compensatory Justice: Over Time and between Groups." *Journal of Political Philosophy* 10 (2002): 392.
Hogg, Peter W., and Mary Ellen Turpel. "Implementing Aboriginal Self-Government: Constitutional and Jurisdictional Issues." *Canadian Bar Review* 74 (1995): 187.

Holmes, Joan. *Bill C-31: Equality or Disparity? The Effects of the New Indian Act on Native Women*. Ottawa: Canadian Advisory Council on the Status of Women 1987.

Horton, Andrea, and Christine Mohr. "*R. v. Powley*: Dodging *Van der Peet* to Recognize Métis Rights." *Queen's Law Journal* 30 (2005): 772.

Isaac, Thomas. *Métis Rights*. Saskatoon: University of Saskatchewan Native Law Centre 2008.

Iyer, Nitya. "Categorical Denials: Equality Rights and the Shaping of Social Identity." *Queen's Law Journal* 19 (1993): 179.

Jacquard, Albert. *Au péril de la science?* Paris: Seuil 1982.

Jaggar, A.M. "Sexual Difference and Sexual Equality." In *Theoretical Perspectives on Sexual Difference*, ed. Deborah L. Rhode. New Haven: Yale University Press 1990.

Jamieson, Kathleen. *Indian Women and the Law in Canada: Citizens Minus*. Ottawa: Advisory Council on the Status of Women 1978.

– "Sex Discrimination and the *Indian Act*." In *Arduous Journey: Canadian Indians and Decolonisation*, ed. J. Rick Ponting. Toronto: McClelland and Stewart 1986.

Jenkins, Richard. *Rethinking Ethnicity*. London: Sage Publications 1997.

Jorde, Lynn B., and Stephen P. Wooding. "Genetic Variation, Classification and 'Race.'" *Nature Genetics* 36 (2004): s28.

Juteau, Danielle. *L'ethnicité et ses frontières*. Montréal: Presses de l'Université de Montréal 1999.

Kaeckenbeeck, Georges. *The International Experiment of Upper Silesia*. Oxford: Oxford University Press 1942.

Kim, Natasha, and Tina Piper. "*Gosselin v. Quebec* : Back to the Poorhouse ..." *McGill Law Journal* 48 (2003): 749.

Kingsbury, Benedict. "Reconciling Five Competing Conceptual Structures of Indigenous Peoples' Claims in International and Comparative Law." In *Peoples' Rights*, ed. Philip Alston. Oxford: Oxford University Press 2001.

Kirk, L.J. "Discrimination and Difference: Race and Inequality in Australian Law." *International Journal of Discrimination and the Law* 4 (2000): 323.

Koubi, Geneviève. "Vers l'égalité des chances: Quelles chances en droit?" In *L'égalité des chances: Analyses, évolutions et perspectives*, ed. Geneviève Koubi and Gilles J. Guglielmi. Paris: La Découverte 2000.

Koubi, Geneviève, and Isabelle Schulte-Tenckhoff. "'Peuple autochtone' et 'minorité' dans les discours juridiques: imbrications et dissociations." *Revue interdisciplinaire d'études juridiques* 45 (2000): 1.

Krosenbrink-Gelissen, Lilianne E. *Sexual Equality as an Aboriginal Right: The Native Women's Association of Canada and the Constitutional Process on Aboriginal Matters, 1982–1987.* Saarbrücken: Breitenbach Publishers 1991.

Kymlicka, Will. *Multicultural Citizenship.* Oxford: Oxford University Press 1995.

– *Politics in the Vernacular.* Oxford: Oxford University Press 2001.

– *Multicultural Odysseys: Navigating the New International Politics of Diversity.* Oxford: Oxford University Press 2007.

Kymlicka, Will, and Alan Patten, eds. *Language Rights and Political Theory.* Oxford: Oxford University Press 2003.

Lavell-Harvard, D. Memee, and Jeannette Corbiere Lavell. "Aboriginal Women vs Canada: The Struggle of Our Mothers to Remain Aboriginal." In *"Until Our Hearts Are on the Ground": Aboriginal Mothering, Oppression, Resistance and Rebirth*, ed. D. Memee Lavell-Harvard and Jeannette Corbiere Lavell. Toronto: Demeter Press 2006.

Lawrence, Bonita. *"Real" Indians and Others: Mixed-Blood Urban Native Peoples and Indigenous Nationhood.* Vancouver: UBC Press 2004.

Le Bouthiller, Yves. "Le droit à l'instruction en français dans les provinces canadiennes à majorité anglophone: Le statut des enfants de parents immigrés." *Revue générale de droit* 24 (1993): 255.

Leslie, John F. *Assimilation, Integration or Termination? The Development of Canadian Indian Policy, 1943–1963.* PHD diss., Carleton University, 1999.

Leuprecht, Peter. "Minority Rights Revisited: New Glimpses of an Old Issue." In *Peoples' Rights*, ed. Philip Alston. Oxford: Oxford University Press 2001.

Locke, John. *Two Treatises of Government.* Cambridge: Cambridge University Press 1988.

Maaka, Roger, and Augie Fleras. "Engaging with Indigeneity: Tino Rangatiratanga in Aotearoa." In *Political Theory and the Rights of Indigenous Peoples*, ed. Duncan Ivison, Paul Patton, and Will Sanders. Cambridge: Cambridge University Press 2000.

MacKinnon, Catharine A. *Feminism Unmodified.* Cambridge: Harvard University Press 1987.

Macklem, Patrick. *Indigenous Difference and the Constitution of Canada.* Toronto: University of Toronto Press 2001.

Macklem, Timothy. *Beyond Comparison: Sex and Discrimination.* Cambridge: Cambridge University Press 2003.

Maclure, Jocelyn. "La reconnaissance engage-t-elle à l'essentialisme?" *Philosophiques* 34,1 (2007): 77.

MacMillan, C. Michael. *The Practice of Language Rights in Canada.* Toronto: University of Toronto Press 1998.

Magocsi, Paul R., ed. *Aboriginal Peoples of Canada: A Short Introduction.* Toronto: University of Toronto Press 2002.

Mann, Michelle M. "Indian Registration: Unrecognized and Unstated Paternity." In *Aboriginal Policy Research: Moving Forward, Making a Difference,* ed. Jerry P. White, Erick Anderson, Wendy Cornet, and Dan Beavon. Toronto: Thompson Educational Publishing 2006.

Margalit, Avishai, and Joseph Raz. "National Self-Determination." In *The Rights of Minority Cultures,* ed. Will Kymlicka. Oxford: Oxford University Press 1995.

Marshall, Ingeborg. *History and Ethnography of the Beothuk.* Montreal and Kingston: McGill-Queen's University Press 1996.

Martel, Angéline. *Rights, Schools and Communities in Minority Contexts: 1986–2002.* Ottawa: Office of the Commissioner of Official Languages 2001.

Martin, Sheila. "Balancing Individual Rights to Equality and Social Goals." *Canadian Bar Review* 80 (2001): 299.

Martínez, Miguel Alfonso. *Study on Treaties, Agreements and Other Constructive Arrangements between States and Indigenous Populations.* U.N. Doc. E/CN.4/Sub.2/1999/20.

Martínez Cobo, José R. *Study of the Problem of Discrimination Against Indigenous Populations.* U.N. Doc. E/CN.4/Sub.2/1986/7/Add.4.

Mathieu, Geneviève. *Qui est Québécois? Synthèse du débat sur la redéfinition de la nation.* Montreal: VLB éditeur 2001.

Mawani, Renisa. "In Between and Out of Place: Racial Hybridity, Liquor and the Law in Late 19th and Early 20th Century British Columbia." *Canadian Journal of Law and Society* 15 (2000): 9.

May, Stephen. "Misconceiving Minority Language Rights: Implications for Liberal Political Theory." In *Language Rights and Political Theory,* ed. Will Kymlicka and Alan Patten. Oxford: Oxford University Press 2003.

McHugh, Paul G. *Aboriginal Societies and the Common Law: A History of Sovereignty, Status and Self-determination.* Oxford: Oxford University Press 2004.

McIntyre, Sheila. "The Supreme Court and Section 15: A Thin and Impoverished Notion of Judicial Review." *Queen's Law Journal* 31 (2006): 731.

McIvor, Sharon D. "Aboriginal Women Unmasked: Using Equality Litigation to Advance Women's Rights." *Canadian Journal of Women and the Law* 16 (2004): 106.

McLeod, Neal. "Plains Cree Identity: Borderlands, Ambiguous Genealogies and Narrative Irony." *Canadian Journal of Native Studies* 20 (2000): 437.

McNeil, Kent. "Aboriginal Governments and the *Canadian Charter of Rights and Freedoms*." *Osgoode Hall Law Journal* 34 (1996): 61.

– "Self-Government and the Inalienability of Aboriginal Title." *McGill Law Journal* 47 (2002): 473.

McRoberts, Kenneth. *Misconceiving Canada: The Struggle for National Unity*. Toronto: Oxford University Press 1997.

Meisels, Tamar. "Can Corrective Justice Ground Claims to Territory?" *Journal of Political Philosophy* 11 (2003): 65.

Mesure, Sylvie, and Alain Renaut. *Alter ego : Les paradoxes de l'identité démocratique*. Paris: Flammarion 2002.

Moore, Margaret. *The Ethics of Nationalism*. Oxford: Oxford University Press 2001.

Moreau, Sophia R. "Equality Rights and the Relevance of Comparator Groups." *Journal of Law and Equality* 5 (2006): 81.

Morin, Jacques-Yvan, and José Woehrling. *Les constitutions du Canada et du Québec du régime français à nos jours*. Montreal: Thémis 1992.

Morin, Michel. *L'usurpation de la souveraineté autochtone*. Montreal: Boréal 1997.

Morris, Alexander. *The Treaties of Canada with the Indians*. Toronto: Belfords Clarke & Co. 1880.

Morse, Bradford W. *Aboriginal Peoples and the Law*. Ottawa: Carleton University Press 1985.

Morse, Bradford W., and Robert K. Groves. "Canada's Forgotten Peoples: The Aboriginal Rights of Métis and Non-Status Indians." *Law & Anthropology* 2 (1987): 139.

Moss, Wendy. "Indigenous Self-Government in Canada and Sexual Equality under the *Indian Act*: Resolving Conflicts between Collective and Individual Rights." *Queen's Law Journal* 15 (1990): 279.

Nagel, Joane. *American Indian Ethnic Renewal: Red Power and the Resurgence of Identity and Culture*. Oxford: Oxford University Press 1996.

Napoleon, Val. "Extinction by Numbers: Colonialism Made Easy."
Canadian Journal of Law and Society 16 (2001): 113.
Native Women's Association of Canada (NWAC). *Aboriginal Women's
Rights Are Human Rights.* Online:
http://www.nwac-hq.org/documents/AboriginalWomensRightsAreHum
anRights.pdf (accessed 8 June 2007).
Newman, Dwight G. "Exit, Voice and 'Exile': Rights to Exit and Rights
to Eject." *University of Toronto Law Journal* 57 (2007): 43.
- "Prior Occupation and Schismatic Principles: Toward a Normative
Theorization of Aboriginal Title." *Alberta Law Review* 44 (2007):
779.
Newman, Warren J. "Understanding Language Rights, Equality and the
Charter: Towards a Comprehensive Theory of Constitutional
Interpretation." *National Journal of Constitutional Law* 15 (2004):
363.
Niezen, Ronald. "Culture and the Judiciary: The Meaning of the Culture
Concept as a Source of Aboriginal Rights in Canada." *Canadian
Journal of Law and Society* 18 (2003): 1.
Otis, Ghislain. "Aboriginal Governance with or without the Canadian
Charter?" In *Aboriginality and Governance: A Multidisciplinary
Perspective from Québec,* ed. Gordon Christie. Penticton, BC: Theytus
Books 2006.
- "Territoriality, Personality, and the Promotion of Aboriginal Legal
Traditions in Canada." In *Indigenous Legal Traditions,* ed. Law
Commission of Canada. Vancouver: UBC Press 2007.
Parekh, Bhikhu. *Rethinking Multiculturalism.* Cambridge: Harvard
University Press 2000.
Parent, Simon G. *Le nom patronymique dans le droit québécois.* Quebec
City: Charrier et Dugal 1951.
Patten, Alan. "The Rights of Internal Linguistic Minorities." In
Minorities within Minorities: Equality, Rights and Diversity, ed.
Avigail Eisenberg and Jeff Spinner-Halev. Cambridge: Cambridge
University Press 2005.
- "Who Should Have Official Language Rights?" In *Languages,
Constitutionalism and Minorities,* ed. André Braën, Pierre Foucher,
and Yves Le Bouthiller. Toronto: LexisNexis Butterworths 2006.
Patten, Alan, and Will Kymlicka. "Language Rights and Political Theory:
Context, Issues and Approaches." In *Language Rights and Political
Theory,* ed. Will Kymlicka and Alan Patten. Oxford: Oxford
University Press 2003.

Perelman, Chaïm. "Égalité et justice." In *L'égalité*, ed. Léon Ingber. Brussels: Bruylant 1977.

Peterson, Jacqueline, and Jennifer S.H. Brown, eds. *The New Peoples: Being and Becoming Métis in North America*. Winnipeg: University of Manitoba Press 1984.

Porter, Bruce. "Twenty Years of Equality Rights: Reclaiming Expectations." *Windsor Yearbook of Access to Justice* 23 (2005): 145.

Preston, Richard J. "East Main Cree." In *Handbook of North American Indians: Subarctic*. Vol. 6, ed. June Helm. Washington, DC: Smithsonian Institution 1981.

Price, Richard, ed. *The Spirit of the Alberta Indian Treaties*. Montreal: Institute for Research on Public Policy 1979.

Proulx, Craig. "Aboriginal Identification in North American Cities." *Canadian Journal of Native Studies* 26 (2006): 405.

Proulx, Daniel. "Les droits à l'égalité revus et corrigés par la Cour suprême dans l'arrêt Law: Un pas en avant ou un pas en arrière?" *Revue du Barreau* 61 (1999): 185.

– "Le concept de dignité et son usage en contexte de discrimination: deux Chartes, deux modèles." *Revue du Barreau* special edition (2003): 485.

Proulx, Jean-Pierre. "Le choc des Chartes: Histoire des régimes juridiques québécois et canadien en matière de langue d'enseignement." *Revue juridique Thémis* 23 (1989): 67.

Purich, Donald. *The Métis*. Toronto: James Lorimer & Co. 1988.

Rawls, John. *A Theory of Justice*. Rev. ed. Cambridge: Belknap Press 1999.

Rayner, Linda. *The Creation of a "Non-Status" Indian Population by Federal Government Policy and Administration*. Ottawa: Native Council of Canada 1978.

Raz, Joseph. *Ethics in the Public Domain*. Oxford: Clarendon Press 1994.

Réaume, Denise G. "Official-Language Rights: Intrinsic Value and the Protection of Difference." In *Citizenship in Diverse Societies*, ed. Will Kymlicka and Wayne Norman. Oxford: Oxford University Press 2000.

– "The Demise of the Political Compromise Doctrine: Have Official Language Use Rights Been Revived?" *McGill Law Journal* 47 (2002): 593.

– "The Relevance of Relevance to Equality Rights." *Queen's Law Journal* 31 (2006): 696.

Réaume, Denise, and Leslie Green. "Education and Linguistic Security in the *Charter*." *McGill Law Journal* 34 (1989): 777.

Rhode, Deborah L. "Definitions of Difference." In *Theoretical Perspectives on Sexual Difference*. New Haven: Yale University Press 1990.

Richter, Daniel K. *The Ordeal of the Longhouse*. Chapel Hill: University of North Carolina Press 1992.

Robitaille, David. "Vous êtes victime de discrimination et souhaitez en faire la preuve? Bonne chance!" *Revue du Barreau* 62 (2002): 319.

Rogers, Edward S., and Eleanor Leacock. "Montagnais-Naskapi." In *Handbook of North American Indians: Subarctic*. Vol. 6, ed. June Helm. Washington: Smithsonian Institution 1981.

Romney, Paul. "Provincial Equality, Special Status and the Compact Theory of Canadian Confederation." *Canadian Journal of Political Science* 32 (1999): 21.

Rosenberg, N.A., et al. "Genetic Structure of Human Populations." *Science* 298 (2002): 2381.

Rosenfeld, Michel. "Equality and the Dialectic between Identity and Difference." In *Multiculturalism and Law: A Critical Debate*, ed. Omid Payrow Shabani. Cardiff: University of Wales Press 2007.

Rouland, Norbert, Stéphane Pierré-Caps, and Jacques Poumarède. *Droit des minorités et des peuples autochtones*. Paris: PUF 1996.

Rousseau, Louis-Pascal. "Les études sur l'ethnogénèse au Canada : Enjeux et horizons de recherche pour le Québec." *Recherches amérindiennes au Québec* 36:1 (2006): 49.

Roy, Gabrielle. *La Détresse et l'Enchantement*. 3d ed. Montreal: Boréal 1996.

Roy, Ingride. *Vers un droit de participation des minorités à la vie de l'État?* Montreal: Wilson & Lafleur 2006.

Royal Commission on Aboriginal Peoples. *Report of the Royal Commission on Aboriginal Peoples*. Ottawa: Canada Communications Group 1996.

Royal Commission on Bilingualism and Biculturalism. *Report of the Royal Commission on Bilingualism and Biculturalism*. Ottawa 1967.

Royal Commission on the Status of Women in Canada. *Report of the Royal Commission on the Status of Women in Canada*. Ottawa 1970.

Rozon, Véronique. *Un dialogue identitaire: Les Hurons de Lorette et les Autres au XIXe siècle*. MA (History) diss., Université du Québec à Montréal, 2005.

Ryder, Bruce, Cidalia C. Faria, and Emily Lawrence. "What's *Law* Good
For? An Empirical Overview of Charter Equality Rights Decisions."
Supreme Court Law Review (2d) 24 (2004): 103.
Sanders, Douglas. "Indian Women: Their Roles and Rights." *McGill
Law Journal* 21 (1975) 656.
Sawchuk, Joe. "Negotiating an Identity: Métis Political Organizations,
the Canadian Government and Competing Concepts of Aboriginality."
American Indian Quarterly 24 (2000): 73.
Schabas, William A. "Canada and the Adoption of the Universal
Declaration of Human Rights." *McGill Law Journal* 43 (1998): 403.
Schouls, Tim. *Shifting Boundaries: Aboriginal Identity, Pluralist Theory
and the Politics of Self-Government*. Vancouver: UBC Press 2003.
Schulte-Tenckhoff, Isabelle. *La question des peuples autochtones*.
Brussels/Paris: Bruylant/LGDJ 1997.
Shachar, Ayelet. "The Paradox of Multicultural Vulnerability: Individual
Rights, Identity Groups and the State." In *Multicultural Questions*, ed.
Christian Joppke and Steven Lukes. Oxford: Oxford University Press
1999.
– *Multicultural Jurisdictions: Cultural Differences and Women's Rights*.
Cambridge: Cambridge University Press 2001.
Sharp, Andrew. "Blood, Custom and Consent: Three Kinds of Maori
Groups and the Challenges They Present to Governments." *University
of Toronto Law Journal* 52 (2002): 9.
Sheppard, Colleen. "Grounds of Discrimination: Towards an Inclusive
and Contextual Approach." *Canadian Bar Review* 80 (2001): 893.
Simmons, A. John. "Original-Acquisition Justifications of Private
Property." *Social Philosophy & Policy* 11, 2 (1994): 63.
– "Historical Rights and Fair Shares." *Law & Philosophy* 14 (1995):
149.
Sioui, Georges E. *Les Wendats: Une civilisation méconnue*. Quebec City:
Presses de l'Université Laval 1994.
Slattery, Brian. "The Constitutional Guarantee of Aboriginal and Treaty
Rights." *Queen's Law Journal* 8 (1982–83): 232.
– "Making Sense of Aboriginal and Treaty Rights." *Canadian Bar
Review* 79 (2000): 196.
Smedley, Audrey. *Race in North America: Origin and Evolution of a
Worldview*. 2d ed. Boulder, CO: Westview Press 1999.
Smith, James G.E. "Western Woods Cree." In *Handbook of North
American Indians: Subarctic*. Vol. 6, ed. June Helm. Washington DC:
Smithsonian Institution 1981.

Spinner-Halev, Jeff. "Land, Culture and Justice: A Framework for Group Rights and Recognition." *Journal of Political Philosophy* 8 (2000): 319.

St-Germain, Claude. *La situation linguistique dans le secteur de l'éducation en 1997–1998.* Quebec City: Department of the Education 1999.

Sturm, Circé. *Blood Politics: Race, Culture and Identity in the Cherokee Nation of Oklahoma.* Berkeley: University of California Press 2002.

Taddeo, Donat, and Raymond Taras. *Le débat linguistique au Québec: La communauté italienne et la langue d'enseignement.* Montreal: Presses de l'Université de Montréal 1987.

Tamir, Yaël. *Liberal Nationalism.* Princeton: Princeton University Press 1993.

– "Against Collective Rights." In *Multicultural Questions*, ed. Christian Joppke and Steven Lukes. Oxford: Oxford University Press 1999.

Tanner, Adrian. "The Aboriginal Peoples of Newfoundland and Labrador and Confederation." *Newfoundland Studies* 14 (1998): 238.

Taylor, Charles. "The Politics of Recognition." In *Multiculturalism*, ed. Amy Gutmann. Princeton: Princeton University Press 1994.

Thornberry, Patrick. *International Law and the Rights of Minorities.* Oxford: Oxford University Press 1991.

Tierney, Stephen. *Constitutional Law and National Pluralism.* Oxford: Oxford University Press 2004.

Titley, E. Brian. *A Narrow Vision: Duncan Campbell Scott and the Administration of Indian Affairs in Canada.* Vancouver: UBC Press 1986.

Tobias, James L. "Canada's Subjugation of the Plains Cree, 1879–1885." In *Sweet Promises: A Reader on Indian-White Relations in Canada*, ed. James R. Miller. Toronto: University of Toronto Press 1991.

Tremblay, André. *La réforme de la constitution au Canada.* Montreal: Thémis 1995.

Trigger, Bruce G. *Natives and Newcomers: Canada's "Heroic Age" Reconsidered.* Montreal and Kingston: McGill-Queen's University Press 1985.

Trudeau, Pierre Elliott. *Federalism and the French Canadians.* Toronto: Macmillan 1968.

Tully, James. *Strange Multiplicity.* Cambridge: Cambridge University Press 1995.

Turpel, Mary Ellen. "Patriarchy and Paternalism: The Legacy of the Canadian State for First Nations Women." *Canadian Journal of Women and the Law* 6 (1993): 174.

Tylor, Edward Burnett. *The Origins of Culture*. New York: Harper &
    Brothers 1958.
Vandenhole, Wouter. *Non-Discrimination and Equality in the View of
    the UN Human Rights Treaty Bodies*. Antwerpen: Intersentia 2005.
Van Kirk, Sylvia. *Many Tender Ties: Women in Fur Trade Society in
    Western Canada, 1670–1870*, Winnipeg: Watson & Dwyer 1980.
Viau, Roland. *Femmes de personne: Sexes, genres et pouvoirs en
    Iroquoisie ancienne*. Montreal: Boréal 2000.
von Gernet, Alexander. "Iroquoians." In *Aboriginal Peoples of Canada*,
    ed. Paul R. Magocsi. Toronto: University of Toronto Press 2002.
Waldron, Jeremy. "Minority Cultures and the Cosmopolitan
    Alternative." In *The Rights of Minority Cultures*, ed. Will Kymlicka.
    Oxford: Oxford University Press 1995.
– "Superseding Historic Injustice." *Ethics* 103 (1992): 4.
– "Redressing Historic Injustice." *University of Toronto Law Journal* 52
    (2002): 135.
Weaver, Hilary N. "Indigenous Identity: What Is It, and Who *Really* Has
    It?" *American Indian Quarterly* 25 (2001): 240.
Weaver, Sally M. *Making Canadian Indian Policy: The Hidden Agenda
    1968–1970*. Toronto: University of Toronto Press 1981.
– "First Nations Women and Government Policy, 1970–92:
    Discrimination and Conflict." In *Changing Patterns: Women in
    Canada*, 2d ed., ed. S. Burt, L. Code, and L. Dorney. Toronto:
    McClelland and Stewart 1993.
Weinstock, Daniel M. "The Antinomy of Language Policy." In *Language
    Rights and Political Theory*, ed. Will Kymlicka and Alan Patten.
    Oxford: Oxford University Press 2003.
Wetzel, Jerry. "Liberal Theory as a Tool of Colonialism and the Forced
    Assimilation of the First Nations of Newfoundland and Labrador."
    Dalhousie Journal of Legal Studies 4 (1995): 105.
Wilkins, Kerry. "... But We Need the Eggs: The Royal Commission, the
    Charter of Rights and the Inherent Right of Aboriginal
    Self-Government." *University of Toronto Law Journal* 49 (1999): 53.
Williams, Colin H. "Recognition and National Justice for Québec: A
    Canadian Conundrum" In *Ethnonational Identities*, ed. Steve Fenton
    and Stephen May. Basingstoke: Palgrave 2002.
Wiseman, David. "Competence Concerns in *Charter* Adjudication:
    Countering the Anti-Poverty Incompetence Argument." *McGill Law
    Journal* 51 (2006): 503.

Woehrling, José. "Minority Cultural and Linguistic Rights and Equality Rights in the *Canadian Charter of Rights and Freedoms.*" *McGill Law Journal* 31 (1985): 50.

– "L'obligation d'accommodement raisonnable et l'adaptation de la société à la diversité religieuse." *McGill Law Journal* 43 (1998): 325.

– "L'évolution du cadre juridique et conceptuel de la législation linguistique du Québec." In *Le français au Québec : Les nouveaux défis*, ed. Alexandre Stefanescu and Pierre Georgeault. Montreal: Fides 2005.

Young, Iris M. *Justice and the Politics of Difference.* Princeton: Princeton University Press 1990.

Zlotkin, Norman. "Judicial Recognition of Aboriginal Customary Law in Canada." *Canadian Native Law Reporter* 4 (1984): 1.

Index